D0871922

THE ARIZONA RANGERS

The
ARIZONA
RANGERS

Edited by

JOSEPH MILLER

Illustrated with photographs

HASTINGS HOUSE, PUBLISHERS

New York 10016

Published simultaneously in Canada by
Saunders of Toronto, Ltd., Don Mills, Ontario

Library of Congress Catalog Card Number: 75–170627

Library of Congress Cataloging in Publication Data

Miller, Joseph,   comp.
    Arizona Rangers.

    "Act establishing the Ranger Force of the Territory of Arizona": p. 245
    "An act repealing the act establishing the Ranger Force of the Territory of Arizona": p. 249
    1. Arizona (Ter.). Rangers. 1. Arizona (Ter.). Laws, statutes, etc. Act establishing the Ranger Force of the Territory of Arizona. 1972. II. Arizona (Ter.). Laws, statutes, etc. An act repealing the act establishing the Ranger Force of the Territory of Arizona. 1972. III. Title.

HV8145.A7M54   363.2'09791   75–170627
ISBN 0–8038–0353–2

Printed in the United States of America

CONTENTS

FOREWORD

THE ARIZONA RANGERS were a colorful group of men, and as the numerous stories in this volume will reveal, were unique in their field. During the rather brief period of their existence, seven and one-half years, a total of one hundred and seven men served with that organization. Some were with them but a short time, and a very few were discharged as being unable to abide by the code of conduct expected of them. A number of the men, finishing out their one-year term of enlistment, signed on again and again. Occasionally a member resigned to accept a position with another law enforcement agency, such as with a sheriff's office as a deputy, or as an officer on a police force in one of the frontier towns, or with the U. S. Marshal's office. On the other hand men sometimes left one of these agencies to join the Rangers when an opening occurred.

As the Spanish-American war came to its conclusion in 1898, Arizonans returning from Cuba to their homes fresh from combat duty with Roosevelt's Rough Riders, gave the Rangers' organizer and first captain, Burton C. Mossman, a choice of high grade men perfectly suited to the need. Expert horsemen all, mostly cowboys by profession, trackers and trailers by experience, with a great knowledge of the country and a natural ability to handle firearms, quick on the draw, this was a way of life for them, and they fitted perfectly into the Ranger force.

A Ranger's prime duty was to get his man and turn him over to the nearest law enforcement officer or agency. Sometimes a suspect was trailed for hundreds of miles before finally being caught by one of these men who never gave up, and whose bounds of rendezvous was unlimited. Once the man was apprehended the ranger's job was about finished except for an appearance as a witness before a grand jury or at a court trial of the suspect.

In a letter written in 1935, from Burton C. Mossman to Will C. Barnes, an Arizona historian, the closing paragraph reads as follows:

"After my day the Rangers were in distinctive garb; wore a conspicuous badge, bristled with weapons, and were so widely and systematically press agented, they soon achieved a dubious fame with the old timers and passed on to a natural and inevitable Falstaffian reward."

A letter written in 1925 by the then state librarian Con Cronin to Harry C. Wheeler, the third and last captain of the Arizona Rangers, giving his opinion on the abolition in 1909 of that organization, had this excerpt:

"I believe that the greatest factor in the repeal of the law was the most active opposition and bitter hatred of the sheriffs of the several of the lower tier of counties of the territory, especially Cochise, Pima, Santa Cruz, Gila, Pinal and Graham. These men all had friends in the legislature, who were pledged to repeal the Rangers."

The stories of the Arizona Rangers in this volume are accounts taken, for the most part, from the Arizona newspapers of the time of their occurrence. No attempt has been made to change the wording or style of writing, hopefully to retain the "flavor" of the period. Although there seemed to be a never-ending series of incidents in connection with the activities of the Arizona Rangers, only the more interesting and exciting episodes, in our opinion, have been included.

To Marguerite B. Cooley, Director, Department of Library and Archives, State of Arizona, my special thanks for the encouragement, and also for the availability of official documents, photographs, early newspapers and other facilities, which has made this volume possible.

Joseph Miller

1

THE ARIZONA RANGERS

FOR YEARS the Southwest has been the synonym for daring, recklessness, and wild freedom; the haunt of the stage robber, the wild marauding Indian, the cattle rustler, and the smuggler. Driven from the states west of the Mississippi, the desperate elements of these thinly settled regions had been driven south by the relentless progress of a higher civilization until they foregathered among the mountain fastnesses and wild tablelands of Arizona and New Mexico, and made the Mexican border a by-word.

Arizona towns scattered along the border were the daily scenes of murders and fierce personal encounters, and the smugglers and cattle rustlers were grown so bold as to ply their business openly. The great Sulphur Springs Valley and similar open stretches, covered for the most part with mesquite, now covered with prosperous towns, railroads, and other evidences of progress, were roamed over by countless herds of cattle, and seldom visited by any save the cowboy. The proximity of Mexico furnished a never-failing protection to the desperado, who, making some sudden foray into the cattle country, would, in a single night, round up a thousand head and escape across the border with his booty.

Today this is changed. The immense copper deposits discovered among the hills, and the extension of irrigation in the valleys, have been tremendous civilizing agents, but to the Arizona Rangers more than to any other thing may be traced the passing of the bad man.

In the spring of 1901, things had come to such a pass along the border that the smaller cattle owners were almost driven out of business. Banding together in well organized, well mounted troops, the cattle rustlers had become so bold as to openly boast of their deeds, and disclaiming the protection of night, drove the captured herds across the mountains in broad daylight. Added to this the remoter, more mountainous sections of the territory were infested by desperadoes of various sorts, and smuggling along the line had become a recognized trade. So well organized were these men that the few civil officers and scattered troops of United States Cavalry were powerless against them. They openly derided the former, and scattered at the approach of the latter, gathering again in some chosen mountain fastness only to descend upon some other valley long before the troops could reach them.

At this point a bill was passed by the Territorial Legislature which was destined to put to an end the wild, free days of the brigandage. On March 21, 1901, a bill was passed at Phoenix empowering and directing the governor to create a body of officers to be known as the "Arizona Rangers," to consist of one captain, one sergeant, and twelve privates. The bill further provided that the personnel of the force should be chosen from the pick of the cattlemen and law officers on the border, and that skill in roping, shooting, riding, trailing, and in general knowledge of the country, together with a rigid physical examination, should determine the fitness of applicants for the positions. They were to operate in all parts of the territory, but especially along the border, in the cattle country.

Fourteen men to cover a country where some of the smaller states of the Union could be hopelessly lost! The cattle thieves and other desperadoes of the territory jested about the new force. They were to learn, however, in a few short months, that "he laughs best who laughs last."

Burton C. Mossman, of Bisbee, was the first to hold commission as captain of this unique, semi-military organization. Under his direction the new force was recruited, but owing to the generally demoralized state of affairs in the territory the personnel of the Rangers was kept as secret as possible for strategical purposes. They were empowered to act as general officers of the peace, and in addition to their duties in riding the ranges and putting down the most desperate elements of outlawry, they could also be called upon by town and county officers in case of need. Usually they went in pairs, passing as cattle men. Mounted on the finest horses that money could buy, and directed by their commander in ways known only to themselves, their mobility reached the uncanny. Notorious bad men and enemies of the law generally found themselves in the iron grip of the Rangers before they were aware that there were law officers within a hundred miles. Two plucky Rangers—more often one—walking coolly into the remotest, wildest haunts of the cattle rustler or smuggler, where no law officer had ever yet dared come, would, by their very daring, paralyze the enemy, who before they could fairly recover from the shock, frequently found themselves, bound and weaponless, on their way to Tombstone, Tucson, or Phoenix, whence their journey to the penitentiary or the gallows was swift and certain.

The desperadoes began to find that they had overlooked two all-important factors in the situation—moral courage and discipline. The Rangers operated so secretly, were so fearless, could mobilize or scatter so silently and quickly, that the outlaws began to entertain for them an almost superstitious fear. Stronghold after stronghold was invaded, and band after band of horse thieves, cattle rustlers, smugglers, murderers, burglars, illicit whiskey sellers, "bunco" gamblers, and others who had long plied their trades fearlessly, found themselves behind the bars.

In March 1903, a revision of the former act of the legislature empowered the governor to increase the number of Rangers to a total of twenty-six men; one captain, one lieutenant, four sergeants, and twenty privates. With this large increase in its numbers, the Rangers were now able to operate more openly, and to cover some of the more remote sections of the territory which had hitherto been neglected.

Meanwhile, in September 1902, the command had passed from the hands of Captain Mossman to those of Captain Thomas H. Rynning, to whose years of experience on the ranges and among the mountains of Arizona had been added the military knowledge and skill in handling men gained as sergeant in the United States Cavalry and as lieutenant of the Rough Riders in the Cuban campaign of 1898. Rynning at once moved the headquarters of the force from Bisbee, where they had been located, to Douglas, a new town just then in the making. The accession of the new captain to the command added to the prestige of the Rangers, for Rynning's bravery, experience, and army history were known far and wide in the Southwest.

No sooner had the new captain fairly recruited the force to its limit than the Rangers were put to one of the severest tests of courage which they had yet experienced. The town of Morenci, in the northeastern part of Graham County [now Greenlee County, since 1909], among the mountains, was largely dependent upon the mines and smelters of a certain copper company. Here in June 1903, the rumblings of discontent among the Mexican miners and other foreign elements in both the mines and smelters suddenly took shape in one of the most dangerous strikes in the history of the territory. The town was in terror, and the sheriff and his few deputies powerless to quell the disturbance. Led on by irresponsible agitators and maddened with liquor it was feared that the Mexican element, actuated by their well-known hate of the "gringos" would commit the worst of outrages, and that many lives and much property would be lost before the military could be brought to the town. In this extremity the Rangers were called for, and with their usual celerity they gathered from far and near to the help of the beleagered population, and, with the assistance of the sheriff and the few available deputies, they held a mob of over three thousand strikers at bay, preserved order, and protected life and property until the territorial militia and United States regulars could be brought in. Owing to their presence and their coolness in a deadly emergency not a life was lost, and scarcely any damage was done to property. Later in the same year they settled in fourteen days another dangerous strike at Globe, and were also the means of satisfactorily arbitrating a savage dispute between the cattle men and the settlers in the Mule Mountains, in the southern part of the territory.

The next momentous occasion for the display of the abilities of the Rangers occurred during June of 1906, at the time of the strike at Cananea in the State of Sonora, Mexico. Cananea, though a Mexican town by position, was in fact an American town in every other way. As is usual in all such mining towns in Mexico, the Mexican workmen far outnumber the white population, and it had been known for some time that there was a spirit of unrest abroad among the lower classes of the workmen, but they had paid no great attention to it, as some such feeling is always sure to exist more or less among two different nationalities working together. But the bad feeling suddenly found a vent at the smelter of the company when one of the American bosses became embroiled in a heated discussion with some of the Mexican work-men, and a riot was at once precipitated which for a while bade fair to wipe out of existence the comparatively small American colony, many of whom were women and children. Messages asking urgently for help were wired to Bisbee, seventy miles away across the line in Arizona, also to Douglas and El Paso, for arms and ammunition. The messages of the company were reinforced by those of the American Consul, and the Americans were advised that the occasion called for the utmost expedition in rendering assistance if the American colony in Cananea were to be saved.

The first message arrived in Bisbee, a town of some eighteen to twenty thousand inhabitants, about six o'clock in the evening. On that evening Captain Rynning, of the Rangers, was on board of the train, bound for Bisbee, and in company with two of his men who were going to Cananea on some regulation matter connected with their work. When the train pulled into the station at Bisbee, Rynning found the town in a turmoil. Men were rushing hither and thither with arms in their hands; the great store of the Copper Mining Company and every other source of supply had been denuded of their stock of firearms and ammunition, and all the available men of the town were being whipped into hurried shape for a dash to the front.

Taking in the situation at a glance, Rynning took immediate command of the mob, and with their willing cooperation the discipline of the Rangers again prevailed in a difficult situation to bring order out of chaos. Directing his two deputies to proceed forthwith to Naco, a town on the El Paso Southwestern Railroad, where the Cananea, Yaqui River, and Pacific, the line running to the town of Cananea, touches the Southwestern, about sixty miles distant from Cananea, and on the international line, and telling them to hold carefully in hand the situation at that point, he then turned his personal attention to the organization of the Bisbee forces, not forgetting meanwhile to wire his scattered forces to mobilize at once at Naco, which they did in the short space of thirty-six hours.

Rangers Rollins and Hopkins, arriving in Naco about seven o'clock in the evening, found that already the cowboys, miners, and other handy citizens of the surrounding country were gathering at Naco, and there was strong talk of an immediate invasion of Mexican territory. A small force of Mexicans were guarding the other side of the line, and both parties were prepared for battle. About eleven or twelve o'clock a force of the Americans undertook to employ a stratagem and get across the line unobserved, but fell into a trap which the enemy had placed for them, and one of their men, in the fusillade which followed, was wounded and carried off by the Mexicans. At this opportune time a special train from Bisbee arrived with Captain Rynning and

Sergeant Arthur A. Hopkins

Sgt. Hopkins, who with Ranger Rollins held the situation in hand at Naco during the Cananea trouble

two hundred and fifty volunteers. Rynning at once took command and held a parley with the enemy. The latter, now hopelessly outnumbered, wisely suggested that both sides consider the matter a draw, and on the Americans agreeing they drew off.

Rynning now found himself in a very difficult and delicate situation. Sixty miles to the south a few hundred Americans might even at that moment be making their last stand against hopeless odds, and the situation was made still more urgent by the presence of so many helpless women and children. On the other hand, should the American forces cross the line it would create a very serious situation from the standpoint of international law, as it would be nothing less than the invasion of the territory of a friendly power. His forces were eager for an advance on Cananea, but the discipline of years of army experience prevailed, and Rynning held back his excited followers with an iron hand.

A whistle was now heard from a locomotive, and the headlight of a special was seen approaching from the west. It was a train from Hermosillo, bearing the governor of the state of Sonora. Governor Yzabal, who was well acquainted with Captain Rynning, at once invited him to a private conference. Rynning told the governor that the occasion was urgent, and offered himself and his men as volunteers. Knowing the captain's military experience and the reputation of the Rangers, Yzabal at once accepted and proceeded to instruct him as to the manner in which he should proceed. In order to avoid international complications the Americans were instructed to cross the line as an unorganized mob, and as soon as they were on Mexican soil they would be sworn in as Mexican volunteers by the governor, who held the requisite military authority.

This was done at once, and the Americans were lined up and duly sworn, thus becoming temporarily Mexican troops. Perhaps it was a bit irregular, but necessity is not a nice observer of red tape. The captain was appointed a colonel, and seven of the Ranger force who accompanied him were also given commissions as officers of the new troops. The matter having thus been arranged, the larger part of the force at Naco then proceeded to Cananea.

Ranger Rollins, who was with Sgt. Hopkins at Naco

Troop of Mexican Rurales under Col. Emilio Kosterlitzky

When their train steamed into the beleagured city there was wild rejoicing among the rescued Americans. They found that the Americans in the town had fairly held their own, but no time was to be lost in ceremony at that moment, and the American rescuers hurried from the train and marched at double quick to the points of greatest danger.

The hills surrounding the town were literally black with Mexicans, and as soon as the Americans came into sight there was a cry of, "Los Americanos! Los Americanos!" and a lively scattering for shelter. Charging the ranks of the peons, the Americans soon scattered them, but at this point a detachment of Rurales—

Mexican Rangers—arrived; the advance-guard of the main body of the Rurales, under their commander-in-chief, Colonel Koster-litzky, who himself arrived shortly after the main body of his troops. Captain Rynning at once turned the matter over to him and, with his forces, recrossed the border. The action taken by the governor of Sonora and Captain Rynning was subsequently ratified and approved by both governments.

In making the several thousands of arrests, which they had in the first five years of their existence, the Rangers had lost only one of their men and found it necessary to take life only six times. Probably no body of men of similar size ever made a better record than the Arizona Rangers, for in the few years they had been in commission they had cleared the territory of innumerable objectionable characters; kept the peace in several dangerous strikes and other disturbances; made cattle-raising, which was in danger of annihilation, a safe and profitable business; broken up systematic smuggling along the Mexican border; freed the border towns of the desperadoes who infested them, and made Arizona as safe a place to dwell in as any of the older, more thickly settled parts of the Union.

———

EDITOR's NOTE: The above article, written by Carl M. Rathbun, which appeared in *Harper's Weekly* in 1906, under the title *Keeping the Peace Along the Mexican Border,* is offered as an introduction to this volume. It not only gives a brief resume of the organization and functioning of the Arizona Rangers, but stresses a few important incidents in the first five years of the history of this unique organization—incidents which proved to be tame in comparison to many more which occurred throughout the life of this gallant band of men.

LET US HAVE RANGERS

We have more than once, in these columns, enlarged upon the necessity of some definite course of action for the relief of the stock growers of Arizona from the increasing depredations of pestilent cattle thieves. While our unceasing efforts to promote the growth of a public sentiment in favor of granting to stockmen such protection as could be afforded through the action of the court have not been altogether in vain, it must be admitted that stock stealing so far from being checked has actually increased, the enhanced value of young cattle having encouraged the unscrupulous to take serious chances in accumulating a herd at the expense of others. The number and daring of the thieves and particularly the defiant and threatening attitude which some of them have recently assumed convinces us that only a heroic remedy for the trouble will prove effective. We have reached the conclusion that a force of Rangers is the only means by which to cope successfully with these rustlers.

The Texas Rangers were largely instrumental in bringing order out of lawlessness in the Lone Star State; and the conditions now obtaining in this territory are similar to those which the Texas Rangers had to confront a decade or two ago. In fact, it is undeniable that a good percentage of the men now engaged in crooked work on Arizona ranges were driven out of Texas by its state Rangers. This is not a reflection on the better class of Texans of whom we have many among our best citizens, and than whom none understand better the good work performed by the Texas Rangers.

The force of Rangers to be enlisted in the service of the territory need not necessarily be very large. Probably twenty or twenty-five good men would suffice. They would be of the utmost value, under proper leadership, in pursuing train robbers, dangerous criminals and escaped convicts. They would be the proper parties to send to the Eagle Creek region to teach the outlaws there that they do not yet own the territory in fee simple.

The expense, of course, would be considerable, but yet trifling compared with the loss which will accrue to the territory if protection is denied the livestock industry. Where would two-thirds of Arizona's counties be without the revenue from the stock ranges? Their income would be reduced from a third to a half. Are the stockmen worth protecting? If not, let it be known at once. Prices of cattle are tempting and cattlemen will not be so foolish as to pay four per cent taxes for the support of county and territorial governments which refuse adequate protection.

How can Arizona ask for statehood when outlaws are allowed to threaten the lives of prominent cattlemen because they, for-sooth, have protested against being robbed and are thought to have given aid to the U. S. officials in pursuit of train robbers? What a commentary on our fitness for statehood that a cattle company is compelled to employ distinguished fighting men to protect its employes from assassination at the hands of despera-does harbored by the men whose sole business is preying on the herds of said company.

County authorities seem unable to cope with the situation. The territory must assume the duty of rounding up the brood of criminals or become the recognized resort of outlaws from the older states. To the end that this reproach may not attach to the fair name of Arizona, let every newspaper and person of influence promptly join in the effort to create a public sentiment in favor of protection to the livestock industry. Let us urge upon the members of the territorial legislature soon to be elected the duty and necessity of equipping a Ranger force for this purpose. It is a question of vital importance to the stock growers. Let them bring all their influence to bear and that quickly.

—Willcox *Range News,* 1898

The Phoenix *Gazette* in response to the above, wrote:

The Arizona Range News in a splendid editorial, calls the attention to the necessity for a territorial Ranger organization. There is no question as to the necessity and requirement of such a body of men. Desperadoes and lawless characters have in many instances been such a terror to some sections of our territory, as to drive peaceful men from their homes. The actions of the "Black Jack" gang in the San Simon and other parts of Cochise county in horse whipping and abusing residents in sparsely settled localities who were supposed to be on friendly terms with the officers, so terrorized many residents that it was a subject of common remark that it was as much as a man's life is worth to give an officer any information. Men who stood high in the localities in which they reside have time and again remarked that they could not afford to give officers aid or openly assist them, as in their isolated home the lawless element would murder them. With such conditions, a company of paid Rangers are required to stamp out and destroy the characters that bring about such a state of affairs. Let us have a territorial Ranger service.

Captain Burton C. Mossman, Arizona Rangers
Courtesy of Mrs. John McK. Redmond

2

BURTON C. MOSSMAN

AN ARIZONA HERO

In reporting the conviction of several cattle thieves at the fall term of district court in Navajo county, the *Range News* expressed the belief that this achievement was largely due to the efforts of Burton Mossman, manager of the Aztec Cattle company. We have since learned through personal inquiry that this conjecture was correct. Chairman Will C. Barnes of the Livestock Sanitary Board of this territory, on a recent trip to Denver with a shipment of cattle, gave the Denver *Stockman* some facts concerning Mr. Mossman and his work, and the following from the columns of that publication is the result:

There is a man down in Arizona of whom little has ever been heard outside of the territory and yet he is one who could furnish many columns of exciting newspaper stories or make the hero of the most exciting romance ever written. His name is Burton C. Mossman and he is the manager of the Aztec Cattle company, which owns big ranges in the northern part of the territory. Mossman is well known throughout the Southwest. He is a thoroughbred American and while a handsome, dashing cowboy, ready to shoot or fight or risk his last dollar in a wager, is also an educated cultured gentleman, capable of moving in the best society and attracting attention as a man out of the usual run, no matter in what phase of life he is found.

Mossman has been making a record this year in his efforts to rid the territory of the thieves that have been so expensive to his company. He has already sent seven of the worst thieves to the penitentiary, a good record for that section, where it is usually very difficult to secure an indictment, much less a conviction. Most of the thieves stole calves. Mossman secured twenty detectives and had them right on the range. He and a detective found a corral hid in the timber and watched a gang of thieves for twenty four hours. While one thief stood guard the others went out and rounded up the cows and calves, cut the calves into the corral and drove the cows away. If any cow came back it was killed. They captured 150 calves in this one corral.

Mossman, who speaks Mexican like a native, had himself thrown in jail over night with a Mexican who was suspected, and during the night the Mexican opened his heart and told Mossman about the operations of himself and several others, which led to the arrest and conviction of several bad thieves. Mossman is both feared and hated by the lawless ones of his district. He is absolutely fearless and recently when cornered in the back of a saloon by a tough gang, who threatened to shoot him if he did not promise to let them alone, he laughed at them and told them he was a better man than they and would certainly have them put in the pen. After an hour's discussion, the gang, stung by Mossman's taunts, sat down with him to a game of poker, and he cleaned them out of all the cash they had and went out laughing at them.

Will Barnes tells a good story on Mossman. It was at a roundup that Mossman got into an argument with a stockman over a steer, which Mossman thought had been stolen by the claimant.

The steer was roped and thrown and the matter was finally referred to Barnes as arbitrator. Barnes decided that the steer belonged to the Aztec outfit and while the claimant accepted the decision he did so grumbling. This aroused the anger of Mossman.

"Aw, what's the matter with you? I'm going to have you arrested for stealing that steer anyhow, so what are you grunting about? You are no good."

"I'm as good as you are," retorted the Mexican.

"No you are not. There is nothing you can do that I cannot do better than you. I can outrun you, outshoot you, outride you and I can lick you any way you want."

Stung by these taunts, the Mexican offered to run Mossman 100 yards for $20. Mossman promptly accepted the proposition and won. Then the propostion was made to toss $5 gold pieces. Mossman won again, and then offered to exchange shots with the Mexican at twenty paces, but the man had had enough.

Mossman has had many experiences in his wild life on the border and a full history of his life would make a romance of the most exciting kind.

—Holbrook *Argus,* 1899

A detailed account of the fight and capture of the cattle thieves appeared in the *Argus* earlier in 1899:

A THRILLING EXPERIENCE

Information has on several occasions reached the sheriff's office here that several Mexicans located in and about Water Canyon, near Pinedale, were suspected of killing cattle belonging to the Aztec company. About ten days ago, Undersheriff Bargman, and Burton C. Mossman, superintendent of the Aztec Land and Cattle company, left Holbrook prepared to camp on the trail of the marauders until they were captured. On the 17th of March they proceeded up Water Canyon to the premises of Antonio Baca. Suspecting that there was stolen beef concealed around the premises they requested permission to search. This privilege was accorded them, and nothing was found in the first house. A second cabin stood near by, but this Antonio claimed belonged to his brother, who was then out hunting horses, and he would not allow anyone to go into it until his brother returned. Bargman however, pried the door open and found plenty of evidence to substantiate his suspicion that the parties were the men wanted. Several Mexicans were at the first cabin when the officers arrived, but they began to disappear one at a time, going up the canyon, with picks, axes, etc., pretending to be going to work. As Bargman emerged from the second cabin, the only remaining one, Antonio Baca was racing lively for the timber. Bargman called for him to stop and fired several shots into the air to attract his attention, but Antonio kept going. Mr. Mossman had in the meantime mounted his horse and started after him. He caught him among a pile of rocks on the other side of a little knoll. In a few minutes Bargman appeared on the scene, and they noticed a Mexican coming from the opposite direction towards them. Bargman halted him, but he still advanced. Behind a fallen pine tree he picked up a Winchester which had been placed there by their companions. He still advanced towards Bargman and Mossman keeping in line of a large pine tree between him and the officers. On reaching the tree he fired once at Bargman and once at Mossman, but missed them. Bargman then began to move in a circle so as to make him expose himself to Mossman. The scoundrel discovered this move and struck across a small open space, and disappeared among the rocks, firing two shots at Bargman as he ran, and Bargman returned the compliment, both missing. They then took the prisoner which Mossman had in the meantime been guarding, to camp. In the evening they again invaded the premises and captured Jose Chavez. The next morning they advanced to the premises again, having tied Antonio Baca on a horse and making him ride up to the premises, calling to the others to come out, as they did. Bargman and Mossman covered them with their rifles. They captured three more, making five in all. They took the prisoners before Justice Neils Peterson of Pinedale who bound them over in $1000 bail to await the action of the grand jury in default of which they were taken to Holbrook and placed in jail.

Another nervy piece of work has been placed to the credit of Mr. Bargman. Navajo county no doubt possesses the best officers of any place in the west. Sheriff Wattron and Deputy Bargman have both made splendid records, and are fast stamping out lawlessness in the county. Much credit is also due to Mr. Mossman for his untiring efforts in assisting the officers to run down the gangs who have for years made a business of cattle stealing.

———

Before the District Court at Holbrook, presiding Judge Richard E. Sloan found all the defendants guilty, except Jose Chavez, who turned State's evidence, and against whom the indictment was dismissed. Antonio Baca was sentenced to four years, Adolfo Baca three years, Albino Corillo, two years and Mariano Condelaria, eighteen months imprisonment at Yuma.

MOSSMAN—RANGER CAPTAIN

Burt Mossman, now a resident of Bisbee, in the butcher business, and said to be an old time cowpuncher, was last week named by the governor to raise a company of territorial scouts to be known as the Arizona Rangers. This proceeding was made possible by the last legislature in an act creating the company.

When complete the company will consist of the captain, Moss-man, a sergeant, to be appointed by the captain, and ten privates. Their pay is drawn from the territory and is as follows: Captain, $125; sergeant, $75; and privates, $55 per month. All men are supposed to furnish their own horses, but each is allowed $1.50 a day to board himself and horse, in addition to his monthly salary. Arms and ammunition are to be furnished by the territory. With the authority to arrest any criminal they may find, they are given the entire territory to work in. It is probable that the men for the company will be drawn from the border counties.

If the Arizona Rangers do as much for Arizona in ridding it of criminals as the Texas Rangers did for that state, then their creation will go down in history as one important credit mark to the last legislature. The *Bulletin* has long contended that Arizona needed a Ranger company to hunt down and rid the territory of hard characters, who in the past have maintained headquarters within our borders, to our discredit. With a strong Ranger company, composed of determined, brave men, who know the country, and who can, at the expense of the territory follow a trail indefinitely, will soon make of Arizona an unpopular resort for law breakers.

The Bisbee *Review*, published at the home of Captain Moss-man, contained the following, one day last week, concerning the Rangers:

"Mr. Mossman was interviewed last evening by a *Review* reporter and he stated that he had received his appointment and would take steps at once to perfect the organization, having written to a number of men whom he desires to enlist in the company. He will appoint his own sergeant and now expects to have the company organized, equipped and ready for business within thirty days. Mr. Mossman stated that he had been offered the position twice but refused it on both occasions, and it was only at the solicitation of the prominent men of the northern part of the territory, and well known citizens of this section that he finally consented to take the place and perfect the organization. He has already on the list of his proposed company a number of men who are well known in Arizona. When the full list has been completed it will be published, but for the present Mossman deemed it advisable not to mention any names."

The organization of the Ranger service at this time is not an indication that criminals are growing more menacing to law abiding citizens than in the past. On the other hand, crime is less frequent now in Arizona than it ever has been in the past. The Ranger service is organized as a precautionary measure, to carry terror to the hearts of criminals and finally to reduce to a minimum stage robbing, train robbing, border killings and cattle rustling.

—Solomonville *Bulletin*, 1901

EDITOR's NOTE: All was not smooth sailing in the territorial legislature in the final passage of the Ranger bill. Adverse comment was made by Mr. St. Charles of Mohave county, a newspaper man, said to be a well meaning but erratic liberal, and appeared to be against almost any legislation that cost money. He said he had been quite intimately associated with frontier organizations for the destruction of Indians and train robbers, and that he never knew of but one Indian killed by organized effort—the rest had all met death by irregular and unauthorized methods. The chief business of the Ranger, Mr. St. Charles said, was to go camping around the country making coffee.

The inception of the bill may only be deduced from an analysis of its legislative history. A careful search of the newspapers of the day discloses no agitation of the subject, except in a few isolated instances. It was not mentioned in the governor's message. Local newspapers offered no comment on the measure throughout the session, nor following its enactment. The bill was not introduced until March 13, eight days before adjournment—a date so late that ordinarily it would have had no chance of passage. The silence which surrounded its preparation, and the speed and smoothness of its progress indicated a quiet but definite understanding. An analysis of the bill's support indicates that the understanding was concurred in by the stock, mining, and railroad interests, chiefly in Cochise, Pima and Graham counties, joined by members friendly to these interests from other parts of the territory. It must be concluded that it was promoted by a combination of the above named interests. That it was also looked upon with favor by the administration is indicated by the fact that it was supported by every Republican with the exception of Riordan of Coconino county, who was a detached thinker, not politically minded, but as likely to be influenced by the attitude of someone he liked as by any other consideration.

BURT MOSSMAN

(Biography)

Burton C. Mossman, organizer and first captain of the Arizona Rangers, was born April 30, 1867, of Scotch-Irish parentage. When he was six the Mossman's moved from their farm home near Aurora, Illinois, to Lake City, Minnesota. In 1882 the family migrated to New Mexico, where Burt grew up as a cowboy and ranchman. When he was twenty-one he was made foreman of a large cattle spread in New Mexico, but this outfit eventually went out of business due to a prolonged drought.

In 1893, at the age of twenty-six, Mossman arrived in Arizona and went to work as superintendent for Thatcher Bros. and Bloom at their stock range on the Verde in the Bloody Basin area. Four years later, in 1897, he was named superintendent of the great Aztec Land and Cattle Co., commonly known as the Hash Knife outfit, with its range spreading over more than two million acres and with headquarters near the settlements of Holbrook and Winslow in northern Arizona's Navajo county. Mossman began clearing out the cattle rustlers who had been thinning out the herds on the Aztec's vast domain, and with great success, but the drought was taking its toll to such an extent that in 1900, he was ordered to liquidate the last remnants of the Hash Knife herds. This being accomplished, Mossman severed his connection with that firm and decided to go into the cattle business on his own. He talked it over with his good friend Ed Tovrea of Bisbee, and they went into partnership under the name of Tovrea & Mossman Company, and opened retail meat markets along the border at Bisbee, Douglas and Nogales, as well as markets in northern Sonora, Mexico.

In 1901, when the Arizona legislature, through the insistence of the livestock interests, and other organizations, decided to pass a law organizing a company of Rangers, in an effort to combat cattle rustling. Mossman, who had a reputation of clearing the Hash Knife ranges of cattle thieves, was persuaded to aid in the drafting of a bill to be presented to the legislature for action. After the bill was passed and it became law, Governor Oakes Murphy induced Mossman to organize a company. As he knew many good men for that type of work, he began building, a few men at a time, experienced horsemen, trailers, lawmen and men of proven courage, several of them just having returned from active duty in the Spanish-American war. After a year of effort, the Arizona Rangers had already become known throughout the southwest as a very successful organization. During his service as head of the Arizona Rangers, Mossman and his little band of one sergeant and twelve privates engaged in many desperate fights with bandits, mostly cattle rustlers, and virtually broke up large-scale depredations against the cattle herds on the Arizona ranches and ranges.

Mossman sent in his resignation to Governor Alexander Brodie, the newly appointed governor, effective July 1, 1902. He held the office until the end of August as he had a bit of unfinished business to attend to. That was the capture of the ruthless bandit and killer, Augustin Chacon, a project he had been working on for some time and he was about to close in on this man through a ruse he had conceived of and had underway, and which was accomplished in very short order.

This picture of Burton C. Mossman was taken at the Cattleman's Convention in Phoenix, spring 1936
Courtesy of Arizona Republic

United States Marshal Myron H. McCord (former governor of Arizona), had appointed Mossman a deputy United States Marshal which gave him the added power to arrest almost any class of criminal he came in contact with, and which gave him a free hand and proved a great help in the capture of Chacon, who died on the gallows a short time later.

Thomas H. Rynning relieved Mossman as captain of the Rangers on September 1, 1902, and he soon returned to his first love, that of the cattle business. He eventually entered into a business partnership with Colonel William C. Greene, cattleman and mining tycoon, that of a cattle-fattening business. They bought the best cattle they could procure, from many sources, and fattened them for market. This project was successful and lasted through 1909 when Mossman gave it up as he wanted to get back into the cattle business on his own again. This he did and fought depression and drought until finally, in the early 1940's, he suffered from a very severe case of arthritis, and returned to New Mexico where he made his home in Roswell. On the 5th of September, 1956, the brave and courageous Burt (Cap) Mossman, died at his home at the ripe old age of 89. He was buried in Kansas City.

ARIZONA RANGERS REVIEWED

Captain Burt Mossman of the Arizona Rangers stopped in Tucson Sunday en route to his home in Bisbee. Captain Mossman spent Christmas with his parents at Las Cruces, New Mexico.

Speaking of the work accomplished by the Ranger company since it was organized, Captain Mossman said: "The Ranger company is still in its infancy and we have not as yet had the time to show what we are capable of doing. Already we have driven a number of criminals from Arizona and the presence of squads of our company in different parts of Arizona has had the effect of stopping the depredations of outlaws. Our company is patterned after the Texas Rangers and we only wish that the territorial government of New Mexico would organize a Ranger troop to cooperate with us in this work. With their aid we could soon clear both territories of the fugitives from justice who have sought refuge here and continue to carry on their depredations. A New Mexico company would make work in Arizona much more effective.

"The names of the members of the Arizona Ranger company have not been made public, or at least they are not generally known, but they are the bravest and most daring men in the territory. When the appointments were made, they were kept quiet, hoping in this way to make their work more effective. The men are paid $55 per month with an allowance of $45 for expenses. They must patrol the Mexico and New Mexico frontier, follow and arrest criminals and prevent crime whenever possible. When a criminal is arrested by them he must be turned over to the nearest officer, although the Ranger has the same authority as a sheriff of any of the counties. They are in no way connected with the federal government or its officers.

"There are at present fourteen Rangers in active service who work in small squads and are constantly on the lookout for criminals. If at any time it becomes necessary, I am authorized to deputize any number needed to pursue outlaws. It is a common occurrence for settlers to warn outlaws of the approach of the Rangers. A short time ago we recovered a band of stolen cattle that had been driven from New Mexico into Cochise county and when we raided the camp of the villains, we found that they had been warned and made good their escape into Mexico leaving everything behind. We approached their camp in the night and expected to catch them asleep.

"There is a general impression in the east that a Ranger company was organized in Arizona because the territory is a wild and lawless country overrun by outlaws who terrorize the peaceable settlers, burn their homes and murder their families. They believe that the Indian too is an important factor here and that the Rangers still have to contest with them. They think that the train robber still maintains his camp in the mountains and is made a hero.

"The fact of the matter is that life and property in Arizona is safer than in many of the large eastern cities. The Ranger company was organized to prevent cattle stealing and to rid unsettled sections of the territory from the fugitives from justice who find a refuge there. When the long stretches of country that are at present unfrequented, become settled there will be no hiding place for these outlaws, and a Ranger company will no longer be necessary."

—Tucson *Citizen,* 1902

THE BILL SMITH GANG

The Arizona Rangers have had their first big fight. A telegram from St. Johns, the nearest point to the scene of the conflict, gave but a meager report of the affair. The fight occurred on the

Black River in the northern part of Graham county. This wild mountainous country is the headquarters of the notorious Bill Smith gang of outlaws. The Smith boys had been living with their mother there, but were singled out as notoriously bad characters. Captain Mossman of the Rangers was about two hundred miles south at Solomonville at the time of the conflict. He received the news that one of his Rangers, Carlos Tafolla [pronounced Tafoya], and Will Maxwell, a sheriff's deputy and a member of the posse in pursuit of the outlaws, were both killed in the fight. Two of the outlaws were captured, but it is reported that one of them afterwards made his escape. The rest of the gang escaped, headed south. Three Rangers stationed at Naco, on the Mexican border, Grover, Smith and Page, left there at once in an endeavor to intercept the outlaws who were expected to cross the line, coming through the Chiricahua Mountains, into Mexico.

Black River, the place where the fight occurred, was the scene of a similar conflict two years before, when George Scarborough and Jeff Milton, noted law officers, killed an outlaw named Johnson and wounded and finally captured the notorious Bronco Bill, who was wanted for train robbery, and received a life sentence in the New Mexico penitentiary. Scarborough was afterwards shot from ambush in New Mexico. He was the father of young George Scarborough, now a member of the Arizona Rangers.

Captain Mossman left for the Black River country along with four of the Rangers, after a conference was held and a plan of action decided upon for the extermination of a band of outlaws who had for a long time infested the Black River country.

After returning to Bisbee from the fruitless chase in the White Mountain country, Captain Mossman visited Phoenix, the capital city, and told the Phoenix *Republican* that the outlaws were followed till the trail was lost and that he had since learned they escaped into Old Mexico. His story is as follows:

"A few days previous to October 8, 1901, Bill Smith and his two brothers were seen near Springerville traveling south with a bunch of stolen horses. On or about October 6, the younger brother appeared in St. Johns for supplies and before leaving made casual inquiries regarding the whereabouts of Henry Barrett, a prominent cattleman in that vicinity, who has more than once made it warm for the Smith boys.

"When Barrett heard of the return of the horse thieves with stolen horses he organized a posse to go after them. That posse was composed of Henry Barrett, Hank Sharp, Bill Maxwell, Arch Maxwell, and two of the Arizona Rangers company, Duane Hamblin and Carlos Taffola, who had been stationed at St. Johns to try and keep an eye on the movements of the Smith boys, who lived in the White Mountains country.

"The posse knew full well the men they were going after. Bill Smith, the leader, had broken jail at St. Johns three years previous and locked the jailer in his own cell. They were men who would fight and were sure shots.

"The posse left St. Johns, going to Springerville, and there took the trail of the horse thieves. On the afternoon of the 8th the posse overtook the thieves camped on Reservation Creek, in the northern part of Graham county. In the camp at the time was a bloodhound which belonged to Bill Smith, and at the approach of the posse he gave the signal, when the young brother picked up his rifle and ran up the side of the hill. Maxwell and Tafolla opened fire. The younger brother ran back along the hill about forty feet and laid down behind a pine tree. Maxwell called on the other two men in camp, who had made preparations for supper, to surrender. Bill Smith answered back: 'All right. Which way do you want us to come out?' 'Come right out this way,' answered Maxwell. Bill Smith started toward the posse, at the same time dragging his rifle behind him so that it could not be seen. When he had reached a point directly opposite the posse he dropped behind a tree and opened fire on Maxwell and Tafolla, who were the most exposed of the posse. Then the fight became general. Tafolla and Maxwell were both killed. Two of the outlaws received wounds, the bloodhound was shot and the trees on all sides were filled with bullet holes. The fight occurred just about dusk. Darkness came on and the outlaws escaped, leaving their camping outfit, horses, saddles, bridles, and other belongings behind."

Captain Mossman, who was at Solomonville when the fight occurred, with three more Rangers, went to the scene of the fight as soon as notified. For eight days they kept the outlaws afoot in that country. About dawn of the 17th they appeared at the Thomas round-up camp and made the cook get them something to eat.

A few days later they put in an appearance at Hugh McKean's ranch, in Bear valley, and, exhibiting a roll of bills of large denominations, wanted to buy horses and saddles. McKean refused to sell, and the outlaws took the saddles and horses anyway, saying they had been afoot long enough and were being pushed by the Rangers. Bill Smith said he was sorry he had killed Maxwell, but was glad he had killed a Ranger.

When the posse reached the ranch a heavy storm had set in and all sign of the trail was lost, according to Mossman.

————

The Tucson *Citizen* reported that George Scarborough, the daring young Arizona Ranger, came in from Deming, New Mexico. He is the son of George Scarborough, the noted New Mexican law officer who figured in the big fight on Black River about two years previous, with the Smith gang of outlaws and was later shot from ambush by one of this band.

"If necessary," said young Scarborough, "I will devote the rest of my life to the capture of the Smith outlaws, one of whom is the slayer of my father."

Recently Scarborough traced some members of the Smith gang to Almogordo, New Mexico, but there lost track of them. He is a determined fellow and much like his father. When he joined the Arizona Rangers this fall it was considered one of Captain Mossman's best acquisitions. Scarborough was brought up in the saddle and is an excellent marksman. He don't know what fear is and when he succeeds in coming up with the Smith outlaws, a lively scrap can safely be promised.

————

Harry C. Wheeler, who moved up in the Ranger ranks from private to sergeant, then lieutenant and finally captain in March, 1907, was reminiscing at a later date with a Tucson *Citizen* reporter, and gave this graphic account of the Smith gang affair from information he had gathered from Captain Mossman and others connected with the fight and pursuit:

"Bill was a bad man—bad in nearly every sense of the word. He had surrounded himself with a half dozen companions whose records for deviltry ranked second only to that of their notorious leader.

"At one time Bill had been a cowpuncher—presumably an honest one, inasmuch as there had never been any complaint to the contrary. It was while engaged in that occupation that he became well known throughout southwestern New Mexico and northeastern Arizona, and the fact that he subsequently selected those sections in which to carry out his operations of lawlessness speaks better for his utter fearlessness than for his moral terpitude.

"Cowpunchers as a whole are a curious lot. Usually a brave and courageous set of men, they retain a certain element of crude chivalry in their natures that makes of them seeming paradoxes. Sensitive in the extreme and clannish to the end, a trifle will cause them to abandon lifelong records of toil and integrity, but even after having turned their backs upon law and order and their hands against their fellowmen, they will still cling to remnants of the cowboy's code of honor. Thus frequently we find, in some outcast of the plains, a touch of gallantry, a bit of principle or even a strain of honor coursing through the blood and intermingling with the desperation of his lawless nature that compels a sort of respect and even admiration, however reluctant we may be to admit it to ourselves.

"Such a character was Bill Smith. Once an honest cowpuncher, some trivial incident in his life's history transformed him into the most desperate and dangerous, as well as the most successful, of latter day outlaws. An accurate description of the man's deeds and characteristics would make of him, in the eyes of the average romantically inclined maiden, an intensely interesting personage, endowed with the most heroic qualities. Standing six feet in his socks, with a figure slender but straight as an arrow, firm and regular features, black eyes that flashed with fire, and thick, black hair, he was about thirty-five years of age when he went on the 'scout' back in 1900. Whatever his reason for doing so may have been, he succeeded quickly in gathering about him a band of seven other desperate characters, including three brothers, all of whom would have followed him into the jaws of pergatory.

"In the winter of 1901 the counties along the western and southwestern border of New Mexico experienced a series of crimes, attributed to these men, seldom equalled in the history of all our southwestern country. Post offices were robbed continually, and several persons were killed in the commission of these crimes. Small stores were raided, travelers over the country were held up and divested of whatever money they had with them. Their horses were sometimes taken and several who had the temerity to resist were murdered. The operations of the band finally extended to many ranches. So bold did the outlaws become that these raids were frequently made in broad daylight, choice horses were selected, with saddles, and after obtaining everything of value which they could handily carry away the desperadoes, with a parting volley of shots, would ride away unharmed. This was before the Ranger force of New Mexico was organized. [New Mexico Rangers organized in 1905, following the Arizona plan, but officially called New Mexico Mounted Police.]

"So frequent did these depredations become and the murders so numerous, that even in that sparsely settled country the people became aroused and began the formation of vigilance committees. These committees in the course of time brought together several hundred men in a sole and determined effort to rid the country of the lawless band of desperadoes whose crimes had driven them to desperation, and so warm did they keep the trail of Smith and his gang for a time that the latter were forced to cross the border into Arizona and take refuge in the White

Mountains of the Blue river country, then one of the wildest regions in the territory.

"In the meantime the authorities of New Mexico had asked for the assistance of the Arizona Rangers in stamping out the band. Captain Mossman unhesitatingly detailed a group of his Rangers to head off the marauders. He had already stationed Tafolla and Hamblin at St. Johns to get a line on the gang, if possible, before they could get into hiding, and though it was a fifteen days' ride to the point at which they expected to meet up with the outlaws, they started at once on their long and seemingly hopeless journey.

"The Rangers were soon convinced that the gang had gone into retreat in some hiding spot in the White Mountains, but as the mountains were covered with snow and the New Mexico border was still being patrolled by the vigilantes they had some hope that the members of the gang had not been able as yet to leave their retreat. It was with this hope that the little squad of Arizona Rangers, on the sixteenth day of their ride, arrived in the immediate vicinity of what they believed to be the robbers' retreat—a hope that proved not to be unfounded.

"Sixteen days' travel on horses from Bisbee and Douglas, a mountainous region presenting almost insurmountable obstacles to the travelers, snow from two to five feet deep, a forest of tall pine trees, base-shrubbed with tangled undergrowth of nearly every description, with no human habitation within a radius of a hundred miles, the temperature below the freezing point and absolutely without provisions of any sort, medical or otherwise, constituted some of the troubles of that little force of men who were going into the fastnesses of an unknown country to meet a band of the most desperate characters the West has ever produced and engage them in a combat against odds that meant death for someone as certainly as the sun gave light by day. Unable to take pack animals with them, they had not even bedding in which to sleep, and were practically cut off from the outside world, while hunting down a band of men twice their number—men accustomed to the surroundings, esconced behind a warm camp fire, under shelter and abundantly supplied both with provisions of food, clothing and ammunition.

"On the seventh day of October, which was the fourth they had spent in the mountains, Sergeant Campbell aroused himself from a cold and cheerless bed, penetrated for a short distance the gray gloom of dawn in the sombre, silent mountains and dug from the snow the half lifeless forms of three companions. Benumbed, stiffened in every joint, half starved and almost wholly exhausted, they provided their tired horses with such meagre grass as they could uncover. In the meantime the Rangers provided themselves with a scant breakfast of frozen rabbit and mountain grouse they had killed with sticks. Sergeant Campbell had forbidden the use of firearms. Then the plans of the day's campaign was outlined while men and beasts shivered around the little campfire.

"The sergeant and Greenwood, of the Rangers, were to go west and north, while Maxwell, a member of the posse and Ranger Tafolla were to go east and north, all four of them returning about noon to their place of starting and report any clews, if any were found, as to the whereabouts of the members of the gang. Tafolla and Maxwell had plunged through the forest, scanning the ground. In their anxiety to discover some clew to the robbers' retreat, time passed unnoticed, the sun trying vainly to peep through the shadows overhead. Maxwell was leading when he suddenly paused. The crunching of the snow died with the stopping of the horses, and still reverberating through the mountains was heard the dying echoes of a shot. Soon another was heard, then another, and silence reigned. The Ranger well knew the meaning of those rifle shots. They well knew that Campbell or Greenwood would not be guilty of such indiscretion unless in a fight, and three shots, they knew were not enough to indicate a fight. Both of the men pushed their jaded horses to the fullest possible speed toward the direction from which the sound of the shots came, and less than half a mile had been traversed when they came into a newly made trail. They could see that two men and a horse had been there, and the blood dripping from the horse's sides indicating that he was carrying the carcass of some game recently killed.

"There was no longer any doubt in the minds of these men that they had found the trail they were seeking and that Bill Smith and his bandits were to be located at the end of that bloody path. The two men paused for conference. They concluded there was small chance of finding the two other Rangers that night, surrounded as they were by a wilderness in an unknown region and with the shadows of night creeping quickly over them. Then, if they hesitated there was the probability that a snow would fall during the night and cover up those precious tracks. They turned and took up the trail of blood along the mountain's side. The sun was scarcely an hour high when, arriving within 100 yards distance, the Rangers saw a small basin-like dip in the ground surrounded by a ring of great tall pines. On the outer edge of this dip several men were seen talking and aiding the new arrivals in the unpacking of their horse. Quickly dismounting and leading their horses to a cluster of bushes to one side of the trail they tied them and began silently to creep forward toward the little basin. If only those men would remain occupied a few minutes longer the Rangers believed they could reach a point of vantage among half a dozen tall pines within fifty feet of the outlaws.

"Their hopes were never realized. They might have been if it hadn't been for that curious sense of a horse which permits him to discover a stranger present. The animal the outlaws were unpacking suddenly gave a snort, reared and plunged slightly backward, jerking the men with him. It was sufficient. Glancing about them the outlaws discovered the two strangers in the open and wholly unprotected ground a short distance away. With a scurrying of feet mingled with oaths they darted into the protected retreat of their circle in the pines.

"The two parties were now within forty feet of each other, Tafolla and Maxwell standing wholly unprotected by even a shrub, two dark spots against a snowy background of white. The outlaws were invisible except where each exposed a slight portion of his arm from behind the trunk of a great tree, supporting the protruding rifle barrels which were now leveled at the two exposed men. There was silence for a few moments as the two gazed coolly and calmly into the mouths of the seven guns beaded upon them. Maxwell was the first to break the silence. 'Bill Smith,' he said, 'we arrest you in the name of the law and the name of the territory of Arizona, and call upon you and your companions to lay down you arms.'

"By this time standing erect, their bodies straight and motionless, their minds still cool and calm and their voices without a tremor, the utter fearlessness of the two officers, now wholly at the mercy of the outlaws, must have touched anew a spark of that gallantry in the outlaw chief to which we have already referred. In Tafolla he had recognized a former companion of his days on the ranch, where they had worked together upon the range. Calmly he addressed his words to that officer.

" 'Tafolla,' he said, 'we know each other pretty well, I believe. We have ridden the range together in times past in better days than these—better than any which can ever come into my life again. We have spent many an hour of weary toil and hardships together upon the plains and we have enjoyed many pleasures together. I liked you then and I like you still. For your own sake, for the sake of your wife and your babies I would spare you now. I would also spare your companion. Go your way Tafolla. Give me the benefit of one day and I will leave here and never trouble this country again. But, Tafolla, do not attempt to take me, for by God! I will never be taken—neither I nor any member of my party. Your decision must be made immediately for it is getting dark.'

"There was not the slightest deviation in the tone of Tafolla's voice from that used in demanding the surrender of the men when he made reply to the outlaw chief's proposal. If anything he spoke more slowly and more calmly than he did in the first instance.

" 'Bill,' he said, 'friendship between you and me is a thing of the past. As for offering to spare our lives we may thank you for that and no more. For thirty days we've followed you, half starved and frozen, and have endured untold hardships in trailing you here. Now we stand together or fall together. The only request I have to make of you—and I make that for old time's sake—is that if Maxwell and I shall forfeit our lives here you will send to Captain Mossman the news and the manner of our death. Let him know that neither he nor the other members of the force need feel ashamed of the manner in which we laid down our lives on this spot this day. There is no more to be said; Bill. Merely remember that a Ranger is speaking, and command you for the last time to surrender.'

"There was a brief fusillade of shots and all was over. The forms of Ranger Tafolla and Deputy Sheriff Maxwell lay huddled together in the snow. The men had lived long enough to fight their rifles empty, for Smith for some reason perhaps he could not have analyzed himself, evidently strove to spare the men's lives, who so willingly died in trying to take his life. Dead shot that he was, he had placed three bullets in the hat of each man, just above the scalp, hoping, no doubt, that he would frighten the men into retreat without his having to kill them. But finding that he was dealing with men who had no fear of death, and having himself finally received a wound in his foot, he reluctantly lowered the range of his rifle.

"Thus died Maxwell and Tafolla, and none knew the manner of their death for many days. Sergeant Campbell of the Rangers scouted for a week seeking some trace of his lost companions, but without avail, and was finally compelled to give up the search and return to headquarters. Upon reaching Bisbee he was handed a letter from Bill Smith himself, giving an account of the lonely tragedy in the fastness of the White Mountain wilderness, even to the quotes of the conversation."

Immediately after the killing Smith and his band left Arizona for parts unknown although it was thought they had made their way through the Chiricahuas and into Old Mexico. The bodies of Tafolla and Maxwell were subsequently recovered and buried with all honors. The Arizona Legislature in 1903 made an appro-

priation for the relief of Tafolla's widow. The law in substance:
Whereas Carlos Tafolla was a member of the Arizona Rangers
and while in the discharge of his duty in pursuing fugitives from
justice, the Bill Smith gang, in the White Mountains in Apache
county, Arizona, on the 7th day of October, 1901, was killed by
these outlaws; Tafolla died while defending the lives and property of the citizens of Arizona, and that Carlos Tafolla left a
widow and three small children in destitute circumstances. The
sum of six hundred dollars was appropriated for the relief of
Aceana Tafolla to be paid in monthly installments of twenty-
five dollars per month.

The 1905 Legislature passed a similar bill for the amount of
three hundred dollars at twelve and one-half dollars per month.
The 1907 Legislature continued the appropriation for a similar
amount, and the last Territorial Legislature in 1909 appropriated
four hundred and eighty dollars in monthly sums of twenty
dollars, for the relief of the widow.

The Solomonville *Bulletin*, in November 1901, published this
item:

Thursday morning Rangers Bert Grover, Leonard Page, Dick
Stanton and Tom Holland rode into Bisbee on their return from
a two weeks scout along the border, where they had gone under
instructions from Captain Mossman after the fight which occurred
on Black River. This party was camped at Naco at the time they
received the telegram and lost no time getting into the saddle.

Mr. Grover was complaining yesterday of the lack of secrecy
attending the delivery of telegraphic messages. He and Page
were across the line in Naco, Sonora, when the telegram reached
Naco, Arizona, and he stated that at least fifteen people told
him the contents of the telegram before he ever received it.

After leaving Naco on the night of the 11th instant the four
Rangers went in behind the Huachuca Mountains and then followed along the border, going over into New Mexico. They
failed to see any signs of the horse thieves who had the fight on

Black River, but brought back several stray horses which they found, and will return them to their owners in other counties.

The Rangers had everything but a pleasant ride, and were for most of the time in heavy rain storms, and on the mountains they encountered snow.—Bisbee *Review*.

In December 1901, the same newspaper noted editorially:

The effort last week made by Sheriff Parks of this county, and Captain Mossman, of the Rangers, to apprehend the "Smith gang," who have haunts in the Blue and Black river country, while futile, shows that there is a determined effort to rid the territory of lawless characters. The efforts will no doubt be kept up until these characters either leave the territory or are captured. When a man sets his hand and head against the law of a country his time of freedom is short. There never was a criminal who made a reputation as a desperado who did not come to grief. Some of them have continued at large for a long time and committed many murders, but all alike are brought to justice. There is no escape for such characters. The law and the people of the country are against them. They are sure to be hung or meet a violent death.

The Tucson *Star* in late 1901, reported:

For several months past cattle men in the vicinity of the Swisshelm and Chiricahua mountains have been missing a number of head of cattle, and at other times they have run across the dead carcass of an animal on which the brand had been cut away and a part of the beef taken for food.

Captain Mossman was notified of this fact and detailed two of his men, Bert Grover and Leonard Page, to look into the matter. They spent several days in looking over the field and ran across several suspicious-looking individuals in their rounds, but were unable to secure any evidence until Monday, when they caught two men in the act of skinning a beef.

The Rangers had ridden up into Hunt canyon, in the Chirica-huas, when they noticed two men in the act of catching a steer. They secreted themselves near by and watched the outlaws at work. The beef was killed and the brand on the hide cut off and thrown into a clump of bushes, and the men were in the act of cutting off a hind quarter, when they were met by the command of the Rangers, as they stepped out from behind their hiding places.

"Throw up your hands." The men were then placed in irons, the hide with the brand on it was secured and the party then started for the Lutley ranch. The animal killed was the property of the Cummings Cattle company, of which Mr. Lutley is fore-man. The men were held there over night and were brought to Bisbee yesterday and placed in the city jail. William Lutley accompanied the party and signed the complaint in Judge Wil-liams' court. The preliminary examination of the men will be held this afternoon.

The men captured gave their names as James Head and William Williams. When seen by a *Review* reporter, they re-fused to be interviewed. It is the opinion of the Rangers and Mr. Lutley, that the two men arrested are a part of the gang that is operating in that vicinity. It is said that there is a number of men now camped at what is known as Rustlers Park on top of the Chiricahuas, most of them being outlaws of some sort.— Bisbee *Review*.

The *Review* later reported:

The examination of James R. Head and William Williams, charged with killing a steer belonging to the Cummings Cattle company, was held in Judge Williams' court yesterday afternoon. Realizing the strong proof of the Rangers, they did not put up any defense. Each one was fined $300 or given the privilege of staying that many days in the county jail.

According to the territorial laws as revised by the last legis-lature, the crime of killing cattle, obliterating, removing or destroying the brand thereon, is made a misdemeanor, except where value of the animal exceeds $50. The inability to convict in the district court, where the penalty was made a felony, was the cause of this.

The prisoners will be given a few days respite in which to raise the amount before being consigned to the Tombstone jail.— Bisbee *Review.*

The Tucson *Star* had these three items in late November, 1901:

Special Correspondence Bisbee *Review.*

Naco, Nov. 16.—Bert Grover, the well known Ranger, met with an accident last night at the Ranger's camp, at Naco, and is in bed with a bullet wound in his leg. Dick Stanton, the Ranger, abused Tom Holland, of the same company, last night, and Holland, not wishing to raise any disturbance with Stanton, walked off. Bert Grover endeavored to stop the trouble, telling the men to stop or he would arrest the aggressor. Holland went away at once. Stanton then abused Grover, and tried to pull his six-shooter. Leonard Page, of the company, stopped Stanton from shooting. Grover pulled his gun and threw down on Stanton. Stanton made a fight, and then tried to throw a load in his Winchester, but was prevented by Grover, who threw Stanton down and stood over him. Some one struck Grover's hand down and the weapon exploded, the bullet striking Grover's right leg, inflicting a slight wound. Bert will be up again in a day or two.

———

Naco, Nov. 16.—There is a good deal of trouble and excitement here in Naco, owing to the tyrannical and extraordinary action of Tranquilino Cuen, the Mexican cattle inspector, who is seizing cattle owned by the small American cattle men in Sonora. Friday Bob Giles and Joe Rhodes came into Naco complaining that Cuen had seized a number of head owned by them. They begged the Mexican officer to explain why this was done. In this they were supported by some of the best cattle men in the district. The official refused an explanation, blustered and pulled his revolver. Giles and Rhodes were unarmed. The cowboys came over into Naco and were told that they were virtually outlawed by Mexico. Bert Grover, of the Rangers, got into trouble trying to remove them over across the line, and had a tough time of it, getting away free again. The cattle will be driven to Bocachi, many miles south, and penned up. The chance of seeing them again is considered small indeed. The stock are proved the property of the men, the vendors' names, brands and money paid being readily shown.

———

About nine o'clock last evening four members of the company of Arizona Rangers, under command of Bert Grover, saddled their horses at the O.K. stable, and, armed to the teeth, started on a run for Naco.

While here Grover was in conference with Colonel Kosterlitzky, who has been in Bisbee for several days. The Rangers refused to give out any information as to their destination or who they were after, but their cooperation with the colonel tends to show that the Arizona Rangers and the Mexican Rurales are working together in an effort to rid this section of hard characters. At 11 o'clock last night Grover and Colonel Kosterlitzky had a long talk over the telephone. It is known that the Rangers have received appointments as Mexican officers, and are at liberty to cross the line in pursuit of a fugitive at any time and place.— Bisbee *Review*.

BLUE RIVER RAID

Deputy Sheriff John Parks, assisted by several other deputies and four Rangers, arrested Witt Neil, J. Cook, and Joe Roberts on Blue River, about forty miles from Clifton. They were supposed to be a part of the Smith gang of outlaws and are also wanted in Eastern New Mexico for some very grave crimes committed there a few months since. The outlaws were heavily armed, but the plan of capture had been so well arranged that they offered no resistance.

"We think we have George Musgrove and one man," was the reading of a telegram received by Captain Mossman from Clifton from one of the Rangers at that place. They have for some time been stationed at that point, their endeavor to ferret out certain bandits who lurk in that country, and the recent arrests seem to be the result of their efforts.

In speaking of the arrests, Captain Mossman stated that there was little doubt the boys had the right man. Musgrove was one of the leaders of the celebrated Black Jack gang that for years kept the southwest in terror. Some of the noted bandits composing this company were apprehended some time ago, as well as a few having been killed.

He is one of the gang that went into Nogales to hold up the bank, but was unsuccessful. When they rushed out of town they were pursued by a party which later encountered them and a pitched battle ensued, one man being killed on each side. The leader of the party has been at large since, but it is to be hoped that he has at last been rounded up.

—Tucson *Citizen,* 1902

A few days later the *Citizen* continued:

SOLOMONVILLE, Ariz., March 18.—Deputy United States Marshal Reno and J. H. Campbell, assistant United States attorney arrived here last night from Tucson for the purpose of taking charge of Witt Neil, George Cook and Joe Roberts, who were under the charge of the county officers, and securing their transfer to New Mexico. The men refused to waive their right to a hearing before Judge Doan at Florence. Mr. Campbell had hoped to get them to do this, so that they might be held to the grand jury in New Mexico by the court commissioner here, saving the government the expense of the trip to Florence. Mr. Campbell and Mr. Reno, in charge of the outlaws, left this morning for Florence, where the preliminary hearing will be held before Judge Doan.

These outlaws were arrested about a week ago by a posse composed of officers of Graham county and Arizona Rangers. The officers had been informed that the New Mexico band of outlaws, known as the Musgrove gang, had headed for Arizona. Several days before the capture was made, Deputy Sheriff Parks of Clifton, received reliable information to the effect that several heavily-armed and suspicious characters had been seen in the vicinity of the mouth of the Blue River above Clifton. This information was at once transmitted to Sheriff James Parks at Solomonville and to Captain Mossman of the Arizona Rangers at Bisbee. On receiving the word Mossman proceeded to Solomonville, where he and Sheriff Parks held a council of war, after which both went to Clifton and arranged for a posse to go on a raid after the men who had been reported on the Blue.

The posse of officers left Clifton on March 9. It consisted of Deputy Sheriff John Parks of Clifton, Gus Hobbs and H. D. Keppler of Morenci, and Frank Richardson of Solomonville; Rangers Henry Gray, Fred Barefoot and Pollard Pearson; and Dick Boyle, Clyde Barber, Willie Willis, W. B. Trailer and Ed McBride, special officers.

On the first night Witt Neil, one of the men the officers were after, was gathered in at a house near the Blue. Neil was in bed when the officers approached. In the bed with Neil was a 30–40 Winchester, showing that he was ready for business at a moment's notice; but he was given no notice at all, and was compelled to leave his "bride" in bed and surrender. He had a double belt full of cartridges besides forty or fifty more in his pockets. Neil also goes by the name of "Shorty" Daniels.

Three of the posse returned with Neil to Clifton and the next day the remainder of the posse caught two men giving the names of Cook and Joe Roberts. Roberts lives in the vicinity of where the capture was made. Cook and Roberts were rounding up horses on the range and were driving a bunch of about twenty-five when they were discovered at some distance by the officers. The officers divided into two posses and had Cook and Roberts surrounded and facing Winchesters before they knew of their presence.

Cook carried a Winchester and a revolver besides a double belt of cartridges in addition to about a peck of them in sacks. There is little doubt but that Cook and Neil are members of the George Musgrove desperado gang, and they are believed to have been implicated in a robbery of a store in New Mexico and murdering its owner. Both these men were taken to the Solomonville jail to await the coming of the New Mexico officials. A third man, who had been in the vicinity of where the capture was made, was not seen and probably quit the country in a hurry after he learned of the capture of his companions.

Roberts answers the description of a man who robbed the post office at Fort Sumner, New Mexico, on January 27 last. He held up several people and got away with the post office funds.

The *Citizen* had this story the following day:

Assistant United States Attorney Campbell and Deputy Marshal Reno returned last night from Solomonville where the preliminary hearing of George Cook, Witt Neil and Joe Roberts, the bandits arrested on the Blue, was held, Cook and Roberts waived examination and were held to await the grand jury in New Mexico on the charge of robbing the post office at Fort Sumner.

Witt Neil refused at the last moment, to waive examination, and his hearing was set for April 4th. The witnesses will be summoned from New Mexico and both Mr. Reno and Mr. Campbell will return to Solomonville for this hearing.

All three of the outlaws are still in jail at Solomonville. Mr. Campbell will tonight go to Phoenix, where Judge Doan is, to get an order for the removal of Roberts and Cook to New

Mexico. When he gets this order Mr. Reno will take the two bandits to New Mexico.

Mr. Campbell reports that all of the bandits are tough looking characters. Neil and Cook are about twenty-five years old and Roberts is thirty-three; they all maintain their innocence, but the government officials expect to have little trouble in convicting them.

Burt Mossman is now in Solomonville and the Rangers will continue their efforts to break up the band of outlaws who made their headquarters on the Blue and Black rivers. The Rangers are doing excellent service in that country, which has always been considered the most dangerous in Arizona and they have succeeded already in clearing it of most of the outlaws.

The bandits will probably receive stiff sentences if they are convicted in New Mexico. The law provides that anyone convicted of attempting to rob the United States mail shall receive not less than five years and not more than ten years for the first offense and where dangerous weapons are used to threaten the life of the person in charge of the mails the law provides a life sentence. The circumstances in this instance come under the latter case and it is not improbable that the bandits will receive life sentences.

The Bisbee *Review* printed this story in connection with the affair:

The Orient saloon was the scene Saturday of an exciting incident in which the city police and the Rangers mixed things in a lively manner.

A big poker game was in progress in which Ranger Bert Grover, Captain Mossman and several others were participants. The cards were dealt and the pot in one instance amounted to $400. This was won by a gambler employed in the Fish Pond saloon and occasioned a remark from Grover to the effect that the pot was won by unfair means. One word brought on another and Ranger Grover reached for his gun. At this juncture Captain

Mossman attempted to quiet Grover, who was somewhat boister-
ous and flourishing his six-shooter. The city police who were on
duty, Jennings and Harrington, came through the front door of
the Orient just as Captain Mossman and Rangers Grover and
Page entered the enclosure adjoining the cigar case. In the scuffle
that ensued Officers Harrington and Jennings and Rangers Mossman, Grover and Page piled up on the street in front of the
Orient. Harrington secured possession of Grover's gun and placed
him under arrest, walking him to the calaboose and preferring a
charge against him of disturbing the peace.

Later in the afternoon Ranger Page secured the keys to the
jail, from the office of S. K. Williams, and liberated Grover,
riding with him to his home in Tombstone Canyon. This action
on the part of Page caused the city police to swear out a warrant
for his arrest, but up to a late hour last night it remained un-
served as Page was not to be found.

The incident caused considerable excitement around town and
a crowd followed the policeman to jail when the arrest was made.

RANGERS IN TROUBLE

The scrap between Burton C. Mossman, his two Rangers,
Grover and Page, and the police at Bisbee a few days ago, has
created a profound sensation in the camp.

The affair was the outgrowth of a little poker game between
the Rangers and a couple of gamblers in one of the Bisbee resorts.
The stakes were rolling high, and when an unusually large pot
went by the wayside, Ranger Grover insinuated "it was fixed."
Of course there was trouble immediately, and the city police took
a hand. Captain Mossman tried to prevent his officers' arrest.
The whole affair was, to say the least, disgraceful.

From all appearances the Bisbee people are not disposed to
let the matter drop. Arrivals from the camp today declare that

there is a concerted movement on foot to remove Captain Moss-man and his entire force. A petition was passed around the camp last night to this effect, and at least fifty signatures were obtained in no time. When 200 names are secured the petition will be forwarded to Governor Brodie. It is thought that this number will be secured before tomorrow.

The petition reads as follows:

"To the Hon. A. O. Brodie, Governor of Arizona, Phoenix, A. T.: Sir: We, the undersigned citizens of Bisbee do hereby request that you immediately remove from his present position as captain of the Arizona Rangers, the present incumbent, Burton C. Mossman."

The petition then goes on to state that Captain Mossman has been guilty of conduct unbecoming a public officer.

                                        —Tucson *Citizen*, 1902

Two days later the Tucson *Citizen* reported:

Word was received from Phoenix today that Captain Burton C. Mossman had sent in his resignation as captain of the Rangers. The resignation was accepted immediately by the governor and Tom Rynning was appointed to his place.

This course on the part of Captain Mossman may be said to have been forced in view of the recent disgraceful brawl at Bisbee in which he was a prominent participant. The very day after the occurrence a petition, demanding the removal of Captain Mossman was passed around in Bisbee and was signed by at least 200 people. The petition was then forwarded to the governor at Phoenix. The feeling in the camp ran high against Mossman and his men after the saloon fight, as it was said this was not their first offense of the kind.

Captain Mossman is generally conceded to have made a good record, but he has also made many enemies in so doing. He has held the office for a little over a year.

Tom Rynning, the new appointee, is well known in Tucson. He was a resident of this city for years. He was formerly engaged in business here under the firm name of Parsons & Rynning. He left this city to go to the Spanish-American war. Tom became a lieutenant in one of the Arizona companies of Rough Riders, and saw hard service in Cuba. He is well known throughout southern Arizona, and no doubt will make a very efficient officer. His friends in Tucson will be glad to hear of the appointment.

Captain Mossman sent a telegram to the Bisbee *Review* from Solomonville saying that he had forwarded his resignation to the governor in July.

The Tucson *Star* commented:

A telegram was sent to Captain Burt Mossman at Solomonville, asking him for a statement on his attitude regarding the petition asking for his removal. The following telegram was received at the *Review* office:

"Wm. Kelly, Bisbee: My resignation as captain of the Arizona Rangers was tendered Governor Brodie in July and will be accepted probably August 31st."

The Phoenix *Gazette*, in support of Mossman, had this to say:

Captain Burt Mossman, who recently resigned from the command of the Rangers on account of charges of gambling and incompetency brought against him by his enemies, retires to private life with the endorsement of a large number of the most prominent citizens of Bisbee. A testimonial is being circulated in Bisbee for presentation to the governor which testifies to the confidence reposed in him by the signers, to his efficiency as an officer and his good character as a gentleman.

THE CAPTURE OF CHACON

All during Mossman's reign as captain of the Arizona Rangers, the capture of the noted outlaw and killer, Augustin Chacon, had become an obsession with him. Chacon had been the terror of Graham and Cochise counties for years, and although he was under a death sentence, he managed to escape from the clutches of the law on the very eve of his date with destiny, and had eluded capture for almost five years.

Although Captain Mossman had sent his notice of resignation to the governor in July, it was not readily accepted, his last salary check being for the full month of August, 1902. In the meantime he gave of his time and energy in plotting the capture of Chacon, as it had been rumored the bandit was below the border in Mexico.

At his request, Mossman had been named a deputy by United States Marshal McCord, former territorial governor, so that ostensibly he could have more freedom of movement outside the boundaries of Arizona, and particularly in Mexico. The amiable relationship between the Arizona Rangers and the Mexican *Rurales*, a similar organization below the border helped to the extent that, although Colonel Kosterlitzky, a former Russian army man, and head of the *Rurales*, did not aid in the capture of the Mexican-Indian escapee, he did not interfere with the plans of Mossman which were to unfold. He apparently played a hands-off policy.

Mossman sought the assistance of two notorious outlaws, Burt Alvord, who had been a deputy sheriff under Sheriff John Slaughter in Cochise county, and later was town marshal of Willcox. Billy Stiles, who served as Alvord's special deputy, also was a part of the scheme. In fact Mossman put Stiles on the payroll of the Rangers, despite the official criticism which was sure to come from the governor. He had assigned Stiles to the border area. As Alvord and Stiles were close friends and partners in crime, Mossman played a hunch on their cooperation, which in the end proved successful.

The capture of Chacon was the culmination of a deep-laid plan, using Alvord and Stiles, and which was most successfully executed. Burt Alvord later stated that he effected Chacon's capture in Mexico and delivered him to Cap Mossman through Billy Stiles. The promise of an equally divided half of all reward money to go to the two men should they be successful in capturing Chacon.

Word had been received by Mossman by special messenger that Chacon would make a raid on a horse pasture located about seven miles this side of the Mexican line. Mossman and Billy Stiles awaited his coming, but their vigilance was unrewarded. They retired to a nearby ranch, and on the following night were again in their places, close beside the pasture gate. They did not have long to wait, for about midnight a horseman rode into a small canyon nearby, and instead of making a raid on the pasture at night, this night being very dark and cloudy, evidently Chacon decided to wait until daylight. Stiles and Mossman commanded Chacon, in Spanish, to throw up his hands as he approached the pasture gate. Mossman was close beside him when the command was given and had him covered. Stiles was on the other side of Chacon ready to shoot him if he made a move.

Chacon did not get rattled. He had long since learned to hold his nerve in check in face of danger. He looked up into the face of Mossman, his brows contracted slightly, and fixing those sharp, black eyes on his captor, said in Spanish, "Kill me! Why don't you go ahead and kill me! I know you will kill me!"

Captain Mossman assured Chacon that he would not harm him if he would come along peaceably, and then ordered Stiles to disarm him, which was done and Chacon was relieved of a six-shooter and Bowie knife. Saddles were quickly placed on the horses and with Chacon safely handcuffed, Stiles in the lead and Mossman bringing up the rear, the three on horseback started across the country for the nearest railroad station, which was Naco Junction.

Captain Mossman took his charge to Benson and turned him over to Sheriff Parks of Graham county, who was there on his way to Cochise county, having been advised that Chacon would soon be in the hands of the officers. At Benson Chacon was seen by the writer and was allowed to talk to him by Sheriff Parks. The Mexican outlaw, who knew not the meaning of fear, took his capture in a philosophical manner.

"Where are you going, Chacon?" was asked by the reporter.

"I suppose they are taking me to Solomonville," said the outlaw, "and I want them to kill me this time. I prefer death to a term in the penitentiary."

Chacon had broken rapidly in the five years since his escape. His form was bent and his beard tinged with gray. To be hunted like an animal for five years left its mark on the outlaw, and now to be returned to the jail from whence he had escaped from the hangman's noose, five years before.

In the district court at Solomonville, Augustin Chacon was again sentenced to suffer the death penalty, the new execution date set being November 21, 1902. His lawyers set up the plea that the law under which he was convicted had been repealed, which rendered his sentence void. Judge Doan held that the supreme court had already passed on that question, which left him no alternative but to pronounce sentence. Chacon was hanged on the same scaffold that was to be used five years before. It was left standing awaiting his return. His last words were "Adios Todos Amigos," and the trap was sprung. His life had ended.

—Clifton *Copper Era*, a composite, 1902

Captain Thomas H. Rynning, Arizona Rangers

3

THOMAS H. RYNNING

NEW CAPTAIN FOR RANGERS

Governor Brodie yesterday issued a commission to Thomas H. Rynning of Douglas, Arizona, to be captain of the Arizona Rangers, vice Burton Mossman of Bisbee, resigned. In making this appointment recognition is given a deserving and thoroughly competent man to fill a position the laborious duties of which the territory has not become fully acquainted with.

Mr. Rynning was second lieutenant of B troop of the Rough Riders. He was with Roosevelt and Brodie in Cuba, being in all the engagements from the battle of La Guaymas up to the surrender at Santiago. During this campaign he won distinction for gallant and daring deeds and no doubt his record on the battlefield did much, if it was not his entire influence, toward securing his appointment as the Ranger's captain. Mr. Rynning, although a comparatively young man, has been on the frontier all his life. He knows well the geography of the territory, which knowledge

will be of unlimited benefit to him in performing his official
duties.

Mr. Mossman, the retiring captain of the Rangers, and the
band's first leader, has shown how badly needed by the territory
was such an organization. His record, the making of which he
owes considerable to his men, has been a splendid one. His private interests in Bisbee became such that last July he decided
they needed his undivided attention, and his resignation was
tended to the governor.

The sergeant of the Arizona Rangers is appointed by the captain and commissioned by the governor. It is likely this appointment will be made the first of next week.

—Phoenix *Gazette*, 1902

TOM RYNNING

(*Biography*)

Thomas H. Rynning, second captain of the Arizona Ranger
organization, was born in Christiana, Norway in 1866. He came
to the United States when he was two years old. In 1885, as a
mere boy, he enlisted in the U. S. Cavalry in Texas. That was a
period when a cavalryman had something to do. Young Rynning,
under General Phil Sheridan, was in a campaign against the
southern Cheyenne Indians in Indian Territory. Following that
campaign and still as a trooper in the Eighth cavalry, he served
under Lieutenant Samuel Fountain in Arizona against the Chiricahua Apaches in 1885 and 1886. On account of his reliability
he was detailed to carry dispatches out of the Sierra Madre
mountains in Mexico to General George Crook in Arizona. He
was with Leonard Wood at the capture of Geronimo. With his
command he marched to Dakota territory in 1888, which was
the longest ride by cavalry in the world. There they relieved the
famous Seventh cavalry (Custer's old regiment) and pursued

Captain Rynning

Sitting Bull into British Columbia. He was honorably discharged from the army in 1891 with a record of 17 battles against the Indians.

Rynning then went to California and from there he settled in Tucson, Arizona in 1893 where he became a building contractor.

Having failed to see enough trouble in the military, after four years of successful contracting, along came the Spanish-American war and he could not resist the temptation to enlist with Roosevelt's Rough Riders. He went in as a private, was promoted to sergeant and left as a second lieutenant in Troop B. He went to Cuba with Colonels Theodore Roosevelt and Leonard Wood.

It is not generally known that an exceptional responsibility fell to him in the battle of San Juan. Just before the advance up Kettle hill, when the Rough Riders were deployed in loose formation and impatiently lying in the grass and brush under galling fire, an officer of the regulars passing alone the lines went up to Lieut. Rynning and stated that Capt. "Bucky" O'Neill had just been killed and ordered Rynning to take charge of that section of the line. Just at that moment there was a spontaneous decision of the Rough Riders, officers and enlisted men alike, that they would not await orders where they were but would advance. Under Rynning the charge up Kettle hill began and was carried out with great success. With an enlisted man, Rynning was the first to reach the summit of the hill, and mounting a great overturned sugar kettle (which gave its name to the hill) directed the enlisted men to hold aloft the Rough Rider regimental flag as a rallying point; and it was while the two were standing on that kettle that the famous flag [which now rests in the museum of the Department of Library and Archives in the state capitol building in Phoenix] was riddled with bullets. Following the rally on Kettle hill the Rough Riders and the regulars on each side of them pressed on to victory at the summit of San Juan hill.

Upon his return from the service he resided in Safford and also in Tucson, engaging again in the contracting business.

In 1902, when Alexander O. Brodie, who was a lieut. Colonel with the Rough Riders, was elevated to the governorship of the Territory of Arizona, Tom Rynning was appointed captain of the Arizona Rangers, succeeding Burt Mossman, resigned. At that time he was residing in Douglas, Arizona, and upon taking charge of the Rangers, moved the headquarters from Bisbee to Douglas. Under his leadership the Rangers became widely known for their handling of strikes in the Bisbee and Morenci areas. In 1906 a copper strike in Cananea, Mexico, where Americans as well as Mexicans were employed as miners at Colonel William C. Greene's copper mines there, brought on a bitter conflict between factions over wages. Volunteers were called in and Captain Rynning headed a force of volunteers from the Bisbee-Douglas-Naco area, and as private citizens, put down the rioting and bloodshed with the aid of the Mexican *Rurales* under the leadership of Colonel Emilio Kosterlitzky.

In 1907 Rynning was appointed warden of the territorial prison at Florence, Harry Wheeler succeeding him as the third and last captain of the Arizona Rangers. Rynning supervised the new penitentiary's construction with the aid of convicts brought there from the old territorial prison at Yuma which was being abandoned. He held that post until statehood in 1912, when a Democratic regime took over, but in 1921, when the Republicans came into power again, Rynning was again named to his old job as superintendent of the state prison.

Rynning went to San Diego, California, after his first term as warden at the Florence prison had ended, and was commissioned as deputy United States marshal for the San Diego division in 1934. He also served as an undersheriff there. Tom Rynning died in San Diego June 18, 1941, at the age of 75, and was buried at Fort Roscrans cemetery in that city.

KILLING AT DOUGLAS

A shooting affray occurred at Douglas Sunday night which resulted in the death of one man and the serious wounding of another when Ranger W. W. Webb shot and instantly killed Lorenzo Bass in the "Cowboy" saloon. The coroner's jury decided that the deed was justifiable homicide and exonerated Webb.

The bullet which killed Bass by penetrating his heart, passed through his body and lodged in the abdomen of Ranger Mc-Donald. The physicians in attendance reported that McDonald's chance for recovery was good.

The killing of Bass is considered to have been provoked by him. According to the evidence he made an assault upon Webb with a revolver, and was shot dead instantly before he could make another move. McDonald took no part in the trouble, and was standing near when the trouble took place.

Webb and McDonald entered the saloon together. They stepped up to the bar and were about to take a drink when Bass, who dealt Monte in the place, ordered them to leave. This the men refused to do, and Bass stepping up to Webb, struck him on the side of the face with the butt end of a revolver. Before Bass could make another move he was shot through the heart and was a dead man. The move by Webb was too quick for him and this is believed to be the reason why Bass did not kill the Ranger. It is currently reported that he had made threats to kill Webb on sight.

Bass was between Webb and McDonald when the shot was fired. After passing through his heart the bullet struck McDonald about the waist line and went upward. He fell to the floor, telling Webb to give any of the others the same kind of a dose, if they made any breaks.

––––––

Additional details of the killing of a man at Douglas by Ranger Webb were received at the office of the governor in an official report by Captain Rynning. There is a disreputable street in Douglas known as Sixth street. There was a disturbance on that street and a deputy constable asked Webb to accompany him to make an arrest. They arrested two men and took them away. Soon after that some shooting was heard in that neighborhood and Ranger Webb and the deputy constable went back to see what was going on. On his way back Webb met three other Rangers, Barefoot, Peterson and McDonald, who had just re-

turned from a long trip. They went together into the Cowboy
saloon and dance hall. The proprietor, Lon Bass, who Captain
Rynning says was one of the toughest men he ever met, came up
to Webb and said something about the Rangers coming into his
place without being called. He swore that they could not make
trouble there and his language was very abusive.

Captain Rynning said he had ascertained that Bass drew his
gun, when Webb quick as a flash fired and shot him through the
heart and before he fell shot him in the side. The people of that
street, the captain said, have an animosity against all officers as
he knows by personal experience, having once gone there himself
to put down a disturbance. At the time of the killing all of the
Rangers were perfectly sober. The captain says that there is a
clique of cow thieves along the border and that they stand in
with the lowest divekeepers.

As soon as the killing occurred Webb was turned over to
Constable Dayton Graham [former Ranger] and as there is no
convenient jail there a couple of Rangers were appointed to
guard him. At the time the report was made up a coroner's
inquest was in progress. Captain Rynning believes there will be
no trouble in clearing Webb.

The story of the shooting as gleaned from travelers who arrived here from the south is noticeably different, though it in no
way reflects on the Rangers. The story is that two or three weeks
ago Ranger Webb and saloonkeeper Bass had some trouble but
later patched it up and spoke pleasantly. On the day of the
shooting Captain Rynning and Rangers Webb, McDonald and
Peterson arrested the two men referred to above, in the saloon,
but that when the second disturbance occurred only Rangers
Webb and McDonald went to the saloon to investigate.

As they approached the bar Bass stepped from behind and hit
Webb with the butt of his revolver, whereupon Webb shot him
twice, one bullet going through his heart and the other lodging
in his body. During the shooting a bullet passed through the right
lung of Ranger McDonald and lodged between the lung and the
surface. Though it had been probed for, it had not been recovered

at last account, and Ranger McDonald's recovery was considered very doubtful.

Bass was known as a desperate man and one who bore the scars of many battles. The pitiable thing in connection with the incident is that Bass leaves several orphan children, Mrs. Bass having died some time ago.

The Tombstone *Prospector* had this item:

Ranger Webb was brought over to Tombstone by Sheriff Lewis and Captain Rynning and placed in the county jail where he will be held until Friday the 13th, when he will be taken back to Douglas and given a preliminary hearing. After the coroner's jury had exonerated Webb he was immediately arrested by the officers on a charge of murder and will be given a hearing. In conversation regarding the case Captain Rynning stated that "Webb had to kill Bass or be killed himself," and added, "He is just as anxious as anyone to have an examination held so that he could be cleared of the matter."

Bass had a gun when he came at Webb, and from his actions it was plain he meant to fire. Bass' friends say that Webb will have a hard time clearing himself of the charge of murder, while Webb himself says the shooting was purely self-defense. McDonald's wound which was at first considered fatal, has proved otherwise and the chances for his recovery pronounced very good.

The interesting question is, who shot McDonald? It is thought by some that an employe of the saloon shot him while the other shooting was going on and others hold to the theory that the bullet that passed through Bass entered the body of McDonald.

The Bisbee *Review* later wrote:

When the preliminary examination adjourned, the prosecution had not finished presenting its witnesses. The testimony was strongly against Webb, several of the witnesses stating that the killing of Bass was unprovoked. The strongest testimony was that of Al White, who is employed at the Copper Queen smelter at Douglas, and was present in the Cowboys' Home saloon when the shooting took place.

When the examination closed the outlook for Webb was dark. If the testimony is to be believed he did wrong in killing Bass. The Rangers were not downhearted at the outlook, and say that Webb will not be bound over to the grand jury.

Yesterday the testimony of A. L. White, John Wilton, E. L. Mattix, John Swords, Alex Gilchrist and James Goode were heard. The last two testified that they were drunk when the shooting took place, and are unable to throw any light on the affair.

The only exciting incident of the day was the removal of C. F. Nichols, who acted as stenographer at the coroner's inquest. His place was filled by W. C. Ferguson, formerly of Bisbee, at the request of Attorney English who alleged that Nichols had not taken the testimony verbatim at the inquest.

The testimony of John Swords was even more positive than that he gave at the inquest. He stated under oath that Webb shot without cause. The witness stated that he was in the saloon when Webb and Bass entered. Webb had some words with Bass and then placed a revolver against his side and fired. He fired another shortly after. About four minutes before a shot was fired in the saloon, he stated that he saw Bass make no move as if to injure Webb. He stated that the wound on Webb's cheek was the result of a glass being thrown by one of the girls in the saloon. He swore that he did not see a gun in the hands of Bass.

A. L. White testified that Ranger Barefoot was quarreling with the bartender in the saloon, when Bass entered the front door and wanted to know what the trouble was. He stated that Webb then drew a revolver and shot Bass in the stomach. He fell to the floor exclaiming, "Oh, my God!" Just before the shooting Webb asked Bass what he was going to do, and the latter replied that he would beat the face off him and put him out. The witness was certain that Bass had no gun in his hand. He said one of the women threw a glass at Webb.

John Wilton testified that Bass entered the saloon, and told Webb to "cut it out" and that he would "punch him." Then Webb shot twice and killed him. Wilton was positive that he saw no gun in the hands of Bass and that he did not strike Webb.

E. L. Mattix, who is a miner, was in the saloon when the shooting took place. He said that Bass entered the front door, and asked Webb what was the trouble. Words passed between the two men, and then Webb shot and while Bass was falling he fired the second shot. Like the others he did not see any gun in the hands of Bass.

The courtroom was crowded to the doors during the examination of witnesses. At the request of the defense, all witnesses were excluded from the courtroom while the others were giving their testimony. This is done to prevent any collusion.

Incidently, the fire at Douglas yesterday morning which destroyed the saloon in which the killing occurred, destroys all evidence of a material nature with reference to the assertion that Webb fired a shot into the floor a few minutes before he killed Bass. Outside of this it will have little bearing on the issues of the case owing to the prosecution and defense having witnesses at their disposal who can testify to the condition of things in the saloon, just before and after the shooting was done.

Regarding the fire at Douglas, the Bisbee *Review* reported:

The Copper Belt theatre, Cowboys' Home saloon and restaurant, adjoining the theatre, were completely destroyed by fire Friday. As far as can be ascertained the fire was the outcome of a quarrel between a Mexican prostitute and her lover, who lived in a back room of the Cowboys' Home. During the quarrel the woman threw a lamp at the man. It struck the wall, broke, and set the place on fire. The house being a light frame structure, lined with cloth and papered, the fire spread with great rapidity to a small shack adjoining, occupied as a restaurant; all were soon in flames.

The Cowboys' Home was owned by a man named Coats. It and all the contents were a total loss. This is the saloon in which Lorenzo Bass was killed. The Copper Belt theatre was owned by J. O. Philips. He saved his piano, cash register, cigars and liquors, but all the fixtures were a total loss.

It is not known why, but for some minutes after the hose was attached to the hydrant there was no water with which to fight the fire. Some say it was fully twenty minutes before the water came on in sufficient force with which to fight the fire.

———

EDITOR'S NOTE: The Webb case came to trial after numerous delays, during the district court proceedings at Tombstone, and after a four-day trial, the jury returned a verdict of not guilty and Ranger Webb was discharged and surities on bond released.

Webb was honorably discharged from the Ranger service at the expiration of his one-year enlistment, September 18, 1903. At the bottom of his certificate of discharge Captain Rynning wrote: "Excellent service, honest and faithful. A fearless and reliable officer."

———

MORE RANGERS

The legislature, in 1903, passed a law doubling the number of the Arizona Rangers. It has been claimed that during the last two years it was possible for the Rangers to cover only a limited portion of the territory, because of the small number provided by the original law. The new act doubles the force, and we hope to see the efficiency of the force more than doubled as a result.

One of the results of the Ranger force is to relieve the counties of the territory of much of the expense of hunting down criminals and bringing them to justice, and especially should this relief be desirable in the border counties, where hard characters are most likely to put in an appearance and make trouble.

The Rangers can accomplish much and be more powerful for good, in our opinion, when they work in harmony and in conjunction with the sheriff's office in the various counties of the territory. This has not been done to a great extent lately; on the other hand there seems to have grown up a kind of jealous rivalry between the sheriffs and the Rangers. We hope now that the Rangers have been increased in number, that a new policy will be adopted, and that Captain Rynning will seek to do his work in harmony with the various sheriffs of the territory. The Rangers could be stationed in the several counties, with instructions to hold themselves in readiness to give assistance to the sheriff. This would save much expense to the counties, and the sheriffs could have an equipped force at the expense of the territory.

The doubling of the Ranger force in Arizona we believe will cause cattle rustlers and other hard characters to steer clear of this section, and if this proves to be the result, then the legislature has done well. We believe the Rangers have been a benefit to the territory, and we hope to see the company grow in efficiency until the last cattle thief has been driven out. But the Rangers are by no means entitled to the credit for the good work that has been done by the sheriffs of Cochise and Graham counties in rounding up many hard cases during the past two years in this part of the territory. Sheriffs Lewis and Parks have both been active, and have accomplished much, and they deserve the praise due when duty is well done.

Now that we have an adequate Ranger force, let it be used to the best advantage, and in our opinion harmonious work with the sheriffs of Arizona will be the best plan to adopt. (Editorial)

—Solomonville *Bulletin,* 1903

Badges (photo is actual size) were of solid silver and lettered in blue enamel with engravings etched in blue. Captain's, Lieutenant's, and four sergeants' badges had rank in blue above the word Arizona; badges worn by privates had numbers, one to twenty. In addition, each man carried a warrant of authority and commissions were issued to the officers.

EDITOR'S NOTE: According to the bill there will be twenty privates, four sergeants, a lieutenant and captain on the force. This is an increase of eight privates and four sergeants. The new salary scale for the force is as follows, one of the provisions being that they own and keep their own horses: captain, $175; lieutenant, $135; sergeants, $110; privates, $100. The captain and lieutenants are allowed to ride on the trains free of charge. The remainder of the force must make their moves on horseback.

An added feature of the new law was to the effect that the captain shall provide and issue to each Ranger a badge, uniform in size and shape, with the words "Arizona Ranger" inscribed thereon in plain and legible letters, which badge shall be returned to the captain upon the said Ranger going out of the service.

Arizona Ranger force at Morenci riot, 1903, the only time entire force, except one man, was called out in an emergency.

MORENCI RIOT

The trouble in Graham county resulting from the putting into operation of Arizona's new eight hour law [1903] has finally reached a stage of contest for supremacy between the properly constituted authorities and the disorderly element among the 3,500 striking miners, mostly Mexicans and Italians, at Clifton, Morenci and Metcalf, a trio of mining towns closely clustered in the area.

The Clifton *Copper Era* stated:

For the past week the strike situation at Morenci has been most critical. There were from twelve to fifteen hundred of the

miners, mostly well armed who practically had control of the camp and compelled the companies to close their mines and cease to operate their tramways. Last week Sheriff Parks arrived on the scene with a large number of deputies from the valley, and swore in others until he had sixty men under him. Then twenty-four Rangers arrived, but this force was inadequate to cope with the strikers, who had stationed themselves on the surrounding hills, and by their long range rifles commanded the situation. At one time they had it in their power to capture or kill all the deputies and Rangers, as they were surrounded by twelve hundred armed miners, who jeered the officers and laughed at them, then defied them to advance further. A battle which meant the extermination of the officers, as well as death to many strikers was averted only by the coolness and good judgement of Sheriff Parks, his deputies and the Rangers. Had a gun been fired accidently on either side, there would have been an awful slaughter. It would have been a fight to the finish, because a braver or better lot of officers was perhaps never before assembled in one group than those under Sheriff Parks, and Captain Rynning of the Ranger force, but it would have been of short duration, as the strikers were fifteen to one. Sheriff Parks ordered a halt, and then a retreat, which was accomplished without provoking the fire of the strikers. It was a most trying and critical moment, and had not all of the officers used good judgment a struggle would have been commenced which would have been prolonged for many weeks at the expense of hundreds of lives and the destruction of millions of dollars worth of property.

On Tuesday night the entire Arizona National Guard, 230 men under command of Colonel James H. McClintock, Adjutant General, arrived on the scene, and on Wednesday morning a number of leaders were arrested and placed in confinement, and many of the strikers disarmed. A search was made of all the houses for arms and cartridges, and some were found and confiscated, but it is not thought that the miners were disarmed by any means, as it is known that many of them have cached their arms in the hills.

Last night 280 troops from Forts Grant and Huachuca arrived and tonight as many more are expected from Texas, in all making more than 800 regulars and militia at the scene of the trouble. The deputy sheriffs at Morenci will now doubtless be withdrawn from Morenci and placed at Clifton and Metcalf, where it is possible their services may be needed later.

At one period Deputies Thompson, Birchfield, Epley and Phillips were surrounded by several hundred strikers, and told to deliver up their arms. The deputies dropped on their knees, threw cartridges into their Winchesters and told the strikers to come and get them. The strikers made no further demonstration, and the officers were allowed to depart in good order.

All the citizens of Morenci speak in the highest terms of praise of the deportment, conduct and judgment exercised by Sheriff Parks, when for more than a week with a mere handful of deputies he was able to protect the lives and property of the citizens of the community.

In the same issue of the *Copper Era* was this comment:

Just as the *Era* goes to press it is learned that the striking miners at Morenci have agreed to resume work at the terms originally offered by the company, nine hours' pay for eight hours' work. It is supposed the Metcalf miners will agree to the same terms.

A special dispatch to the Tucson *Star* is as follows:

Clifton, Arizona, June 12, 1903.—Col. J. H. McClintock disarmed the strikers here yesterday. Today the strikers have agreed to accept the company's terms. The strike is therefore now over. Sheriff Parks and his deputies and Captain Rynning with the Arizona Rangers have shown fine generalship throughout this trouble and to them is largely due the credit of averting bloodshed.

JAMES COLQUHOUN

General Sup't. Arizona Copper Co.

EDITOR'S NOTE: Although no mention was found in the newspapers as to any possible effects the unprecedented flood which swept through the Clifton area had on the sudden settlement of the strike and the end of hostilities, it seems there is a possibility it may have, as in the same issue of the *Copper Era* was this startling headline:

Unprecedented Disaster Wreck Devastation and Death Caused By a Cloud Burst in Chase Canyon. Loss of Life from Twenty to Thirty Persons—Only Seven Bodies Recovered—Many Homeless and Much Damage Done—Hundreds of Men Cleaning Up the Wreckage and Streets.

The old saying that "misfortunes never come singly" has again been verified. When the strike situation had reached an acute stage and an armed conflict between the officers of the law and the strikers was momentarily expected, Clifton was visited by the most disasterous flood in its history, sweeping into eternity a score of human beings and causing untold property losses.

In the middle of Tuesday afternoon ominous clouds were seen hovering over the mountains from the New England camp to Morenci, and it was evident that heavy rain was falling. Telephone messages were received from the Longfellow mine and Metcalf to look out for floods, and word was sent up Chase creek, inhabited mostly by Mexican families, and where the principal part of the town of Clifton is located, warning the people to that effect. But few people realized the danger, and but little attention was paid to the warning.

Then the storm broke loose in Clifton, the rain falling in sheets, as if spilled from a mighty reservoir, accompanied by hail as large as walnuts, propelled with force as if shot from a gatling gun. The people ran for shelter to their homes and stores.

In an incredible short space of time a terrifying roar of angry, washing waters, which drove terror to the hearts of those who realized its import, was heard above the roar of the rain and hail and the deafening peals of continuous thunder and lightning, which fairly rent the hills, and reverberated from crag to crag of the narrow canyon which confines the limits of the town.

The flood waters struck the upper end of the town with a breast of from six to eight feet, carrying houses, horses, wagons and human beings on to the Frisco*river with a speed and fury indescribable.

Not until then, when too late, did the people realize their great danger. It might therefore be said that the flood came without warning, as in fact it did to most people. Houses were picked up and jammed against others only to break into a thousand pieces,

* San Francisco river was commonly called Frisco river by the locals.

carrying their helpless occupants for a few hundred feet, when they sank beneath the murky waters never to be seen alive again. In a few moments the happy and prosperous town of Chase creek was partially almost wiped from existence. The scenes of terror as witnessed by many who were fortunate enough to be in the brick buildings, or who had made their escape and were clinging to the rugged sides of the mountains, were indescribable and can never be blotted from the tablets of memory.

Wreckage and debris would pile against a building or block up the narrow street, causing the water to pile up until its force swept everything before it crushing strong buildings, like egg shells, and hurling the debris with still greater violence against another building, which, like its neighbor could not withstand the force of the compact and was lifted from its foundation, and dashed into fragments in a few seconds. And so it continued from the upper end of the town of Chase creek to the Frisco river, a distance of probably a mile. How anyone who was on the creek side of the town escaped is a miracle, but hundreds did escape, many of them being mangled and bruised from head to foot. Had this storm occurred in the night time the loss of life would have been appalling.

Within a few moments the worst was over, but the flood lasted for an hour before it commenced to recede and it was a considerable time after that before any material assistance could be rendered to those whose lives were imperiled in buildings wrecked but still standing.

Owing to the strike hundreds of men were in idleness and on the streets, but insofar as being able to render assistance was concerned, they might as well have been a thousand miles away.

The Douglas *Dispatch* in 1905 carried a story from Phoenix, saying:

Seven of the Morenci rioters were released from the territorial prison last week on the expiration of their two-year terms. One of them, the leader, Three Fingered Jack, sentenced at the same time, was not of the number. It will be remembered that he took part in the last attempted prison break and was sentenced to a term of ten years.

The Morenci strike following the eight hour law which went into effect on June 1, 1903, was succeeded by a riot which was put down by the National Guard, the Arizona Rangers, and the United States troops in July. Several of the more prominent of the rioters were arrested and tried in the court of Graham county the following fall. Eight of them were convicted and sent to Yuma prison. One of the number was an Italian and a member of the Mafia, from which organization he received $5 per week during his imprisonment. He had accumulated about $90 at the time of the release of himself and his companions. They celebrated their freedom by a drunk which has been given a place in the annals of the town of Yuma. Two of the released went to Tucson, two went to Phoenix, and the other three went to the Pacific coast.

JEFF KIDDER IN TROUBLE

Ranger Jeff Kidder, who some time since was doing duty in this section, but recently transferred to the southern portion of the territory, seems to be trying to make a reputation for himself as a bad man, judging from the following from the Bisbee *Review* of July 6:

"Who sent this Ranger in here with his pistol to beat up men on the streets of Bisbee? What provocation is there for inflicting a man with the methods of a thug, bully and butcher upon a community that has the reputation of being peaceful to a degree, excelled by no camp on earth? Is the reputation of a member of the Ranger force to be made and maintained by the muzzle end of a .45 in the hands of a hot-headed man wearing a star? Who gave this man Kidder, wearing an Arizona Ranger badge, the extraordinary powers warranting him to cut men's heads open with the butt end of a .45? Why are not our own officers ample to care for the peace of this community? They have taken care of it in the past; they are still able to do so without the savage assaults of a murderous mind, stimulated with the idea that he's the whole cheese, if he can demonstrate his ability of knocking out men and boys with his ever ready gatling. A sorry affair, indeed, was that on the streets of Bisbee last night. Let the captain of the Rangers come here—fair man as Captain Rynning is, and take this man Kidder out of here, strip him of his star and badge which gives him the authority to 'pack a gun' and use it like a crazy man, unfitted to be an officer by every evidence in the world. The last and most flagrant assault by this man Kidder was made early in the evening, and as far as can be ascertained, and the *Review* man made diligent search for all the facts in the case, was a wicked assault made on a young man named Radebush. He with companion was standing near the front of the Turf saloon, on the sidewalk, and on the curb thereof, when along came the great peace preserver of Arizona, his ever ready shooting iron in his pocket, prepared for business. With a gruff 'You'll have to get off the streets here,' he pushed Radebush off the sidewalk, where he had a perfect right to be. Radebush turned and said: 'Why, what's the matter with our standing here?' This was enough for Mr. Kidder, the big man with the big gun. Arizona had been deadly insulted by a common miner— a peaceful young fellow who works for the Calumet and Arizona company, a young man who by scores of testimony from such men as Lewis Hunt, Mayor Taylor and others state is a steady, hardworker, without a particle of bad blood in him. This dreadfully insulting remark of Radebush was enough for the dignity of the arsenal packer. Out with his side kick, his .45, he immediately smashed poor Radebush over the face with his deadly weapon and knocked the young man cold. As he fell to the sidewalk his forehead struck the cement walk and was cut open. There he lay unconscious, the third victim of this man strapped with a belt full of cartridges and a long tom gun, a new weapon for slashing men brought into vogue in Bisbee.

"So cowardly, so vicious and so brutal was the unprovoked assault that he (Kidder) was soon surrounded by a thousand men, and cries of 'get a rope,' 'hang him,' 'string him up,' came from a hundred throats, and it required but the leadership of one single solitary man to have swept the other officers from the street and strung Kidder to the first pole they came to. The feelings of the citizens was aroused in a high pitch."

The Douglas *American* of July 7th had the following relative to the trouble gotten into by Kidder:

"Ranger Kidder, charged with beating several people over the head with a six-shooter Tuesday evening while about making an arrest on Main street in Bisbee, was arraigned yesterday in Judge McDonald's court at Bisbee on two charges of assault and one of assault with a deadly weapon. In the first two cases he asked for a change of venue, which was made to Tombstone, and in the third waived examination, being bound over to the grand jury in the sum of $1,600. There is a great deal of feeling over the matter in Bisbee. Strong assertions is made by the men attacked and their friends that the attacks were unprovoked and the work of an officer who exceeded his authority. Rangers here expressed themselves yesterday and today as deeply deploring the affair because of the reflection it cast upon the Rangers as a body and as desiring the matter thoroughly sifted. If Kidder is guilty as public sentiment appears to indicate, they want him to receive the limit of punishment."

The above item, which was reprinted in the Williams *News*, carried the following item two weeks later:

Last Wednesday at Tombstone Ranger Kidder was convicted in the justice court on a charge of assault and battery committed on the person of a man named Fagan in Bisbee on the evening of

July 5th. The jury was out only a short time, when they brought in a verdict of guilty as charged, and the justice imposed a fine of $50.

The case against the Ranger for assault upon Graham was dismissed on account of witnesses of the prosecution not being present. Kidder must answer another charge for assault upon Radebush. This case will come up before the grand jury.

The Tombstone *Prospector*, in November 1904, reporting the district court activities, listed the Territory of Arizona vs. Kidder, plead not guilty. In December this paper noted: Mr. Radebush, a witness in the case of the Territory vs. Jeff Kidder, is in town today. He is one of the parties whom Kidder is charged with having beaten up. In June 1905, the *Prospector* said: The case of the Territory vs. Jeff Kidder, for assault with a deadly weapon has been transferred to Pima county upon the motion of the attorneys for the defendant filing affidavits to the effect that by reason of biased and prejudiced published reports of the case the defendant could not secure a fair and impartial trial in this district. This is the sensational case of alleged assaults made by the officer at Bisbee on July 4th of last year.

————

EDITOR'S NOTE: In checking through various newspapers, no further mention was found in the case. The Douglas *Dispatch* in November 1905 said: Ranger Jeff Kidder, who is stationed at Naco, is in the city to transact official business and to call on friends. He reports everything quiet in the vicinity of Naco.

"WILD WEST" IN TUCSON

"Hands up!" was the command uttered by a masked brave at 11:30 o'clock last night in the Palace saloon, and the seven men who were congregated in the place suddenly realized that the crisp order meant business and that the days of the Wild West were not altogether gone as six of them obligingly filed into the back room at the right of the rear of the saloon and stood there with uplifted paws.

For the seventh man, a carpenter named M. D. Beede, had cut and run for it as soon as the would-be holdup made his appearance. And to that fact Proprietor Kane of the saloon probably owes the fact that he is still in possession of his "bank roll" today.

At the time narrated, Decker, the night bartender, was standing at the end of the bar; Lincoln, the crap dealer, and Johnson, the roulette dealer, were behind their respective games, while Beede, Matt Fayson, a miner, E. O. Smith, one of the city's typos, and the colored porter were variously disposed about the room engaged in conversation.

Suddenly there appeared through the back door a man of ordinary build, dressed in a long, faded coat, blue overalls, a dirty slouch imitation Panama hat, and with a red bandana handkerchief covering his face, through the punched eye-holes of which glittered a pair of restless black orbs.

"Throw up your hands!" was the command of the desperado, "and march into that side room," an order obeyed by everyone except Beede, who was already out of the front door like a flash.

The victims could not help observing, in spite of their rather nervous condition, that the bandit was in an equally nervous state, judging from his repeated jestures to "hold 'em up higher," as he gradually edged toward the coveted crap table money. This he would have reached in a few seconds at the rate he was progressing when suddenly—"crack!" went a pistol shot, followed by two others in rapid succession, and the gentlemen who had been doing the living picture act suddenly got busy dodging bullets, but the seance was very short, for as the smoke cleared away Sergeant Harry Wheeler, of the Arizona Rangers, was seen standing in the front door with a smoking revolver, while the holdup artist lay on the floor with blood flowing from a wound in his head and another in his right breast.

Carpenter Beede had run into Wheeler immediately after making his hurried exit, and thinking the latter was about to go into the saloon, hurriedly ejaculated: "Don't go in there—there is a holdup going on!" to which the Ranger answered: "All right; that's what I'm here for," and cautiously advancing to the saloon door, he opened it and at the instant was descried by the robber, who pointed his big .45 Colt's at him and pulled the trigger, but just a trifle too late, for the Ranger's gun had spoken first and the bullet had grazed the right side of the bandit's head, staggering him and undoubtedly destroying his aim. As it was his bullet whistled harmlessly past the Ranger, who thereupon fired again, this time with better effect, as the ball took effect in the man's right breast, effectually putting him out of business for the time.

As he sank to the floor with a groan the crowd closed in on him, seeing that there was no further danger, and soon Dr. Olcott was called and was on the scene, doing what he could for the man, who was seen to be very badly if not fatally wounded. He was promptly removed to the hospital by the doctor's orders, and at 10:30 a.m. today had very slight chances of recovery. His name was ascertained to be George Anderson, and he came here from Locust Grove, Georgia. Just who he is, or how long he had been here no one seemed to know.

From the evidence of people on the sidewalk during the shooting there was a fourth shot fired, evidently at Mr. Wheeler from across the street, by a confederate of Anderson, although neither Wheeler nor anyone in the saloon could vouch for this. The fact remains, however, that a bullet went by Wheeler which embedded itself in the leg of the roulette table and which, from the line of firing, obviously must have been shot by somebody outside.

Sergeant Wheeler is a small man, but he proved his right to his office thoroughly. "I am sorry that this happened," said he to a *Citizen* reporter this morning, "but it was either his life or mine, and if I hadn't been just a little quicker on the draw than he was I might be in his position now. Under the circumstances, if I had it to do over again I think I would do exactly the same thing." This was said without the slightest air of bravado, and merely as the plain statement of an officer. The sergeant had just arrived from Willcox last night, where he is stationed and was leaving Wanda's restaurant when he met Beede.

Ranger Wheeler telegraphed to Captain Rynning, who was in Benson at the time of the shooting, and who took the first train here. He went out to the hospital this morning in company with a representative of the sheriff's office, in order to secure an ante-mortem statement from the wounded man, in case his injuries should terminate fatally.

In one of the foregoing paragraphs, wherein the names of the occupants of the saloon were mentioned, the name of "Policy Sam" Meadows was inadvertently left out. Sam was there—very much so, according to his version, which is undisputed by others.

It appears that the bartender Decker, thought the matter was a joke at first, or else he is gifted with a superabundance of nerve, for when the bad man first issued his command to elevate the "digits," Decker jokingly held up first one finger and then two, at the same time asking his robberiets if that was enough. But he was soon undeceived as to the man's mission, for that worthy told him to "get a move on" in no uncertain terms, whereat he complied.

At 2 o'clock Dr. Purcell, the county physician, who went out to the hospital to attend the wounded man, reported that his chances for living were practically nil, as he was shot through the right lung as well as in the forehead above the right eye, although the latter wound is not, of course, fatal. The right eye is powder burned, according to the doctor, which supports the theory advanced by some that the man shot himself, but this is scouted by nearly all the eye witnesses of the affray. The Ranger is almost positive that his bullets inflicted both wounds.

Bandit George Anderson finally passed away, breathing his last at 3 a.m. today.

By the time the readers of this paper are glancing over its

columns, the true name of the bandit who was shot last Sunday night by Ranger Wheeler may be known, for the coroner's jury will then have been in session over an hour and the information may have been elicited from some witness. For the present, though, it remains unknown as far as the people are concerned. The story of the dead man whose remains have been viewed all day long as they lay at the Reilly undertaking parlors, is a trifle out of the common with regard to the usual lawbreaker of his class.

A week ago last Friday afternoon a man well dressed in a dark suit, with a derby hat came into the San Augustin hotel and asked proprietor Hall for a room for an indefinite period, particularly wishing a room only, which is contrary to the rules of the house. His request was granted, however, as he occupied the apartment Friday and Saturday nights and was seen in the room early Sunday evening by the domestic, but when the chambermaid went to make up the bed Monday she discovered that the room had not been occupied the night before.

After waiting a day or two, Mr. Hall, thinking at first that in spite of the good appearance of the guest, he had simply been done out of a little rent, took possession of the neat traveling bag left there and locked the door. Subsequently he remembered that the man had spoken of being pestered for money he owed by people outside of this town, and putting two and two together, with the reading of the story of the hold-up and the mysterious bandit's refusal to give his true name, at least as given out, he opened the grip and discovered that its contents consisted of numerous letters, telegrams and documents, in addition to a few articles of clothing.

These documents clearly established the fact that the man was named Walter F. Stanley, and that he was the advance contracting agent for the Independent Carnival company. One of the letters is an introduction from Maynard Gunsul, secretary of the recent Albuquerque fair, in which he commends both the man and the show. Another letter establishes the fact that he recently entered into a contract with Douglas people, including the

Douglas band, for a date for his show there. He had very evidently worked west from Denver, Pueblo and other Colorado points, as the telegrams showed.

When, therefore, the man died yesterday, Mr. Hall promptly reported his knowledge to the authorities and turned over the grip and its contents. The man's wife is evidently in Denver, and there is nothing to indicate that there are any children. There was no money found in the grip and the man probably didn't have any, or else he would have paid for his room in advance.

Now, however, comes the fact that he had evidently made up his mind to commit the crime for which he paid the penalty with his life, for as the readers of this paper will recollect, in the story of the shooting, it was stated that there was undoubtedly a shot fired at Ranger Wheeler from across the street, probably by a confederate.

The night following the shooting a man in a box car of an east bound freight told his brother hobo travelers that he had a wounded partner in Tucson. His information reached the authorities and Ranger Wheeler took up the trail of the confederate and at the time of the bandit's death, was twenty miles east of Lordsburg, New Mexico, hot in pursuit. Then he was wired for by the officials here to come back for the inquest today. Hence he had no choice but to report here, which will probably result in the fellow's escape for good.

As a final chapter, it is known positively that the name Walter F. Stanley was an assumed name. The man came from Locust Grove, Georgia, as has been stated, and it is understood that Undertaker Reilly is in communication with parties there—in fact, he received a wire today from that point, but the contents have not been made public at this writing. They may, of course, be brought out in the evidence before the coroner's jury.

LATER—This afternoon telegrams were received by Mayor Schumacher, and Undertaker Reilly from the father of the dead man, ordering him to be buried here, which will probably be done tomorrow afternoon.

His real name is Joe Bostwick.

—Tucson *Citizen*, 1904

ARIZONA RANGERS

Arizona is by no means the domain of the bad man. The burglar insurance people give lower rates there on bank safes than they do in New York and yet with its vast area, nearly thrice that of New York, policed by twenty-six men, the Arizona Rangers, it would seem to be open to the highwaymen of the country. But the Rangers are doubly efficient. They know the lay of the land. They can track a man with all the skill of the Indian with scant clews through a desert where few desperadoes could find their way.

Captain Rynning, the head of the Ranger force, has his office at Douglas to be near the border, where much of the Ranger work is done. The organization is secret. The men are not generally known, so that they may work in a town without their presence being suspected. Last year they found it necessary to kill but one bad men, and this is certainly a record to be proud of, for they covered 10,140 miles on their ponies and arrested 455 men. For a little army that is doing about as well as the Arizona taxpayer could expect.

Along the Mexican border the Rangers co-operate with the Mexican Gendarmes Fiscales, a body of frontiersmen, skilled Indian fighters, and enemies to desperadoes, headed, strange to say, by a square jawed Russian, Amelio Kosterlitzky, who came to the Mexican border years ago from the Russian army in search of adventure, which was not then to be had at home. He is dreaded by the border scoundrels, for the law in Mexico and its administration gives him plenty of leeway.—Brooklyn (NY) Eagle.

—Douglas *Dispatch,* 1905

TIBURON ISLAND TRAGEDY

Land of mystery and intrigue and home of the primitive Seri Indians. Lure of the adventurous and sometimes doom for those less fortunate in coming back alive from its haunting environs.

The Douglas *Dispatch*, in May of 1905, tells of the return from Tiburon [tē-vōō-rôń] Island, of Arizona Charley and his party after an uneventful trip. He tells of their having no firearms; that their weapons are the primitive bow and arrow and wooden spear. He related that the Seri were expert in spearing fish, which they eat raw; no evidences of cooking or of fire were seen. From the indications, fish was about the only food of the Seris, as there were no signs of agriculture or gardening, nor were there any nut or fruit trees to be seen.

Physically, the Seris were said to be much like the Cocopah Indians in Arizona—strongly built and symmetrical in form, but apparently nothing warlike about them and that it might be possible they were cannibalistic, as is often rumored, but there was no indications of it.

The island itself showed unmistakably that it is of volcanic origin, the surface being generally rough and mountainous, and, though not barren, there is a sparse vegetable growth in a few small valleys. There is a small tree on the island that resembles the sycamore, the largest one noticed being not four inches in diameter.

Tiburon Island is said to contain about 20,000 acres, but it is thought that this estimate was too great, and there is nothing especially attractive or inviting about the place.

———

The Douglas *Dispatch*, later in the month, had this item:

Thomas Grindell and G. Olin Ralls leave this morning for Bisbee, where they are joined by Messrs. Hoffman and Ingraham, and leave Wednesday for Nogales. They leave for Magdalena, Sonora, and spend Friday with Colonel Kosterlitzky, who is assisting them in their trip to the Tiburon Island. He will furnish them with soldiers if they so desire.

From there they leave for Altar, where they buy horses and outfit for the trip. They go first to Libertad and then skirt the coast to Cape Tepapa, where there are ruins of an old monastery of the Seri Indians. They go south from there to a strait about a mile and a half long at low tide and the water is very rough. This is crossed by means of Indian boats called "belsas," being made of pine. From this point they get on land four miles and explore the island. The island is twenty-four miles by twelve miles.

Mr. Grindell visited the savage Seris last year, but found them the most peaceable people on earth. Many of them were so poor that they could hardly navigate and lived on a very plain diet, such as fish and turtles. They do not cook their food and do not use knives, but simply in a very primitive manner tear the food asunder and eat it raw.

The women are supreme in tribal government and the older they are the greater their power. The party will be gone about six weeks and will go into the Yaqui country before returning.

The following month, the *Dispatch* had this item:

Ed P. Grindell arrived in this city Sunday from Cananea. He is very much worried about the continued absence of his brother Tom, superintendent of the Douglas schools, who left with Olin Ralls of the Copper Queen smelter and four others for Tiburon Island in the Gulf of California, at the close of the school year.

The party was to have returned on August 1st, almost a month ago, but no message has as yet been received since they left Guaymas for the island. He says he is almost certain something must have happened to the party to delay their return for so long a time. The Seri Indians who inhabit the island are not especially warlike, but they have no particular love for the white man and the Grindell party may have gotten into straits through their treachery.

———

And later this story:

There were several rumors on the streets yesterday that the bodies of Tom Grindell and the members of his exploring party had been found at the mouth of the Colorado River, the report being brought here by a man who returned from the Altar district yesterday. There is but little doubt here that Grindell and his party have met death either at the hands of treacherous Indians or by drowning, the waters of the gulf being fully as treacherous as the Indians in that section are said to be.

Reports from Nogales state that E. P. Grindell, a brother of the lost explorer, is prosecuting his search, but there is little hope that the party will be found alive. The report of a grewsome find by vaqueros in the employ of a ranchman in the Altar district may lead to some conclusive evidence as to the fate of the explorers.

The Nogales *Oasis* says:

Sunday evening E. P. Grindell came here from Hermosillo, where he had been for several days, en route to Tucson on business; but has since returned and gone to Altar where he will organize a party to go out to the gulf coast and Tiburon Island, to search for the missing exploring party headed by his brother T. F. Grindell, which passed Caborca on the 9th of June, with the intention of going to the island, and has not since been reported, when at the time of departure from Altar the plan was to return to Hermosillo not later than the 15th of August.

At Hermosillo Mr. Grindell was given by Governor Ysabal letters to the prefect in Altar, and a general letter calling upon all to whom presented to afford every attention possible to aid Mr. Grindell in his search. He will outfit at Altar and follow out the trail of the missing party so far as possible.

While in Hermosillo Mr. Grindell met a man who has a cattle ranch near the coast who stated that his vaqueros had reported finding a deserted camping place occupied but shortly previous where there had been left a sheet iron camp stove. Everything belonging to its owners, but that, had been carried away. Upon a stick or post planted in the ground near the stove were nailed four human hands. If upon investigation at Altar it is learned that the missing party took such a stove, the searching party will try to locate the place where it was seen and thoroughly scour the surrounding region for further traces.

The missing men are four in number, T. F. Grindell and Olin Ralls of Douglas, Dave Ingraham of Bisbee and Lieutenant Hoffman, who had a commission in the rough riders. They are all young, active men, well capable of caring for themselves, and has anything untoward occurred to them, it has been through unavoidable accident or treachery.

Magdalena, Sonora, October 16, 1905

Captain Thomas H. Rynning, Douglas:

My Dear Captain: Your esteemed favor dated the 11th instant reached me yesterday morning. I immediately got three men ready to go with your sergeant and as he did not arrive on yesterday's train, I took train for Nogales and no one seems to know when he will return. I returned here this morning and will go again to Nogales this afternoon with the hope of finding your sergeant, as I think not a moment ought to be lost in hunting for the Grindell party. For my part, I am ever ready to be of service to you.

How unfortunate is this affair! If Tom Grindell would have minded and heeded my advice, he would be all right today. When he went on his expedition he and Ralls stayed with me one day. I cautioned them against the trip—that is, the route they intended to take, as I know too well the country. I insisted on them going by way of Guaymas, but all to no avail. Tom was bull-headed about the thing, and it was impossible for me to get him to change his mind. I pictured to him the things as I experienced them once, and for no money in the world will I undertake a like job. Instead of getting Tom to desist, he became more determined.

It was my intention to get my orderly trumpeter to go with them in case the Guaymas route, but I would not permit the trumpeter to join them on the one they took. Before they left Douglas, when Ralls indicated to me the intended trip and outlined the road by letter, I even then advised him not to take this road. I do hope my letters will be found among Ralls' effects at Douglas so that you may see how hard I fought with them to desist.

I am also positive that the poor fellows died for want of water, for after the Papago guides left them they no doubt wandered in a demented state of mind superinduced by thirst, until one by one they gave out and lay down to die; but then as long as their bodies are not found there is hope, and most sincerely do I hope that they will yet turn up sound and well.

EMILIO KOSTERLITZKY.

Douglas, Ariz., October 10.—The following taken from the Nogales *Oasis* is the latest information received from E. P. Grindell, who is heading a searching party for his brother:

There are now indications that the exploring party headed by Thomas Grindell may have been murdered by their guide. E. P. Grindell of Tucson, who is searching for his missing brother and his companions, was in Nogales yesterday. He had been to Altar, where, through the efforts of Antonio Ramirez, presidente of the municipality, he succeeded in finding the Papago Indian guide who left that place with the party last June and later returned without them. The guide told of leaving the party on the coast. He said they found the four hands mentioned by the Mexican cowboy some weeks ago, before he left the party. He also told Mr. Grindell that the missing party intended to go to the Escalantes ranch, about thirty-five miles from the coast, where he left them. He said they had camped one night at a place where there was no water and had turned the horses loose. The horses scattered, and two of the men, with himself, went to find them. The entire day was spent in hunting for the animals. He then left the party and returned to Caborca. He offered to take Mr. Grindell to the place where he left them, telling him the country was dry and sandy and they could find tracks that had been made six months before. Mr. Grindell agreed to take the trail with the Indian, but the night before they were to depart, Arturo Furken of Caborca accosted Mr. Grindell and told him that the man he was to start out with was of shady reputation, and offered to accompany them. When the Indian was told that Mr. Furken would be one of the party, he demurred and did not want to go. Later he agreed to go if he could take two of his brothers with him. He was told that his brothers could go along. Next morning there was no Indian guide to be found. He had secured a fresh horse during the night and fled the country. His flight has caused Mr. Grindell to believe that the man let the horses of the missing party scatter and while the men were separated hunting for them, the guide murdered them one at a time. He also believes that had he gone alone with the guide as he had intended, he would have never returned.

Wednesday Mr. Grindell was in Hermosillo and told his story to Governor Yzabal. The governor said that they would have to get that guide, and assured Mr. Grindell that he would get him. Mr. Grindell has gone to Tucson, where he will remain a few days, while the Mexican authorities are seeking the guide. If they do not find the Papago he will go back to Sonora and employ men to assist him in the search.

Washington, January 5.—The department of state has received a letter from E. P. Grindell, dated from Hermosillo, Mexico, and giving a detailed account of his search for his missing brother, Thomas Grindell and the members of his party. The letter is as follows:

Hermosillo, Sonora, Mex. Dec. 9.

Robert Bacon, Assistant Secretary of State, Washington, D. C.

Sir:—Mr. Hostetter, the American consul here, informed me you have written him regarding four Americans lost in the vicinity of Tiburon Island last July; namely, Thomas Grindell, Olin Ralls, David Ingraham and Jack Hoffman. Mr. Hoffman, however, has since been found, and you no doubt have heard his story. He says the other boys likely perished for want of water.

Now I have been searching for this party since the 5th of September, giving my entire time to the matter, but have failed to find any of them. I have, however, found their trail and have followed it for over one hundred miles, but the recent rains have entirely obliterated their trails. So now I have nothing to work on but the general location. I found the boys' camp deserted. I found four or five animals dead. I trailed Mr. Ralls over forty miles, where he went alone with one mule. A sudden rain forced us to stop following the trail for the day, and next day the trail was gone. But one of the Indians found, about ten miles further on, a dead mule. The mule had the pack saddle still on its back and a rifle and bucket still fastened to the saddle, which led me to believe that Mr. Ralls had fallen between this and the point where I last had his trail. I searched the country thoroughly, but could find no trace of the men.

I had with me five to twelve Papago Indian trailers and one American companion. We searched the entire coast of the mainland in front of Tiburon Island for a distance of one hundred miles, and back into the mountains for from twenty to thirty miles, and I think I have covered every place where bodies might reasonably be expected to be. We rode over eight hundred miles on horseback.

I have given up ever finding the boys, but as a last resort I have offered a reward to the Papago Indians of $200 for each of the bodies they find. It is my opinion that the boys wandered in their frenzied condition away back into the mountains, into places where they never will be found. Everyone here has been very kind to me in the search, especially Louis Hostetter, the American consul. He has been very considerate, and helped me many times. I trust this information will be of value to your department. Very truly,

E. P. GRINDELL.

Yesterday afternoon the *Review* was in receipt of the following telegram from J. A. Naugle, superintendent of the New Mexico & Arizona Railway with headquarters at Guaymas, Sonora. The telegram is the first information received from the exploring party which left Douglas last June, headed by Prof. Thos. Grindell, consisting of five members, for the purpose of exploring Tiburon Island in quest of a gold mine which was reported to be fabulously rich.

Guaymas, Mexico, Oct. 25.

Mr. J. E. Hoffman, who was with Professor Grindell and party, appeared in my office this morning and states that the party became separated near the crossing to Tiburon Island about June 29th, and that he continued along down the coast, arriving here yesterday. He thinks the party has probably perished for want of water and food. He states that the Papago Indian guide was all right. In case it is desired to find them or recover their remains, the party should start from Guaymas by boat. Hoffman offers to accompany the rescue party. He is without funds. Advise us if we can render any assistance from this end.

J. A. NAUGLE.

Upon receipt of the telegram the *Review* immediately called up Thomas Rynning at Douglas, captain of the Rangers, but

Mr. Rynning was in Mexico. Lieut. Hopkins of the Rangers was notified of the contents of the telegram, and he at once notified the Mexican consul at Douglas, who in turn communicated with the Mexican State authorities at Hermosillo and Magdalena. It is expected that when the Mexican officers at Hermosillo learn of the arrival of Hoffman at Guaymas they will immediately send a courier after the rescue party, which left that place on October 17th, traveling in the direction of Caborca and Port Libertad.

In addition a telegram was sent to Mr. Naugle stating that Mr. Hoffman was to be furnished with expense money and to have him wait for the arrival of the rescue party headed by the brother of Professor Grindell.

Almost five months have passed since Thos. Grindell, who last year was the principal of the public schools at Douglas, organized a prospecting party for the purpose of exploring Tiburon Island, off the west coast of Mexico, in quest of a rich gold mine. Mr. Grindell visited the island in 1904, and it was for the purpose of prosecuting his search still further during his summer vacation, that the party was organized the first part of June. After leaving Caborca, a settlement about half way between the railroad and the coast, no trace of the party has been had. They were then on their way to Port Libertad, where they expected to find boats which would afford them transportation to a point opposite the island. Instead, they found Port Libertad deserted, and the party then started down the barren and desert coast on foot. The Papago guide refused to go into the desert and returned, but the intrepid party pushed on south hoping to strike fresh water, and were never heard of since until Mr. Hoffman, of the original party, arrived in Guaymas yesterday after a journey on foot lasting from June 29th.

Judging from the Hoffman story the party became lost and separated, and the possibilities are that he was the only surviving member.

—Bisbee Daily *Review*, 1905

J. E. Hoffman, who is supposed to be the only survivor of the

Grindell expedition, which left here for Tiburon Island last spring, has arrived at Magdalena, according to reports received here, and will accompany the searching expedition headed by Captain Thomas Rynning over the trail taken by the Grindell party. They are expected to leave today for Altar.

Previous to leaving Guaymas for Magdalena, Mr. Hoffman wrote a brief history of his trip to the coast, and it was just received here. The following is the story written for the *Dispatch* by Mr. Hoffman:

"We left Bisbee June 1st for Nogales, where supplies were secured and from there went to Santa Ana, Sonora, by train, where Grindell and Ralls left their surplus baggage; thence by stage to Altar, where we secured more supplies, one horse and a burro; thence to Pitiquito also by stage, where we bought one horse and four burros, with two pack saddles. At Pitiquito we packed our burros and started for Terno Rancho. Before reaching there, however, two dry camps were made and more water was secured at the second camp from a ranch about four miles distant. At Terno Rancho we secured a Papago guide. We then started for Coyote Springs, two or three camps being made on the way, the first one in the mountains, where a fresh supply of water was secured, the last we had.

"Then our hardships began. We were out of water long before reaching Coyote Springs and exceedingly thirsty. We stopped there a few days and then started for Tiburon Island pass, but at Coyote Springs we got the last water we ever had. Before reaching Tiburon pass, where our last camp together was made, we made three camps, one of which we made on account of the intense heat. Before reaching the third camp we were out of water, or rather nearly out, as Grindell and Ralls still had a little in their canteens. Dave Ingraham and myself were completely out, although Dave and I were in good shape. I was about played out and drank seven cups of sea water and two cups of coffee made out of sea water. You know the effects. The next morning I could hardly navigate, with about eight more miles to go to reach Tiburon pass.

"However, I dipped my head, arms and breast in sea water about every half mile or so and felt better right along. The reason that I played out was that I was the packer and the cook and did lots of sweating, although the boys helped all they could.

"We arrived at Tiburon pass, where Grindell and Doc Ralls took the animals and water cans and started to cross. In the meantime I was distilling water and distilled about ten tincups full. Dave and I drank seven. I continued to distill water, Ralls having given up the attempt to cross to the island and having started out for the San Antena Rancho with about half a gallon of water (distilled). He did not return for two days and we were forced to do something, distilling not furnishing water fast enough for three.

We started out for the San Antena Rancho on or about June 28th. We ran across a strong trail and followed it, thinking that it would bring us to the ranch. After traveling twenty or thirty hours the trail proved to be a stock feed and water trail in wet weather. We stayed here in the shade the rest of the day, before starting for anywhere else. Dave and I were played out, but Grindell took the canteens and continued on; this was the last seen of Grindell. We rested all night and started back for the gulf the next morning.

"We found a shady spot to rest on the way back, but there was not shade enough and we were partly in the sun all day. The next night we continued toward the direction of the gulf and traveled two more nights together. We quenched our thirst by chewing the pulp of the water plant (cactus). The fourth night Dave could not go any farther and the fifth night I was forced to leave him, and made the gulf the next morning, weak and exhausted. High tide had covered our former camp and had done considerable damage. I found three or four bunches of matches which were not wet and started to distill water, but it took me all day to get some water.

"Olin Ralls had returned without water, as I found a plate with some fried bacon from which he had taken the grease and mixed it with flour and eaten part. It took me five days to regain strength enough to return to the mountains for Dave. I got out as far as we were or farther, but got so weak had to return without seeing anything of him. Stayed in camp three or four days more and, decided that the only way to save my life was to travel south for Guaymas. I left about July 14th or 15th, taking with me bacon, shotgun, the only gun left, the rifles and six-shooters being left on the desert, flour, baking powder, two pair blankets, *coal oil* and cooking utensils, making two loads.

"It took me until October 24th to reach Guaymas. I had to make detours of twenty or thirty miles around some of the swamps. I had too many troubles in regards to water, food, sore feet, etc., to bother you with.

J. E. HOFFMAN.

After the statement of Hoffman, the Douglas *Dispatch* reported that Governor Kibbey had granted a leave of absence to Captain Tom Rynning and four privates in the Rangers for thirty days to join a search party. Captain Rynning was supposed to start from Nogales with Sergeant Old and privates Stanford, Kidder and Burnett, all of whom go as private parties and not in their official capacity. They will be joined by a squad of men detailed from the Mexican Rurales by Colonel Kosterlitzky, and will leave as soon as possible for Altar, where the trail of the missing party will be taken up.

The next issue of the *Dispatch* reported that the action of Governor Kibbey in giving leave of absence to Captain Rynning and four of his men to join the search for Tom Grindell was very favorably commended on.

RYNNING REPORTS FAILURE

After an unsuccessful attempt to find the missing members of the Grindell expedition to Tiburon Island or to recover the bodies of the three lost Americans, Captain Tom Rynning of the Rangers, who had been petitioned to head the relief party, returned to Douglas yesterday morning. With the exception of finding the decomposing remains of animals used by the party and a portion of their outfit, no trace of Tom Grindell, Dave Ingraham and Olin Ralls was discovered.

Captain Rynning was seen last evening at the Ranger headquarters by a *Dispatch* reporter and gave the following story of his trip:

"The party which was organized at Guaymas to go to the relief of the missing explorers left Guaymas at noon November 2nd in the power boat Lolita of twenty tons. In the party were John F. Hoffman, the survivor of the ill-fated expedition; Dr. Frank Toussaint of Guaymas, Rangers Tip Stanford and W. A. Old and myself. The crew of the Lolita comprised the captain and a crew of five Mexicans.

"Dr. Toussaint is formerly of Milwaukee, Wisconsin, and is engaged in mining near Guaymas. He is a warm friend of a sister of the Grindell boys and took a personal interest in the search. In addition to the money which I took from Douglas, the doctor advanced me $100 to outfit for the trip and to charter the boat. We found out on our return that the message from Walter Douglas requesting me to draw on him for $500 was received at Guaymas two hours after our leaving for the island. If we would have had that amount we might have stayed longer and continued the search for the bodies further in the interior. I never drew on Mr. Douglas for any money.

"We arrived at Tiburon Island the next evening, the distance being about 125 miles. We did not disembark until the next morning at 9 o'clock. Although we sailed completely around the island the only human habitation we saw were five deserted Seri villages and two dogs. All of the natives had probably gone into the interior of the island.

"The captain and sailors on the Lolita evidently were well informed as to the Seri Indians or else had been intimidated by the stories they had heard of the cruelties practiced by the natives as they absolutely refused to leave the boat. No amount of gold could have persuaded them to set foot on Tiburon soil.

"After the trip around the island we landed on the mainland and Hoffman guided us to the last camp of the party. There we found two dead horses and a half mile below the last camp we found a dead burro, three coats, an overcoat, two blankets, an ax, a burro bell, saddle and two pack saddles. We also found a camera which belonged to Mr. Grindell. It was hidden in the brush some distance below and there we also found a quantity of bacon, flour and other provisions and about 300 rounds of ammunition.

"Hoffman led us to the place where he assured us was the spot at which he left Dave Ingraham to die, but no trace of him could be found. Hoffman found his buck-handled knife near this place. All of the statements made at Guaymas by Hoffman were corroborated by what we found, but no trace whatever could be found of the bodies, dead or alive, of the missing explorers.

"Going further inland we found the trail of what we supposed was the other relief expedition, which is led by Ed Grindell. The trail of the horses showed that they were shod, which convinced us that it was Ed Grindell's party. The trail seemed to come down from the north and went back that way, only further to the east. One of the trails was nine miles from the camp of the missing party and the last was about fourteen miles from the camp.

"Considerable apprehension was felt by the members of our party for the other rescue party, as it was feared that they were making a dangerous trip and they are likely to meet the same fate that Grindell and his companions are supposed to have met.

"Realizing that nothing further could be done in that vicinity, we re-embarked and left for Guaymas, where we arrived yesterday morning. Hoffman expected to leave last evening for Bisbee and will probably be there tomorrow.

"Hoffman is almost completely recovered from the results of his awful trip down the coast to Guaymas. The trip that we made in twenty-four hours it took him ninety days to make, and when he arrived in that city he was in horrible shape. His body was almost completely covered with running sores and he was almost crazed by his experiences. His face was almost as black as that of a negro owing to the exposure to the sun and weather, and persons who knew him before he left on the trip failed to identify him. In some instances he was requested to repeat parts of conversations he had with some of these people to prove his identity.

"Parts of his story were not given much credence in Guaymas, but the trip to the island convinced us that he told the truth in every instance. His experiences in that trip down the coast would make an interesting but exceedingly harrowing tale, and that he is alive today is the best proof of his story to those who know the country through which he went.

"As to Grindell's fate and that of his companions, it would be hard for me to give an opinion. It is the general belief, however, that if they were not actually killed by the Seris, their bodies were disposed of by them. The stories concerning the habits of this tribe regarding their cannibalistic tendencies we found to be true. It is a fact that they eat all of their meat raw and that they have been known to partake freely of human meat.

"Of course, there may be a chance that the members of the party escaped, the absence of any trace of their bodies leaving some hope of that, but it is beyond me where they are if they are alive, with the possible exception that they are prisoners in the interior of Tiburon Island, but there seems but little hope of that. The other relief party under Ed Grindell may have discovered something more, possibly the bodies of the missing men, and nothing further can be done until they return."

———

A telegram was received by the *Dispatch* from Hermosillo yesterday stating that Ed Grindell and Ralph Colvin of this city had arrived in that city after a fruitless attempt to locate the former's brother and his two companions; the third organized attempt to find the missing explorers. The message stated that the party had just returned from the coast, but the search was absolutely fruitless, as the recent heavy rains had obliterated all trails and traces of the party which had previously been found. The telegram which was sent to the *Dispatch* by Mr. Colvin states that Ed Grindell had given up all hope of ever hearing anything from his brother and that it would be useless to continue the search.

There is this satisfaction, however, that everything was done within human power to locate those whose fate will always be conjecture and this will, of course, be some consolation. Mr. Grindell has spent his time and money and did not give up the hunt till it was found that all efforts were in vain. The many friends of the men who were lost showed the right disposition in helping in a material way in every necessary manner and now that the search is at an end they will feel that everything was done that could be done.

CAPTAIN RYNNING TO RESIGN?

There is no little surprise as well as disappointment expressed by many people because of the failure of Governor Kibbey to appoint Captain Rynning of the territorial Rangers superintendent of the territorial prison, says the Tucson *Star*.

It was generally understood that Captain Rynning was going to receive the appointment. This because of his peculiar fitness and qualifications for the very important office, which is charged with most responsible if not dangerous duties.

It was expected Captain Rynning would receive the appointment because he had justly earned the promotion and official recognition. Captain Rynning had made a good record as a Rough Rider in the Spanish-American war. He has made a splendid record as captain of the territorial Ranger force. It was the presence of mind, the indomitable courage and quick action of Captain Rynning that quelled and brought to naught the riot of the strikers during the Clifton strikes two years ago, in which by his courageous timely action he saved much bloodshed and destruction of property.

For this service to the territory Captain Rynning is entitled to recognition and official promotion. That promotion should have been superintendent of the territorial prison, because of all men in Arizona, outside of Ben F. Daniels, he is peculiarly fitted for this heavy trust.

Captain Rynning is a giant in frame and strength, an athlete in action; he has had much experience with criminals, having been in the Chicago police force, and has managed the range duties of Arizona with marked skill, prudence and unstinted courage, and with much credit to the service.

The *Star* has ever maintained that public honors and promotion in the public service should follow well performed public service. That qualification should be the most important consideration, linked with integrity and good citizenship, and when sustained by a record of public service there should be nothing to defeat the right of public recognition.

Captain Rynning meets every one of these requirements and for this particular official station. It is to be hoped when Jerry Millay resigns or if he refuses to accept the appointment, that Governor Kibbey will see his way clear to appoint Captain Rynning superintendent of the territorial prison.

—Douglas *Dispatch*, 1905

Rynning Has No Complaint.

Captain Tom Rynning of the Arizona Rangers, who returned last evening from a trip to the territorial capital, said to a *Dispatch* reporter that he had no intention of resigning, as was reported by the Phoenix papers.

The head of the Rangers was asked concerning the superintendency of the Yuma penitentiary, for which he was prominently mentioned before the appointment of Jerry Millay. "I have no complaint to make," he said, "although I did think that the appointment would be offered me. Governor Brodie made me a promise of the office on the resignation of Mr. Daniels, which was expected some time ago, but I learned from Governor Kibbey that Colonel Brodie had never mentioned it to him, due undoubtedly to the stress of official business which occasioned his leaving the executive office of the territory and his subsequent hurried trip to the Philippines. Governor Kibbey told me that had he known of Colonel Brodie's promise he would have offered me the appointment, but thinking that he knew the facts in the case I never sent in an application for the place."

—Douglas *Dispatch*, 1905

Two or three Arizona newspapers are camping on the trail of the Arizona Rangers, with the evident intention of impairing the usefulness of the organization by diminishing its numbers, says the Nogales *Oasis*. The plea is made that when the Rangers were organized cattle thieves were numerous along the border and the services of the Rangers were necessary; but that the evil has been so greatly lessened during the past few years as to render the maintenance of the company at its present strength unnecessary.

The reason advanced for the proposed diminishing of the force is hardly a logical one, from the viewpoint of a man in the cattle country, and right on the border, as well. It is a fact that cattle stealing has become less popular in this section, but the cattle thieves have not all been killed off by any means. Some have been sent to Yuma; some have been driven out of the country and others have sought less dangerous vocations.

This condition is due to the energetic services of the Arizona Rangers. They are experienced cattlemen, trained to the rugged life that an active Ranger must lead and knowing the trails of the country and the habits of the cattle rustler. It is fear of these men that has stopped the depredations of the cattle thieves. Abolish the Rangers and the abolishment of the organization will be the signal for which many are undoubtedly waiting to resume their raids. Cut the force in two and the danger of cattle stealing will be sufficiently diminished to tempt many of the old timers to again start in business with a horse, a riata and a branding iron for capital.

The *Oasis* has been in Arizona for many years. It knows the Rangers as an organization of fearless and efficient officers. It knows of their work and in the interest of the cattle industry and other industries it stands for the maintenance of the Arizona Rangers. They have done good work and the fruits of their labors should not be undone.

—Douglas *Dispatch*, 1905

The editor of the (Clifton) *Copper Era* has worked himself up into a great state of nervous excitement over the Ranger force. He is greatly worried for fear some member of the force will arrest some lawbreaker within the sacred precincts of the Cliff town. He writes as one inspired and constantly reminds the Rangers and the public that the local officers can take care of all the criminals who come within their jurisdiction. It is the duty of every Ranger to respond to the call of the local officials, whether it be in Safford, Clifton or Phoenix. If he did not do so he would be derelict in his duty.—Safford *Journal*.

—Douglas *Dispatch*, 1905

THE ARIZONA RANGERS. That is the caption of an editorial defense of Captain Rynning's men in the last issue of the Safford *Journal*, the latest addition to Graham county newspapers, and from the same it seems that the Rangers are not without friends in Graham county, where most of the agitation against them begins. The *Journal* says:

A few, and we are glad to note that it is only a few, of the Arizona newspapers are advocating that the force of the Arizona Rangers be reduced in numbers. Investigation shows that the agitation was started by the *Copper Era* of Clifton. There is a reason for all things and if we examine this particular question we will find that the reason for the attitude of the *Copper Era* is that at one time, not very long ago, when there were several notorious hop joints running in Clifton which the local authorities were either incapable or incompetent to close, the assistance of the Rangers was called for—and the joints closed. This action undoubtedly made some powerful enemies for the Rangers in ' Clifton and the *Copper Era* is their mouthpiece.

Under the circumstances it is safe to say that very little attention will be given to the frenzied wailings of the *Copper Era*. No body of men has done more to rid this territory of notorious cattle thieves, thugs and highwaymen than the Arizona Rangers. This organization was created for the purpose of making this territory a fit place for peaceful and industrious citizens. How well it has succeeded is evidenced by the fact that now there is being raised a cry for a decrease of their numbers. Perhaps the Rangers are not kept so strenuously active now as in the early days of their existence—we hope so, anyway. "Eternal vigilance is the price of peace." A reduction in the numbers of the Rangers force just at present would be inviting a return to the old days when every man who went twenty miles from home had to pack a gun and be a law unto himself.

The Rangers are all right. They have done and are still doing good work. Let us keep every one of them.

—Douglas *Dispatch*, 1905

PLUNKETT AND KENNEDY MURDERED

Word comes from Phoenix of the horrible murder of two well-known ranchmen who resided near Livingston. Sam S. Plunkett and Edward A. Kennedy, the murdered men, were found with their bodies terribly mutilated and their skulls crushed. It was evident from indications that the murder had been committed forty-eight hours previous to the finding of the bodies.

Rangers and Indian scouts are searching the surrounding country for the murderers with some hope of success. The Phoenix *Enterprise* says of the crime:

It is more than likely that before another twenty-four hours have passed the murderers of the ranchers will have been apprehended and landed in jail. This statement is made on information brought to town by Sheriff E. P. Shanley of Gila county, who is in Phoenix today.

Regarding the murder little further information is available, but the scouts, Al Sieber and Ranger Peterson, who at once took up the trail when the crime was discovered, run their men within ten miles of Globe. There the trail was lost. The men had been traveling on foot. At that point where the trail was lost, it is thought they were picked up by someone traveling on horseback, for such were the indications on the road.

There the men discarded a butcher knife which was all covered with blood and which was no doubt the same knife with which the lone ranchmen were stabbed. They also changed their shirts at this point and discarded clothing showed blood stains.

Adolph Ludwig, who has been employed at Roosevelt, arrived in Phoenix this morning from that camp which he left Saturday morning. He says that when the news of the murder was received at Roosevelt, Mr. L. C. Hill, project engineer for the Roosevelt Dam construction, left at once for the scene of the murder with two Indian scouts.

—Douglas *Dispatch*, 1905

Three months later, in October, 1905, the *Dispatch* reported:

The mystery which surrounded the murder of Plunkett and Kennedy, and which has baffled the police of the whole southwest, has finally been solved, but the brutal murderers of the two ranchmen will probably never be brought to justice. The mystery has been solved by the shrewd work and detective ability of Lieutenant Harry Wheeler of the Rangers, who secured the first clue to the identity of the perpetrators of the crime at Willcox during a visit there.

Several days ago the *Dispatch* published a story from the Globe *Silver Belt* of the arrest of a Mexican bartender at Globe on the charge of being an accessory to the murder after the crime had been committed. The information was never supposed to have been published by the paper, as the publicity given by the publication will probably give the murderers an opportunity to get further away, but it leaked out somehow and the officers are doing their best to land the criminal with this handicap.

The clue for which the officers had for months been searching came from a Mexican girl who had been the lover of the Globe bartender. She told a friend that this man had harbored for several days the two men who had killed Plunkett and Kennedy. She told this when she learned that two innocent men brought from Alamogordo, New Mexico, were in danger of being hanged for a crime which they had never committed. She said that the bartender had helped the murderers dispose of their bloodstained clothes and had secured new ones for them and that when they left for Mexico he had cashed a check for them. One of them was arrested as a vag the night after he reached Globe, but was released the next day. They are now at Mines Prietas, Sonora, but it is improbable that they will ever be brought to justice unless Ortega, the bartender gives them away. The latter is in jail at Globe, and every effort is being made to wring a confession from him. He seems to be the only man who knows their names and their description.

Harry C. Wheeler as a lieutenant in the Arizona Rangers.

Lieutenant Wheeler, who recently returned from Globe, where he caused the arrest of Ortega, went to the scene of the murder, and he says that from the indications and from what he could learn of the crime it was one of the foulest ever committed in this territory. He said there was little hope of the real criminals ever being caught unless Ortega confesses, and it is very likely that he will be kept in jail until he does.

Following is the *Silver Belt* story as mentioned above:

P. Ortega, a Mexican who has tended bar in Mark Cheever's place for many months, is now in the Gila county jail charged with being an accessory after the fact on an alleged confession obtained from him by Mrs. Cheever at the insistance of local officers.

The story told in this connection by Ortega is as follows: Officers visiting the saloon in question noticed that when one of them entered the place in connection with their official duties Ortega seemed very uneasy and furtively watched them closely. Mrs. Cheever was asked who he was and what he had done to make him so sensitive to the approach of the officers.

She questioned the man who replied that he was not aware that he had committed any offense unless it was because of the fact that he had kept the two Mexicans who had killed Plunkett and Kennedy in hiding for a couple of days and helped them out of town. It is said that he kept them at the Cheever boarding house for two or three days, bought them new clothing and got a pay check cashed for them.

He told Mr. Cheever that they were friends of his and after they had gone he advised her to have the rubbish cleared out of the open space under the building because of the danger of fire. She employed another Mexican to do the work and is now convinced that Ortega's object was to have the blood-stained garments worn by them and hidden in the rubbish burned with the trash to remove all evidence of the crime so far as they were concerned. Mrs. Cheever says that one of the men had three knife wounds on one of his legs which were attended to by Ortega. They had plenty of money, but kept very closely to the premises while here. She is very confident of her ability to identify them if they were brought before her because she saw them at each meal while they remained in Globe and had good opportunity to become acquainted with any peculiarity of features.

She further says that Ortega admits having received letters from the escapees dated *Minas Prietas* where they were at last writing. If this story is true all clues have been at fault and of the dozen or more suspects examined all were undoubtedly guiltless of the murders. If Filipe Sanchez would tell what he knows there is little doubt that the identity of the much sought murderers would be fully established. Whether they can be secured or not is another story and it is highly improbable that they will ever be made to answer for the crime even if they were conclusively proved to be the men wanted. Ortega will have a preliminary hearing within a few days when it is expected that much important evidence would be brought out. Ortega made similar statements to others and to one woman to whom he confessed his story is on the way and will be here to testify.

The Douglas *Dispatch* noted:

It is expected that a squad of Rangers will go to *Minas Prietas* in Mexico, accompanied by Rurales the coming week to secure two Mexicans who are suspected of being the murderers of Ranchmen Plunkett and Kennedy near Livingston several months ago.

The *Silver Belt* had this to say regarding developments:

Pantaleon Ortega, the man who told Mrs. Cheever and others that he had assisted the murderers of Sam Plunkett and Ed. Kennedy to make their escape from this city was placed under bonds of $2000 for appearance before the next grand jury on a charge of being accessory after the fact. It will be impossible for him to secure bail. Steps have been taken to secure the presence of the witnesses at the time. The man suspected of being one of the two who committed the crime, placed under arrest last week, was released as there was no evidence to show that he had anything to do with the case. It is believed that if Ortega and Sanchez would tell what they know that the full story would be disclosed and the identity of the murderers clearly established.

In 1910, ex-Ranger Captain Harry Wheeler was reminiscing and told a Tucson *Star* reporter this story of the search for and subsequent capture of the Plunkett and Kennedy murderers:

"It was in 1905, shortly after I had become a commissioned officer in the Ranger service, that all Arizona was horrified by the story of the Plunkett-Kennedy affair—one of the foulest and most brutal crimes ever perpetrated in the territory. Sam Plunkett and an aged companion, Ed. Kennedy, living on a small ranch on Pinto creek within one mile of the village of Livingston, in Gila county. This town is located about thirty miles from Globe, on the road to Roosevelt. The crime had been committed on a dark, rainy night, the motive being robbery. Two days after its commission an awful sight met the eyes of those who discovered it. Plunkett had been murdered in his bed, his body showing sixteen knife wounds and his head being crushed in with some blunt instrument. His companion had been killed in a similar manner, the body showing knife wounds and the head being crushed beyond recognition.

"Two Mexicans, formerly employed by Plunkett had disappeared and no trace could be found of them. This, coupled with the finding of a bloody shirt belonging to one of the men, led the officers to suspect the Mexicans of the crime, and their trail, leading straight to the mountains, was taken up by the Rangers. This trail was followed to Globe, and when the northern Rangers had traced the men to that point the chase was given up for the time being. The Rangers had no allowance in the matter of expenses for pursuing the criminals to a railroad point, hence we adopted our usual plan in such cases—that is, every Ranger was furnished with as complete a description of the men as was possible to secure and orders were issued to keep an eternal vigilance for the men wanted. And it must be said to the credit of the Ranger force that, as in other cases, for long and weary months after the commission of this crime had left the minds of most Arizonans, the Rangers continued to work quietly upon the case. We finally secured information that the men were in Sonora, Mexico, where they had been seen at several mining camps. One informant stated that the men seldom remained more than two weeks at any one place.

"Upon receipt of this meager information, Rangers Old and Hickey, and Eugene Shute, deputy sheriff at Roosevelt, who by the way was related to Plunkett, and myself sought permission of the governor to enter Sonora and seek the men wanted. This permission being granted we arrived at Nogales in December 1905, and were soon on our way into the interior of the state.

"I will doubtless be pardoned for mentioning here that this trip was made at the joint expense of the Rangers named and the relatives of the murdered parties. The territory contributed no part to our endeavor to secure the guilty parties.

"After searching Magdalena we visited Colonel Kosterlitzky and sought his aid in our quest for the fugitives. The only encouragement he gave us was to warn us against the Yaqui Indians, then engaged in fierce warfare against everyone who entered their country. We then went to Santa Ana, where we took a stage for a distant mining camp. After searching this latter place we returned to Santa Ana and made our way by rail to Ortiz. There we expected to take a rig overland to La Dura, some ninety miles distant and located in the heart of the Yaqui country. We were surprised early next morning after our arrival as we were about to start when a Mexican officer approached us and positively forbade us taking the trip. He said the Yaquis were within ten miles of Ortiz, where a cavalry squadron was encamped, and even declared that the roadway for that distance was unsafe unless the travelers were accompanied by a military escort. This latter he promised us, but failing to get it we determined to make our escape from the military. Consequently before daybreak next day we quietly hitched up our horses and, having bought a few provisions, drove cautiously out of the sleeping encampment.

"After traveling about twenty miles we were surprised to see coming toward us a troop of cavalry, some of the soldiers wearing bandages about their heads and others wearing their arms in slings. Others were leading horses with empty saddles, and when we saw these the true import of the cavalry dawned upon us. The troopers looked like veterans and their leader had grown old in the service. We were halted, and even before he spoke he appeared surprised to see us. A terrible fight with the Yaquis, he said, had taken place the day before, with great losses to the Indians. Seemingly of a kindly disposition he told us of the dangers of the Yaqui country and endeavored to pursuade us to retrace our steps. Being in charge of the little squad of men with me I called him to one side and explained to him the situation. We were all soldiers, I told him, and soldiers in our country were as loath to turn back as soldiers in his own. Gravely he listened to all I had to say. Gravely he saluted me. And gravely he called his troop to attention and resumed his way.

"We made good progress the remainder of that day and struck camp in a cluster of mesquite trees. It was extremely cold and as we had no blankets and did not dare make a camp fire we suffered considerably. With dawn, however, came additional troubles, for following a clatter of horses' hoofs we were quickly surrounded by a troop of cavalry and placed under arrest. For our own good, we were told, we were to remain guests of the military until such time as other arrangements could be made. In vain I informed the officer in command that we were Americans; that we had done no evil and that we were perfectly willing to go on our way and take all responsibility for the dangers to which we were subjected. The captain ordered his men to take us in charge and we were marched to a block house about five miles distant. Here we found another small garrison of soldiers and were given good quarters and plenty of food. The best of all, though, was that we had a comfortable bed.

"On the fourth day of our enforced habitation of the fort we were gladdened by the arrival of dispatches from Ortiz, ordering a safe escort for us to the point of our destination. About ten days were required in making the trip to La Dura and return, a careful search of the camp having failed to reveal the presence of our men. We went to Guaymas and were met with the same disappointment. Then we returned to Empalme, then in the first stage of its growth, and took up our search along the right-of-way for the new road then building. After riding over the twenty miles of completed roadway we proceeded on foot. Mile after mile we trudged through cold and dark, with not a single human habitation within the next 100 miles, guided only by the open space cleared for the right-of-way for the road. We had been told there were several parties of laborers at work along the line, and it was among them that we hoped to find the men we were seeking.

"The next morning after beginning our ling hike across country we ate our last morsel of food and put ourselves on short rations of water, and the close of the day found us footsore and terribly hungry. Hickey's feet got so sore that he had to take off his shoes. We laughed, in spite of our desperation, as we trudged along, his shoes tied about his neck. The next day, however, we were all in the same condition—four straggling Rangers, all nearly starved, with canteens which no longer held a drop of water. Around the neck of each dangled a pair of shoes tied with a string. Things were desperate indeed by this time. We were compelled to rest every ten minutes, and no one spoke. We knew we could not go back and we knew not how far it was to the first gang of workmen. Fully fifty miles had already been covered by us.

"We had now passed three days without food and two without water. Hope was giving place to despair, but I determined that we should travel that night. It seemed that hours had passed when Hickey uttered an exclamation. 'That's a house,' he said, and pointed out to us a faint flicker of light. Pressing onward we finally came to the little adobe shanty, which we found to have but one door and a few portholes opening into its single room. Rapping on the door we were astonished to hear several voices, a scurrying of feet and a voice cry out, 'Get your pistols, boys. Kill the Yaquis.' This, spoken in a high pitch of the voice, was evidently meant to intimidate us, the inmates having mistaken us for the terrible Yaquis. After a short consultation we decided to take the chance of being shot and force an entrance into the building, for we were in no condition to proceed further on our journey that night. Pandemonium broke loose within when we went to the door in a body and again demanded admittance. I scarcely ever heard such yelling. Cries and curses mingled with prayers. It was in vain that we hammered on the door. We could not make ourselves understood in that noise and confusion. The only thing left was to break through the door and risk being shot down. Starving men, however, will take chances. We broke through the door. By this time the room was dark. Lighting a match, our eyes were greeted with a sight impossible to describe. The Yaquis went up in our estimation several hundred per cent when we saw what consternation and terror they had created among those Mexicans. Seven men, three women and half a dozen children were huddled in one corner. The women were holding their childen to their breasts while they knelt on the hard floor. Children were whimpering and clutching at their mother's dresses. The men, terror stricken and kneeling, had nevertheless placed themselves in front of the women and children, evidently intending to be the first to die. Not a weapon had they.

"It was with some difficulty that we finally succeeded in convincing them we were not the dreaded Yaquis, but when they saw we made no move to injure them they finally became quiet, permitting us to explain. After that they could not do enough for us. They washed and bound up our injured feet and made us as comfortable as possible on their crude pallets. They then brought us water, giving it to us first in small quantities, increasing the allowance gradually until we were allowed all we wanted. In the meantime, the women went to work cooking for us, and soon tortillas of flour, with beans, coffee and goat's milk cheese, were ready. They permitted us to sleep until three the next afternoon. After again attending to our needs our benefactors told us the main body of the working crew on the new railway had gone ten miles farther on, but was expected to return within a few days. We decided to remain where we were until the crew

returned, which it did on the third day. We again failed to
locate our men, however.

"Our feet now being well again we struck out on our return
trip to Empalme, and from there went to the famous mining
camp of *Minas Prietas*. Here we discovered our first clew to
the men we were seeking. Men answering their description perfectly had left the camp a few days before that, stating that they
were going to Nogales.

"For Nogales we started at once. There we separated and other
Rangers were sent for. All Arizona was systematically searched
for these men. After separating in Nogales I went to my territory
in northern Cochise county, while other Rangers scoured the
camps in the Helvetias, Silverbell, Mammoth, Washington,
Mowry, and a dozen other places, for the word had gone out to
the Rangers that the murderers were again in Arizona.

"It so happened that I was destined by chance to pick up the
fugitives. It happened at Willcox. The constable there for a long
time had borne the reputation of being such a terror to the lawless that he and his town were usually given a wide berth by
criminals of all kinds. Hence when two Mexicans considered it
more advisable to remain outside the town, even in a terrific
downpour of rain, than to show themselves there in daylight,
I became suspicious. I found them sitting alongside the railway
track, in a perfect deluge of rain. When I approached they
attempted to move away, and upon being informed of their
arrest, the larger man, named Gonzales, drew a big, murderous-
looking knife. The smaller of the men, named Ascension also
slyly opened a smaller knife which he had concealed in his
pocket. The descriptions were perfect, and I knew I had the
men we had so long sought.

"In jail that night the larger of the two men walked to and fro
in his quarters until daylight. 'We will be hung in Globe,' he
urged repeatedly, addressing his remarks to Ascension.

" 'No,' the latter would reply. 'They will hang you but not me.'

"Ascension, little more than a boy, later told us how the other
man had committed the foul murders on the lonely little ranch

near Livingston; how Gonzales had compelled him to witness the deed and how the money had been divided.

"Both men were bound over to the grand jury of Gila county. The smaller one was subsequently released and the sheriff in some manner, allowed Gonzales to escape and he afterwards committed suicide.

"However, the Rangers' work had been completed; they had done their duty well and the company, at least, knew that the territory had been ridded of two of the most undesirable criminals. Over nine thousand miles had been traveled in order to capture these men. Every conceivable hardship and danger had been endured uncomplainingly. Rangers drawing $100 per month, with absolutely no expense allowance, had readily and willingly spent their own wages, month after month, in the performance of their duty. I know of no other peace officers in the territory who have done this.

"Hence arises the question:

"Were the Arizona Rangers patriots or fools?

"I leave it to the questioner."

Captain Rynning will leave this morning on his big gray horse for a trip over the territory, which will take about a month of his time. He goes provided with bedding and supplies and will take along a pack horse to carry the outfit. The first stop will be at Bisbee and from there the captain will push on toward the west. He expects to cover about 1,500 miles before returning to Douglas and during his absence his duties will be attended to by Lieutenant Wheeler, though the captain will keep continuously in touch with headquarters.

—Douglas *Dispatch,* 1905

Some weeks later the *Dispatch* had this story:

To spend six weeks in the saddle and cover thirteen hundred miles is not what an ordinary man would care to do. Captain

Thomas Rynning has just completed such a ride, and without any ill effects.

Captain Rynning is spending today in Phoenix on his way from his headquarters in Douglas to Prescott and the northern part of the territory, where he will be for a few days on official business.

This morning Captain Rynning visited with his superior officer, Governor Kibbey, and together they discussed matters that concern the Arizona Rangers and the work they are doing along the southern and eastern borders of Arizona, as well as at interior points.

With becoming modesty Captain Rynning consented to tell some of the features of his long ride. In the telling he did not appear to think it had been much of an exploit, though to almost anyone else it would be an event of a lifetime.

Investigation of cattle killing cases was what took the Ranger captain from Douglas on horseback to the extreme northeastern portion of Arizona. Indians have been giving the cattle owners considerable trouble by killing their cattle.

Rynning's first ride was from Naco through Santa Cruz and Pima counties and back a distance of about 500 miles. He saw nothing exceptionally startling on the trip, but wherever he found a Ranger, gave him instruction. After returning to Douglas, Rynning got a fresh horse and started north, going through Cochise, Graham and Gila counties and into Pinal county. At one time he was within seventy-five miles of the Tonto Basin reservoir. From there he continued north into Navajo and Apache counties.

In the White River country Captain Rynning met a party of Bisbee hunters who were out for a vacation. He had the pleasure of acting as their guide.—Phoenix *Enterprise.*

RANGER KIDDER

In order to save the life of Ranger Kidder, yesterday afternoon, Deputy Sheriff Sparks drew his revolver and shot a hobo at Naco who was attempting to make an assault with a dagger. A free-for-all fight was taking place there yesterday evening, brought on by about fifteen tramps who were drinking and raising a disturbance just west of town on the railroad track. Officers Kidder and Sparks were called to settle the trouble when the hoboes assaulted them. Both officers were knocked down and badly, but not seriously injured. As Ranger Kidder arose one of the tramps drew a dagger and attempted to assault him, when Deputy Sparks drew his revolver and fired, the bullet taking effect in the assailant's hip.

All the rioters were arrested and landed in jail. A warrant will be sworn out in justice court charging the one who made the knife play with assault with intent to kill, and others on a charge of disturbing the peace. The man who was shot will be sent to the county hospital at Tombstone, where he will remain under arrest. The fight was witnessed by a large crowd of people.

—Bisbee *Review*, 1906

CANANEA RIOT

Awful Reign of Terror in Greene Camp at Cananea, Mexico— At Least Fifty Men are Killed and Wounded—Prominent Americans Shot Down in Cold Blood—The Town Set on Fire and the Mines Burning—Men, Women and Children Flee for Their Lives —Pitched Battle at Naco.

"For God's Sake Send Us Armed Help at Once" was Colonel Greene's Message to the United States.

———

Naco, Arizona, June 1.—Forty-five American Miners killed and more than twice that number wounded and dying—Fifty Mexican miners and four policemen killed and many more wounded —the town burned—citizens fleeing for their lives to the hills, stores being looted, and machinery being dynamited. Soldiery rushing in from across the American line.

———

The above glaring headings greeted the readers of the Douglas *Dispatch* on the morning of June 2, 1906, and the newspaper went on to reveal:

This in brief was the situation at Cananea at one o'clock this morning. At noon yesterday the Mexican miners, about 5,000, left their work at the Capote and adjoining mines and appeared on the Mesa or public square and demanded of the foreman that their wages be raised from $3 to $5 per day, Mexican money, and eight hours per day, and stated that if this was not complied with at once that they would strike. After a half hour conference, they called on Colonel W. C. Greene, who appeared from his sick room, and addressed them from the veranda of the mining company's office. He explained to them that he could not raise their wages without the consent of the governor of Sonora, but that he would do this as soon as he could hear from the governor giving his consent.

This did not satisfy the Mexicans, who immediately went on a strike and called all their men off the works and instituted a state of rebellion. They said that if they could not get their demands granted, the Americans could not work and at once armed themselves and began to make a wholesale warfare on the Americans.

The American miners being unarmed at work were taken by surprise and were swept down before the ruthless fire of the

Col. William C. Greene, Cananea mines owner, talking to Mexican strikers. In background are American miners, ready to cut loose if trouble starts. Man in derby hat at Col. Greene's left is Gov. Yzabal of Sonora. His military aide, Gen. Luis Torres, seated in back seat, extreme right.

Mexicans. The Americans made as good defense as possible and soon returned fire under fearful disadvantages, killing and wounding as above stated.

Col. W. C. Greene at once appealed to the Americans and Governor Yzabal at Hermosillo, who at once started with Mexican Rurales, arriving at four o'clock this morning. Here they were joined by Captain Thomas Rynning of the Arizona Rangers and five hundred armed miners of Bisbee. A special train carrying Rangers, special officers and armed citizens, left Douglas at eight o'clock making the run of thirty-five miles in thirty-five minutes. They joined the governor and his forces. A train passed through Douglas from El Paso at two o'clock, having 1000 rifles and ammunition on and were joined here by officers and armed citizens.

At 10:15 a long train pulled into Naco, carrying nearly one thousand, principally women and children, who passed through to Bisbee. They were in a state of terror and many of them were without hats and anything, but the clothing they had on their backs. They were sitting on the floor of the baggage cars, and seats were taken out to make more room for the crowd which was jammed in as tightly as possible. The train stopped about seven miles out of Cananea to pick up a great many of the refugees who had flown from the town on foot seeking to gain the international line.

At 10:30 another train came to Naco having two coaches loaded with women and children, who were hungry and half starved. They were at once fed by the people and wandered about the town eating at the lunch wagons and getting whatever there was to eat. They had left all of their possessions behind them and fled for safety. They were all terrorized and told harrowing stories of the fearful conditions which they had left behind them.

NACO, (11:30 p.m.—Special.)—The town is swarmed with men armed, walking to and fro doing sentinel duty. The country around swarms with riders coming in from all directions, ready to join the armed forces which is to cross the international line in the next hour. Ranger Arthur Hopkins is in charge of the situation, and all under arms must report to him. The Arizona Rangers, twenty-four in all, are present and prepared to cross the line as soon as the Bisbee contingent joins them. Tremendous excitement prevails and every minute news reached here by telephone giving fresh information of the alarming condition. The officers have little to say as to their plans further than they are ready at the proper time to cross the line.

NACO, (11:45 p.m.—Special.)—A party of mounted men have just arrived from Bisbee in advance of the train which will arrive here in about an hour. These cavalrymen reported at once to Ranger Hopkins. The boys here have just completed organizing a special company to take a special train to Cananea and will leave in a few minutes.

The Mexicans have refused to permit the soldiers to pass the line and a skirmish is expected to take place at this juncture. It is the idea of the Bisbee men to ride the line and prevent the Mexicans from making an attack on the train. Everyone is prepared to make the attempt to cross the line, no matter what is in advance. There are horsemen arriving all the time and swelling the ranks and it is believed that a strong cavalry force will be in readiness in a few minutes.

NACO, (12 p.m.—Special.)—Just now a pitched battle took place near the stock yards, just east of town, where over 200 shots were fired as fast as possible. Two Americans were shot off their horses and several Mexicans were killed and wounded. A courier ran into the center of the town having been chased by a posse of Mexicans who were determined not to let them pass the line. The Americans are scouting for an opportunity to cross and the fighting continues all along the border for several hundred yards. There is great consternation prevailing here, and it is feared that the Americans are taking too many chances in trying to cross the line. The special train is waiting on the line to make the crossing and a telegram from Cananea is just received urging the troops to hurry.

NACO, (12:15 p.m.—Special.)—There was a company of twenty-five horsemen riding along the line just now when they were fired upon from ambush by a large number of Mexicans. Two men were shot. They are shooting now all along the line.

NACO.—The telephone from Cananea is in charge of B. A. Packard and other Americans, who are keeping the Americans on this side of the line in touch with the progress at that point. They

The lumber yard fire at Cananea, Mexico, set by the rioters

report that everything is burning and that the mines are burning at several places and that all work has been abandoned and the smelters are shut down. There is no working going on and a large number of Mexicans are marching up and down the streets carrying flags and making a tremendous noise. They have no order and there seems to be very little leadership among the strikers. Every one but the strikers have left the streets and are in hiding or are fleeing to the hills.

NACO, June 2.—In the midst of the turmoil and confusion, Col. W. C. Greene passed through the crowd in his automobile, crowding the way through the strikers. He was not molested by any one and made a last effort to quell the mob and to send them to their homes. This was without avail, and after passing through several of the main thoroughfares he returned home and gave up, seeing that his efforts were futile. Greene was cautioned to remain under cover, but this had no effect upon the copper king, who did all in his power to allay the storm.

As the train pulled out of Cananea loaded with the large number of refugees, an American was attacked by three Mexicans, all armed. Before the eyes of the spectators, the American put up the great fight, killing all three Mexicans and escaping with his life.

———

NACO, June 2.—(12:45—Special.)—A telephone message was just received from B. A. Packard, which was sent by Colonel Greene. It says: "FOR GOD'S SAKE SEND US ARMED HELP." This struck terror into the very hearts of all, and it was hard to keep the men from rushing across the line in a forced march to Cananea. It seems now that the very American forces are being annihilated and are utterly helpless. What the morning will bring forth no man can say, but it looks now that not half the terrible butchery and destruction can be told. There is terrible consternation reigning here and death and destruction seems rampant. Five hundred fighters strong left Bisbee at 12 o'clock sharp and are expected every minute.

———

NACO, June 2.—(Special)—Three Mexicans have been killed in the skirmishes on the line. One was shot through the head and killed immediately; one was shot twice and the third was shot through the bowels, which proved fatal. Three others are reported wounded.

———

NACO, June 2.—(9:30 p.m.—Special.)—A telephone message from W. C. Greene, president of the Cananea Consolidated copper company to Col. B. A. Packard, says forty people are killed. Buildings have been set on fire by the rioters. The American consul, Galbraith, has wired Washington asking that troops be sent from Fort Huachuca, Arizona, to protect the American citizens.

EDITOR's NOTE: The foregoing headlines and special bulletins give some idea of the excitement and turmoil which took place at Naco and Cananea, and after considerable revaluation of the situation, it was discovered that the loss of life and damage of property was not as great as was first reported. Captain Rynning did show a great deal of poise and in his handling of the riot and coordination with Colonel Kosterlitzky, he showed himself possessed of a good quality of diplomacy.

A resume of Captain Rynning's diplomacy in connection with the Cananea riot is contained in a later article appearing in the Phoenix *Republican,* in part as follows:

Rioting by the Mexican miners was in progress and they showed themselves especially hostile to Americans, of which there were some 300 men, women and children in the camp. Word came to Bisbee of the situation and citizens appealed to Rynning to lead a rescue party to Cananea. He replied that it would probably mean his losing his job as captain of the Rangers, but he would lead the proposed expedition; and he asked for armed volunteers to the number of 300. The number required followed him immediately to the border town of Naco, where they proposed to entrain for Cananea. At the Mexican line Governor Yzabal of Sonora met Captain Rynning and forbade his entrance into Mexico, pointing out that permission could not possibly be given to an armed party of Americans to come into his country. Captain Rynning replied that they were not going in as a party but as individuals; that they were going on a peaceful mission to Cananea to protect and rescue Americans in peril and they were going on that train. Governor Yzabal made the best of the situation and went along. He afterwards lost his job when it was represented to President Diaz that he had permitted Captain Rynning to cross the line.

Arriving at Cananea with his armed Americans, Captain Rynning was met by Colonel Kosterlitzky, the famous Russian commander of Sonora Rurales, who had just arrived with some hundreds of Mexican soldiers. Captain Rynning anticipating some controversy with the colonel, already had ordered his men to proceed to a hill which commanded the town, and when the interview began the Americans were assembling on the hill. The colonel pre-emptorily ordered Captain Rynning to return to Naco with his men, and added that he was there to protect life and property, that the Americans were a menace to peace, and he broadly intimated that if his orders were not obeyed there would be trouble. Captain Rynning, in his slow, quiet voice, suggested to Colonel Kosterlitzky that he direct his gaze to the neighboring hill. "My men are up there," Captain Rynning said, "and you can see that they command the situation. I am going to see that the Americans here are protected until they can be taken out of town and across the American line. We don't want trouble, but if you want it we can accommodate you."

Kosterlitzky, like Yzabal, put the best possible face on a disagreeable situation. A considerable number of rioters were killed after the arrival of the Rynning party, and it has always been understood that the Americans did their share toward putting down the riot—but there was no conflict between the American and Mexican soldiers, and in due course the American residents were escorted out of town and across the line.

As soon as possible thereafter Captain Rynning reported personally to Governor Kibbey and advised him of all he had done. It is understood that the governor said to Rynning, "You deserve to be severely punished for what you have done and I will try to make the punishment fit the crime—how would you like to be superintendent of the prison?"

When Governor Kibbey told President Roosevelt of the Mexican exploit of his former Rough Rider lieutenant, "Teddy" gave one of his famous chuckles and said: "Tom's all right, isn't he?"

LIEUTENANT WHEELER AND HIS HAT

That General Luis E. Torres will not permit any discourtesy on the part of Mexican officials to any American citizen and that he is desirous of retaining the most cordial feeling between the two republics is shown by the following incidents and correspondence:

Some time during the early part of last week a rancher on the American side of the line near Naco lost a bunch of goats, a portion of which strayed over into Mexico. The rancher secured permission from one of the Mexican officials at Naco by the name of Jiminez to go over into Mexico to search for his goats. He also requested Lieutenant Harry Wheeler of the Arizona Rangers to help him in his search. While on the Mexican side of the line the rancher, although having previously had permission to cross the line, was arrested by this man Jiminez and thrown into jail.

Wheeler on hearing of the occurrence proceeded to the office of Jiminez for the purpose of securing the man's release if possible. On entering the office Jiminez was found with his hat on, but requested that the American Ranger immediately remove his headpiece. This Wheeler very courteously refused to comply with unless Jiminez would accord him the same courtesy.

On the refusal of Lieutenant Wheeler to remove his headgear, Jiminez is said to have started for the Ranger lieutenant, but for some unknown reason stopped before he reached him. Wheeler eventually left the office of Jiminez and still had his hat on. The lieutenant immediately reported the occurrence to his superior officer, Captain Rynning of Douglas, who took the matter up with General Luis E. Torres, who wrote as follows:

"Captain Thomas Rynning,
    "Douglas, Arizona.

    "My Dear Friend: Your very kind letter has been received and
I thank you very much for helping us watch the border for the
bandits who were reported to be heading toward the boundary
line.

    "I deeply regret the lack of courtesy shown by the adminis-
trator of the customs service at Naco toward my friend, Lieutenant Wheeler, and I have reported the case to the proper officials.
I wish to apologize myself for the lack of good behavier on the
part of Mr. Jiminez, and I wish to say further that I work at
all times to keep the best of relations between the people of our
two countries.

    "Believe me, my dear captain, truly your friend.

                                    LUIS E. TORRES.
                            —Douglas *Dispatch*, 1906

RANGER KIDDER GETS HIS MAN

DOUGLAS, Dec. 31.—A running fight in which five shots were
exchanged occurred here this afternoon between a man suspected
of being a desperate character, and Jeff Kidder, a member of the
force of Arizona Rangers, and as a result the suspect lies fatally
wounded.

    For several weeks past the local police and the Rangers have
been receiving reports of hold-ups and house-breaks, and in
every instance have been unable to secure the slightest clue as
to the identity of the perpetrators of the crimes.

    During the past few days a number of strange men have been
noticed in the city, who have had no visible means of support,
and the police officers determined to watch them, thinking that
this might be the explanation of the crimes. The Ranger force
was divided up and have been patrolling certain places where
these men were in the habit of congregating.

While riding his beat this evening, which took him in the direction of the railroad roundhouse, Jeff Kidder, a private in the Ranger force, noticed a man start up in front of him about forty yards, and he immediately shouted to the fellow to halt. Instead of stopping the man redoubled his speed, and Kidder shot over his head. At this the suspect turned, and drew from his hip pocket a six-shooter, and fired three shots at the Ranger, none of which took effect, Kidder, who is one of the crack shots of the Ranger force, drew down on the fellow and the first shot passed through his head.

The Ranger went to the man's assistance at once and picked up the revolver, which was a 38-calibre on a 45 frame. In one of the man's pockets he found an ordinary sock filled with 38-calibre cartridges, and outside of this there was not a thing whereby the man could be identified.

A doctor soon arrived on the scene and administered restoratives to the wounded man, but up to a late hour tonight the fellow had not recovered consciousness, and the physician stated that there is no possibility of his recovery.

————

DOUGLAS, Dec. 31.—The man shot by Ranger Kidder died at the C. & A. hospital at 11:45 tonight. No one has yet appeared who can identify the man.

————

DOUGLAS, Jan. 10.—(Special)—After hearing the testimony in the case against Ranger Kidder, who was charged with killing a stranger near the roundhouse one night last week, Judge Ben Rice this morning discharged the prisoner on the motion of Assistant District Attorney Ross. The warrant charging Kidder with murder was sworn out against Kidder at his own request, he desiring that the case have a full investigtion in court.

George Campbell, who was with Kidder at the time the killing occurred, was the first witness. He testified that he went with Kidder on the evening of the trouble and that they followed a man across the railroad track; Kidder called on him to stop, saying that we were officers and desired to look at him. At this the man fired a pistol, the bullet whizzing close to my ear. Then Kidder fired three shots; the man's gun lay about four feet from him when he went to him.

Christian Nelson, machinist, testified that he was on the ground and saw the deceased after he was shot; deceased was lying on his back with blood coming out of his head, but he was not dead. He saw the gun.

Leslie Kyle, roundhouse foreman, said Kidder came to the roundhouse and asked for a 'phone, stating that he was an officer and had shot a man and wanted to 'phone for the coroner, which he did. I saw the deceased with a gun lying three or four feet from him; also a pipe; deceased had a bullet wound in his eye.

F. E. Smith, machinist, was at the roundhouse on the occasion of the shooting and saw the injured man when the wagon came after him; did not see his wound.

Con Jones, boilermaker, said a man was killed near the roundhouse and he saw him and a gun lying close to the dead man.

W. C. Copeland, boilermaker, testified: "All I saw was the dead man, 50 or 60 feet this side of the roundhouse. I think he had a hole in his head. I think he was still alive; know nothing about the shooting."

Jacob Smith, boilermaker, stated that he saw a man with a hole in his head, ready to turn in his checks, southeast of the roundhouse about nine o'clock; did not see the pistol until after it was picked up.

M. F. Knechtel, boilermaker, said: "I saw the man 15 or 20 steps southeast of the roundhouse. He was shot over the right eye. I heard no shots. He looked like he was still alive; saw him dead since at Ferguson's undertaking parlors."

Albert Ryan: "I was not at the shooting; I saw a body at Ferguson's undertaking parlors and recognized him. I knew him in Texas and knew him as Tommy Woods; I knew him in Douglas. I glanced at his face and he was dead." Ryan, when cross-examined, admitted that he told three men that he had not seen deceased for five years.

Lee Thompson testified to *corpus delicti* at the undertaking parlors: "I knew the deceased as Tom T. Woods for three years; he worked for me twice, then opened up a saloon on Ninth and G." Cross examined he stated: "He always carried a gun. I have heard him say he would not give his gun up to an officer or anybody else. I am not sure that I told Kidder about this before the shooting."

Campbell was recalled and stated that he had seen the man's body at Ferguson's undertaking parlors.

Ryan, on being recalled, admitted that a few days ago he had declared that he did not know the name of the deceased. At this point, on motion of Assistant District Attorney Ross and without objection, the name Tom T. Woods was substituted instead of "John Doe."

The gun was produced in evidence; also Kidder's gun. Constable Shropshire identified Kidder's gun and stated that Kidder offered to give it up the night of the shooting.

Young Davis testified: "I am E. P. and S. W. night watchman. Went over with Judge McDonald and found the man; he was alive. I picked up the gun and examined it; it was three feet from the body and had been fired once; the body was taken to the Calumet hospital. I knew him by sight for three years, but did not know his name.

Davis cross examined: "I examined the gun by sticking my little finger in the muzzle and smelling of it; identified the gun.

The defense called Officer Shropshire who identified the gun as the one Davis gave him; he found a stocking containing 38–40 smokeless cartridges in dead man's hip pocket; also a couple of skeleton keys. The gun had been freshly fired. One shot had been fired out of it. The gun was a 38 on a 45 frame.

Witness Campbell, for the defense, stated that Kidder asked him to go down on Sixth street, which they did. They came back near Happy Jack's place and went down on Railroad avenue to investigate a robber's nest; went to the window. Thought there were three men and a woman. They were talking about a watch and money. Deceased came out of the back door and came up the street. We followed him on suspicion. We split and followed him across the railroad yards; it began to rain. Kidder was ahead of me; I think I was within 30 or 40 yards of him. Kidder called to him in a loud tone, "Hold on there, Jack, we are officers and want to look at you." Deceased fired as previously stated.

Kidder's statement corroborated Campbell's statement regarding Sixth street, and the hobo headquarters; also in regard to the shooting. He hailed him as stated by Campbell; deceased replied with a shot and I went to shooting back. I fired three shots, then saw him on the ground. I left and went for an officer. I was a territorial Ranger at that time. I was and I am here under orders from the captain of the Rangers.

The prosecuting attorney moved the court to discharge the defendant. The position of the prosecuting attorney was fair in the extreme and his remarks to the court as well as the evidence fully vindicated Kidder. The court found that Kidder killed Tom T. Woods in the proper discharge of his duty.

—Bisbee *Review*, 1907

INSANE FIT OF JEALOUSY

BENSON, Ariz., Feb. 28.—In an insane fit of jealousy, J. A. Tracy, aged 38, a resident of Vail Station, where he is the agent for the Helvetia Copper Company, attempted to kill D. W. Silverton and wife yesterday at Benson, and would have succeeded had it not been for the interference of Lieut. Wheeler of the Arizona Rangers.

As a result of the murderous attempt, Tracy is dead and Wheeler is carrying two wounds to the Tombstone hospital for treatment, one in the left leg above the knee, and another in the right foot.

Tracy was shot four times by Wheeler. One ball entered the left breast, another through the neck, the third in the shoulder and the last shot fired by Wheeler passed through the left hip.

Back of the murderous attempt made by Tracy to kill Silverton and wife is a story shrouded in mystery relative to the relations existing between Tracy and Mrs. Silverton before she was married.

Mrs. Silverton refuses to give her maiden name, but says she knew Tracy, first in Nevada about a year ago and later in Arizona. She says she knew Tracy in Tucson and also Vail Station where she was a resident at the time Tracy lived there.

When taking her deposition before the justice of the peace she swore Tracy was nothing more than a friend. Later, to a *Review* reporter in disconnected statements, she said:

"This is all a one-sided affair you know. We were doing our best to avoid trouble, and I don't see what they want us to stay over here for. Tracy is nothing to me. I have never been married to him. I first knew him in Nevada about a year ago. He was always wanting me to come to him."

Again she said: "He was crazy jealous."

What Mrs. Silverton was doing in Nevada, Colorado, Tucson, Vail Station, and other points in the West, she does not state, and is very careful to guard her maiden name. She takes this course upon the advice of her husband, who declares he does not care what transpired between his wife and Tracy in the past; that she is his wife now and he proposes to protect her.

D. W. Silverton Jr., is a son of Col. D. W. Silverton, of Louisville, Kentucky, a prominent family of that city. Col. Silverton has been in Cananea on several occasions as the guest of Col. W. C. Greene. Young Silverton appeared worried yesterday as to just how his father would receive the news of the incident at Benson, in which he and his newly wedded wife played such an important part.

When pressed by the reporter for the name of his wife before she was married, Silverton gave as an excuse for refusing to answer, that his wife was well connected in Colorado and that he did not wish her folks to learn of the affair.

Mrs. Silverton admitted to a *Review* man that she had lived in Colorado and Nevada, and that her mother still lived in Colorado, but that her father was dead. When pressed for more details concerning her life and movements, prior to her marriage to Silverton, she evaded the questions, saying she could not see how that could interest anybody.

Mrs. Silverton is good looking. Rather tall and well formed. Large black eyes, brown wavy hair, and seems partial to turquoise jewelry. Two large turquoise rings are worn on the left hand and she wore ear rings with set turquoise stones. She gave her age as 25 and said she had been in Arizona about a year and a half.

Young Silverton is a son of one of the oldest families in Kentucky. He is a graduate of a school of mines and says he is in the West to see the practical side of mining. He says he first met his present wife about eighteen months ago in Nevada and that they had corresponded at intervals since that time. He says he wrote his wife to leave Vail Station and go to Phoenix, where he met her and they were married six weeks ago by an evangelist named McComa, who was traveling through Phoenix at the time.

With the marriage of Silverton and this girl, whether for cause or not, Tracy's jealousy was aroused. He learned that the couple were in Tucson on their honeymoon. He followed them there and at one time had an interview with Mrs. Silverton. She says he wanted to make her a present of a diamond ring which she refused. Tracy made no threats at this time, but in order to avoid meeting him again Silverton and his wife took an automobile ride through the country around Tucson. Tracy returned to his business at Vail Station, but the next day, according to Mrs. Silverton, she received four threatening letters from Tracy.

Tiring of Tucson, Mr. and Mrs. Silverton decided to visit Bisbee, Cananea and Douglas. They boarded the train for Benson at 2:30 p.m., Wednesday afternoon and arrived at Vail, a way-station, about one hour later. As the train stopped at the depot, Mrs. Silverton looked out of the window and saw Tracy standing on the depot platform. She pointed him out to her husband who hastily left his seat, and jumping down from the car steps, he introduced himself to Tracy as the husband of the woman to whom he had written the threatening letters. Just what passed between the two men is not known. The meeting was not pleasant and as the train pulled out of Vail Station for Benson, Tracy attempted to catch the rear car but failed.

Mr. and Mrs. Silverton arrived in Benson an hour later and took rooms at the Virginia hotel, being assigned room 14. During the night, Tracy arrived from Vail Station armed with a .45 Colts pistol. He remarked to a comrade, who rode with him on the freight train, that he was "going to Benson to get a couple of people." Silverton evidently thought that Tracy might follow him and his wife to Benson and secured a negro porter to watch for Tracy and inform him if he arrived. When Silverton arose early Thursday morning, preparatory to leaving for Bisbee with his wife, he learned that Tracy was in Benson. To make sure he stepped out on the front porch of the Virginia hotel and saw Tracy standing beside the train which was about to depart for Bisbee. Upon seeing Tracy, Silverton immediately entered the hotel and asked Castenada, the proprietor, for a gun, as he feared a man standing over by the train intended to do him harm. Castenada advised that instead of getting a gun, that he report the matter to an officer, and summoned Lieut. Wheeler of the Rangers, who was stopping in the hotel.

After listening to the story of Silverton and searching him to make sure he was not carrying a concealed weapon, Wheeler walked towards the train, for the purpose of preventing trouble, and to disarm Tracy, should he discover he was carrying a gun. As Wheeler left the hotel, walking across the street to the railroad tracks, Tracy was standing on the car steps of the cafe parlor car. As Wheeler approached Tracy, and was within a few feet of him, Mr. and Mrs. Silverton left the hotel also, to go to the train. As Tracy saw the married couple leave the hotel he jumped down from the steps and as he did so attempted to pull a gun, and had the gun half out of his pocket, when Wheeler stepped up close, saying:

"Hold on there. I arrest you. Give me that gun."

For reply Tracy whipped out a revolver and fired, the shot entering the side of Wheeler's coat, passing through without doing any damage. As Tracy fired the first shot, Wheeler got his own gun into action, and the next two shots were fired almost together, Wheeler continued to advance upon Tracy, commanding him to halt; that he was under arrest, and to surrender his gun. Tracy kept firing and Wheeler returned the fire. When Wheeler had fired four shots, all of them taking effect, and the men were standing in the middle of the street, Tracy said: "I am all in. My gun is empty."

At this announcement, Wheeler threw his gun down on the ground, and walked toward Tracy, commanding him to surrender. At this time Wheeler was shot through the leg and Tracy was shot four times in the body above the waist line, though he was still able to stand on his feet.

Tracy's gun was not empty. As Wheeler advanced toward him, Tracy fired at him twice, one of the shots taking effect in the Ranger's foot. Nothing daunted, Wheeler gathered up some rocks and began throwing at his man (his own gun was several feet behind him) and finally, after Tracy had shot at him six times, Wheeler walked up to him and disarmed him, turned him over to a lone Benson officer, went back and picked up his own gun, and then was so weak from pain and loss of blood that he had to be assisted into the hotel.

Tracy was able to walk with assistance. From the nature of his wounds, it was thought best to send him to a hospital at Tucson. He died on the way, at Mescal Station.

Capt. Rynning, who was in Benson at the time, took a deposition from Tracy, but could not get him to say much beyond the fact that there was a woman in the case.

Wheeler was taken to the hospital in Tombstone yesterday by Capt. Rynning. He will be confined to his bed for about a month.

When seen by a *Review* man at Benson, Wheeler regretted the occurrence and was sorry when he learned that his assailant had died while being taken to Tucson.

There is little doubt that Tracy came to Benson for the purpose of killing Silverton and his wife, and but for the prompt and plucky action of Ranger Wheeler, there was very little doubt that he would have accomplished his purpose.

LIEUTENANT WHEELER MADE A GOOD FIGHT

(Editorial)

The affray at Benson Thursday morning resulted in the display of unusual bravery by Lieut. Wheeler of the Arizona Rangers. The circumstances of the encounter with the man Tracy disclosed the fact that the brave officer, while acting in the defense of his own life, had no desire to take that of his assailant when he made the claim that his pistol had been emptied of bullets.

It is quite evident that only for the presence of Wheeler in Benson, Tracy would have killed the man Silverton and perhaps his wife also. Tracy was acting like an insane man and had undoubtedly followed Silverton and wife to Benson with the purpose of satisfying an insane jealous hate.

Wheeler has shown that as an officer he is all right. He was no doubt taken unawares when Tracy began shooting at him, but he was not stampeded; he was there to prevent murder which had been threatened by Tracy and he did so by risking his own life.

Lieut. Wheeler is to be congratulated on his narrow escape from more serious harm and also on the fact that he did his duty as an officer, and while the death of Tracy will be regretted it no doubt saved the life of Silverton.

———

PHOENIX, March 1.—D. W. Silverton, who stated to a newspaper reporter at Benson on Tuesday that he and his wife had been married in Phoenix six weeks ago, will find he is unable to prove this assertion by the records of the probate court in this county.

A newspaper correspondent called on the probate judge here today and that official informed him that a marriage license had never been issued in this county to D. W. Silverton to wed anybody.

The story told at Benson to the effect that he had been married by a traveling evangelist is also evidently a fabrication, as no one ever heard of a traveling evangelist by that name. The persistency with which Silverton refused to give the maiden name of his alleged wife, and the failure to find any marriage license on record in this county, surrounds the tragedy enacted at Benson Thursday with additional mystery regarding the relations of Tracy with the woman in the case and also her relations with Silverton.

———

Now that the excitement attending the killing of Tracy by Ranger Lieutenant Harry Wheeler has subsided, little side stories which throw a melodramatic air about the episode are coming to light.

It is related by a bystander who was so close to the shooting that he had to move lest he get out of luck and into range of some of the flying missiles from the guns of the combatants that as both men lay on the ground at the end of the affray, at a time when Wheeler is said to have refused the comfort of a chair, preferring that it be given his erstwhile antagonist, the man who would have taken his life had his aim been true, Wheeler turned his head toward the man near him remarking: "Well, it was a great fight while it lasted, wasn't it, old man."

"I'll get you yet," said Tracy, with the faintest kind of a grim smile. He reached for Wheeler's proffer hand. But little did the wounded man realize that it was his last threat. He expired but a few hours later on his way to medical attendance at Tucson.

—Bisbee *Review*, 1907

GOVERNOR KIBBEY REPORTS

In his biennial message to the territorial legislature in 1907, Governor Joseph H. Kibbey had this to say about the Arizona Rangers:

"Although expensive to the territory, the Arizona Rangers proved so often their usefulness that it seems impossible to recommend the repeal of the law authorizing the force. The area of Arizona is vast, and there are so many remote sections in which the county peace officers do not ordinarily travel—the remoter sections being the favorite haunts of criminals of the most desperate class—that the Rangers to a large extent perform functions that can not well be performed at all by sheriffs or their deputies. The Rangers are traveling almost constantly, and as their identity is kept hidden except when necessary to reveal it, they are enabled to make many arrests of great importance. During the biennial period ended June 30, 1906, the Rangers made a total of 1,756 arrests, of which 451 were for felonies. In addition to these arrests, they made many others in conjugation with local officers, the Rangers being quite frequently called upon for assistance by sheriffs and police officers.

"During the past year one of the most notable achievements of the Rangers was to detect a conspiracy which was forming in Arizona by Mexican citizens to start a revolutionary movement against the government of Mexico, to arrest the ringleaders of the revolutionists, and to aid in their deportation or conviction. When the officers of the Rangers brought to my attention the facts they had learned as to this conspiracy, I at once laid all the available facts before the United States District Attorney, and also advised the State Department at Washington. The projected revolutionary movement was effectively suppressed, and for their efficiency in this matter the territorial authorities have been warmly thanked by both the Mexican Government and the United States Government.

"The total cost of maintaining the Ranger force during the fiscal year 1905 was $33,354.46. During the fiscal year 1906 it was $33,054.17."

———

Captain Tom Rynning of this city has received the appointment of superintendent of the territorial prison at Yuma, succeeding Jerry Millay, who resigned on account of bad health. The appointment was announced yesterday by Governor Kibbey.

This leaves open the position of captain of the Rangers and it is rumored that Lieutenant Wheeler, who is next in line in the Ranger force, will be given the appointment.

The news of Captain Rynning's appointment is a source of much gratification to friends in Douglas and elsewhere over the territory. It has been predicted that Deputy Sheriff Hopkins, formerly sergeant of the Rangers, will be offered the lieutenancy and that in the event of his declination the position will be up to Ranger Kidder who is now stationed at Douglas. Should the lieutenancy come to Sergeant Kidder it could not be given to a more deserving officer. He has been very active in the hunting down of criminals for the four years of his connection with the Rangers. He has always been a careful, courageous and zealous officer and the people of Douglas would be pleased to hear of his promotion.

—Douglas *Dispatch*, 1907

EDITOR'S NOTE: The immediate appointment by Governor Joseph H. Kibbey of Lieutenant Harry S. Wheeler as captain of the Rangers and confirmation by the Arizona Legislature which followed on March 22, 1907, gave the organization its third, and what proved to be its last captain.

Sergeant William A. Old was appointed to the lieutenancy by Governor Kibbey, and the appointment was confirmed by the legislature.

———

Captain Harry C. Wheeler, Arizona Rangers

4

HARRY C. WHEELER

HARRY C. WHEELER

(Biography)

HARRY C. WHEELER, one of the most noted peace officers of the entire Southwest was born in Jacksonville, Florida in 1876. He had attended a military school, and it is said, he was rejected by the United States Military Academy because of his not being quite tall enough, much to his distress. He descended from a family of fighting men, his father, William B. Wheeler having served with distinction in the Spanish-American war. Harry Wheeler also served in the Philippine war with the first United States regulars from Oklahoma. It is said he was discharged from the cavalry because of injuries he sustained when his horse kicked him causing severe injury.

Wheeler came to Arizona in 1900 and settled in the border town of Bisbee. In July 1903, Wheeler enlisted as a private in the Arizona Rangers. Three months later he was promoted to sergeant. In July 1905, he was commissioned lieutenant and in March 1907, was elevated to the captaincy, upon the resignation of Thomas Rynning, who had been named prison superintendent. Wheeler remained with the Rangers as their captain until the legislature abolished the organization in February 1909.

In September 1909, he was appointed deputy United States marshal for the Tucson district and at the end of that year resigned to become a line rider in the customs service in connection with the Douglas custom house.

Wheeler was elected sheriff of Cochise county when Arizona attained statehood in 1912 and was re-elected and served until he enlisted in the army during World War I, when he turned in his resignation. He was commissioned a captain and was stationed at Hoboken, N. J., in charge of several hundred recruits, later being transferred to Camp Merritt, N. J., where he remained for several weeks. He sailed for France in March 1918, having been assigned to the Signal Corps of the Aviation Division, much against his wishes as he felt he wasn't fitted for that particular branch of the service.

Three months later Wheeler was ordered back to the United States to face law suits and indictments brought against him as the result of the deportation of the I.W.W. (International Workers of the World) and their sympathizers from Bisbee in July 1917. He was anxious to return to Arizona to take whatever may be coming to him, as he put it, in connection with the deportation of 1186 men from Bisbee. As sheriff of Cochise county he directed the deportation, deputizing the men who assisted him, and assuming all responsibility of these men being loaded into cattle cars and shipped to Columbus, N. M.

Wheeler had been released on a short furlough to dispose of these personal matters. Just before leaving he received his transfer from the Signal Corps to the infantry for front line duty in France, having made application for the change some time before. He embarked at once for the United States, landing in New York the latter part of July, going directly to Washington.

Wheeler as a younger man

From there he secured additional orders and proceeded to Tombstone, Arizona, as he had been ordered to report at nearby Fort
Huachuca temporarily or until the suits pending against him
were disposed of. He was sent to Nogales in charge of a machine
gun troop in the interim.

The Bisbee Deportation case dragged on. Wheeler was originally named as one of the defendants, having been bound over
for trial at his own request. When the preliminary hearing was
called in September 1919, it was revealed that no information
was ever filed against him in the superior court. However, the
case was finally settled and all defendants, hundreds of them,
being found "not guilty" by a jury of their peers within a matter
of a very short time.

The war was then over and the pioneer, soldier, Ranger,
sheriff, and good citizen that he was, died on December 17, 1925,
at the Calumet and Arizona hospital in the mining town of
Warren (Bisbee), following a short illness which ended with
pneumonia, at the age of about 50 years. Harry Wheeler was
buried there.

RANGERS STOP STEER TYING

With the action taken by Ranger Captain Harry Wheeler yesterday at Don Luis in preventing the exhibition in which steers were to have been roped and tied, and "Nigger" Pickett was billed to throw a steer with his teeth, the end to cruelty to animals in Arizona, whether in an exhibition or otherwise, was marked, the last and most thrilling of wild west feats had received a quietus and the only vestige now left of life on the plains remains in the simple and monotonous stunt of the cowpuncher who may continue to mount the hurricane deck of the untamed broncho and be jolted to his heart's content.

The Twenty-Fourth Legislature said that cruelty to animals in the guise of feats of skill and exhibitions must stop. Captain Wheeler seconded the enactment of the law, and so far as known, Sunday, April 13, 1907, was the first time in the history of this territory that cowboy sport was peremptorily called to a halt under threat of imprisonment.

For the past three weeks O. C. Nations and Clay McGonnigle, both famous throughout the west as steer tiers and broncho busters, have been conducting weekly exhibitions of their ability, and as a side line "Nigger" Pickett, of Texas, a black cowboy, has been throwing a steer by catching the animal's lip between his teeth after mounting the running steer from the back of a fleet pony, and throwing the beast. To the morbid this has proven a most interesting feat and crowds have gathered expressly to see this part of the performance. There will be no more of it wherever there is an Arizona Ranger, or for that matter any other officer of the law who is conversant with the latest statute covering this feature of exhibitions.

Sunday's was the second exhibition scheduled to be conducted for the edification of the Bisbee public, the first having been conducted without interruption.

The management of the affair offered no resistance to the

orders of the officer of the law, but substituted instead of the steer tying and the "Nigger" steer contest, a whole lot of rough riding which seemed to catch the crowd and serve to appease them.

The officers would not even permit the riders to throw a rope about the cattle which they had secured for the occasion, but owing to the foresight of the management a large number of unbroken bronchos were on hand and the exhibition that followed was sufficient to satisfy the crowd that had gathered.

—Bisbee *Review*, 1907

The law referred to above is as follows:

AN ACT

To Prohibit Exhibition of Steer Tying and Steer Tying Contests Within the Territory of Arizona.

Section 1. That it shall be unlawful for any person or persons to engage in any steer tying contest or exhibition of steer tying within the Territory of Arizona.

Section 2. That it shall be unlawful for any person to cast, rope or throw any animal of the horse, cow or other kind, either his own property or the property of another; Provided that nothing in this Act shall apply to necessary work done on the range or elsewhere in the handling of such animals.

Section 3. Any person or persons violating the provisions of the Act or aiding and abetting in the violation of the provisions of this Act shall be guilty of a misdemeanor and upon conviction thereof shall be punished by a fine of not less than Fifty Dollars or more than Two Hundred and Fifty Dollars or by imprisonment of not less than thirty days nor more than one hundred and eighty days.

Section 4. This Act shall take effect and be in force from and after April first, 1907.

Approved March 18, 1907.

EDITOR'S NOTE: The Arizona Legislature in later years liberalized the above law making it possible to resume the sport which is so popularly known today as the "Rodeo."

Tucson, Ariz., May 6.—Lieut. "Billy" Old, of the Arizona Rangers, is in the city preparing to go to the northern part of the territory, where he will command the movements of a bunch of Rangers in a war against a band of horse thieves that have kept the stockmen of that part in constant terror for several years past.

The first work of the Rangers will be in that part of Arizona lying east of the Colorado River, which is one of the wildest parts of the United States. This little neck of rough country has served as a safe rendezvous for cattle and horse thieves for years. It is almost imposible to reach it from the west on account of Death Valley and owing to the difficulty in getting across the canyon of the Colorado the outlaws have practically run things as they please.

Following the same tactics in most every theft, the thieves cross the river, secure their hoofed booty and drive them back across the canyon. For a small number of officers to follow the thieves into their own country has always been considered futile and owing to the country preyed upon by the outlaws being very sparsely settled, the getting together of a number of men large enough to follow the thieves has been impossible. The territorial government was finally appealed to by the ranch owners, and the work about to be commenced by the territorial Rangers is a result of this appeal.

—Douglas *Dispatch,* 1907

Democrat, Phoenix: On their way to Prescott, where they will make their headquarters, Lieutenant Old and Ranger McGee of the Arizona Rangers stopped over in Phoenix today before continuing north. In the past they have been at Nogales. Lieutenent Old will have charge of the Rangers in the northern part of the territory. He states that Captain Harry Wheeler, who succeeded Prison Superintendent Rynning, will be here in a few days on a tour of inspection of the whole territory. Old states that conditions are normal along the Mexican border, with an occasional bad man breaking out and demanding the attention of the officers.

—Douglas *Dispatch*, 1907

Lieutenant Billy Old who has charge of the officers in the northern part of the territory is a visitor in Tucson today and says that he has secured an almost entirely new force. He said:

"Four of the officers from Southern Arizona who were detailed for work in the northern part were unwilling to remain there and they were given the alternative of doing work where they were assigned or resigning, and four of the force decided that they preferred to get out of the service. They did not like the wintry blasts and the many snowstorms. However, new recruits have been secured from the northern part of the territory and the quota is complete again."

—Tucson *Citizen*, 1907

SARABIA KIDNAPPING CASE

Probably never in the history of Cochise county were the citizens of any community worked into such a frenzy as was evident in the city of Douglas on the first day of July, when it became known that a prisoner had been kidnapped from the city jail, probably by the cooperation of two police officers of Douglas, and taken forcibly across the international boundary line into Mexico, which was the last heard of him. A monster mass meeting was held, at which those in attendance made speeches denouncing in the most vigorous terms the outrage which had been committed, because it had been learned that the prisoner who had been taken in such a brutal and crude way, was not wanted for murder, as was alleged, but was wanted on the other side because he with some associates had criticized the existing government of the Southern Republic.

During this time excitement was at a white heat, and even the sheriff of Cochise county, Jack White, and District Attorney Shelley were abused, because they had not prevented the outrage. It was seen, however, when reason was given a place in the affairs, that both of these gentlemen had been most unjustly criticized and abused, and apologies were rendered to them.

Resolutions were adopted calling on the President of the United States, and the President of Mexico, to right the wrong, and even demanded the immediate removal of the Mexican Consul at that point, who was alleged to have been implicated in the affair. Complaints were also sworn out against Ranger Sam Hayhurst, Constable Shropshire, Consul Maza, Jailer Lee Thompson and Special Guard Dawdle, the last of whom was never arrested, as he is believed to have left the country. The absolute injustice of the complaint against Hayhurst, however, will be apparent from the statement of the prisoner himself, now a free man, the only ground on which the complaint had ever been sworn to being that he was the arresting officer; and it is now clear that he acted under orders and in the best of good faith, discharging his duty as a fearless officer.

About two months ago Captain Ramos Bareras called upon Captain Harry C. Wheeler, of the Arizona Rangers, coming as a representative of the new border force lately instituted by the Mexican government, which, however, is separate from the Rurales under the command of Colonel Kosterlitzky. At that time he asked for the arrest of Adolpho Garcia, wanted in Mexico for various alleged crimes. Nothing ever came of this visit. About three weeks ago Bareras again called on the chief of the Rangers and asked for the arrest of one Manuel Sarabia, whom he said was wanted in Mexico on a charge of inciting revolution. The American officer informed the Mexican that under the laws of the United States Sarabia had committed no offense, and therefore could not be arrested.

"But," added Bareras, "this man is a murderer. Don't you arrest men in the United States for murder?"

To this Wheeler replied that we did. The Mexican then stated to the captain of the Rangers that Sarabia had commited murder at several different places, naming them. He was assured that if the man were found he would be held by the American authorities, but that Mexico would have to secure extradition papers. The various Rangers were notified to watch for Sarabia and place him under arrest, awaiting papers, but nothing came of this.

On June 29, Captain Wheeler and Ranger Sam Hayhurst boarded the train leaving Bisbee for Douglas, having been here at the time of the big fire on that day. As the two officers walked through every coach before taking a seat in a train, Captain Bereras met them in the Pullman coach, and told the head of the Rangers that he knew where Sarabia was, showing the man's description, address and everything else connected with him, showing that he was in the city of Douglas. Hayhurst was on the road to Douglas at that time, and Captain Wheeler, out of the courtesy due from an officer in the service of one nation to that of another, told Bereras that his subordinate would arrest Sarabia, holding him on this side of the line until the customary extradition papers were regularly made out, served, and it was shown that there was probable cause to think the prisoner guilty of the offense charged. Then in accordance with the story told him by Bereras, Captain Wheeler told Hayhurst that the man wanted was reported to be a murderer, and to be careful, as he might be desperate. With these instructions the Ranger went to Douglas.

The ordering of the arrest of Sarabia by Wheeler is in accordance with the courtesy of the two friendly nations. However, there has never been an instance where the captain of the Arizona Rangers turned over a prisoner to Mexico until extradition papers were issued no matter how guilty the accused might be known to be. An instance of this is the case of Trujillo, the infamous Mexican murderer, cutthroat, assassin and outlaw, whom Wheeler refused to give to Mexico a few months ago, although he had him on this side of the line in custody, until the regular papers were issued in accordance with law. The Mexican officials, however, would not get extradition papers, even for the infamous Trujillo, claiming it was too expensive and laborious a task, and in consequence Wheeler gave the prisoner his liberty.

With this usual courtesy, the captain of the Rangers in the Sarabia case ordered the arrest of the accused, subject to instructions. Hayhurst carried out instructions, and there is no doubt that within a couple of days the prisoner would have been freed had it not been for the scheming of the subordinate Mexican officials, who were looking for a reputation, and Americans having no regard for honor and integrity.

Despite the fact, however, that violence was used to betray the confidence which the head of the American Ranger force placed in the word of a man who was supposed to be a soldier and a gentleman working for a friendly nation; despite the fact that men perporting to be American citizens connived and conspired to help the treachery; yet today the victim of the outrage is free, and on American soil. This result is due solely and alone to the efforts of Captain Wheeler in bringing the matter to the attention of General Torres in an informal way, and not only Arizona, but the United States, has reason to be proud of this man, whose bravery has been established on a solid foundation; whose integrity as a gentleman can not be questioned; and who in the last instance has shown himself a diplomat of the highest ability in bringing about a result in his characteristically modest and quiet way, that could not have been achieved by the federal state department itself, without complications. Throughout the entire affair he has displayed the courtesy and gentlemanly bearing, backed by the highest sense of justice, that justifies the pride of everyone who knows him to think that he is an American citizen.

When Captain Wheeler brought the affair to the attention of General Torres, commander of the northern military zone of Mexico, and governor-elect of Sonora, the latter at once made a thorough investigation of the affair, and on his return to Hermosillo immediately opened the doors of the prison, thus making Sarabia a free man to go whither he would. This was done entirely in an unofficial manner, so far as international relations were concerned, so that when Sarabia chose to come back to the United States on the same train Wheeler did, he did it of his own free will, and was at no time under arrest nor is he now. In his action General Torres displayed the high sense of justice, which has done much to foster the friendly feelings existing between the United States and Mexico.

When Sarabia stepped from the train at Naco last evening he was met by a *Review* reporter. The man accused of many murders, but who is now known to be guilty of no offense, but that of criticizing the Mexican government, stands about 5 feet 3 inches in height, weighs 130 pounds; is 24 years of age, has a small black moustache, a heavy suit of black hair on his head, dressed in natty clothing, and would give one the impression of being a college student.

The reporter asked Sarabia for a detailed statement, and the following is the substance of his replies as he only speaks broken English. He was born in the City of Mexico, and educated there. After finishing his studies six years ago, he became a member of a group of men who disliked many of the features of the Mexican government, under the presidency of Porfirio Diaz, and banded themselves together for the purpose of bringing about reforms. The name of this organization was, and is, the Junta Liberal Mexicana. This group entered the newspaper field, believing that they could bring their ideas to the attention of the people of the republic most effectively in this manner. In this enterprise he was associated with Ricardo Flores Magon, who was editor in chief of the publication which they called the *Regeneracion.* The troubles of the newspaper were many, the plant being confiscated on several occasions, and the editors thrown in jail. Finally they arrived at the conclusion that they could best serve their interests from the United States, and on January 22, 1904, arrived at Laredo, Texas, in company with several of their associates. Sarabia remained at Laredo for two months, and went from there to San Antonio, where the publication of *Regeneracion* was again attempted, and carried on for several months, but was finally prevented by the intervention of the government of Mexico on technical charges. From San Antonio the headquarters of the Junta were removed to St. Louis, Mo., where the work was carried on for several months, when the Mexican government again, through Esperon Y'de la'Flor, brought trouble upon the heads of the editors, which finally resulted in their leaving St. Louis. Sarabia went to Chicago, thence to Hammond, Ind., from there back to Chicago, from there to St. Louis, and finally back to Texas, where he visited and worked in various cities. In all of these different cities, Sarabia said he worked from three to four weeks. On June 1, 1907, or thereabouts, he arrived in Douglas and secured employment in the office of the Douglas *International-American* under the name of Sam Moret, fearing that if he used his real name, some such incident as lately occurred might happen.

On June 30, at about 10 a.m., he walked to the railroad depot intending to mail a letter on the through train, and was suddenly told to throw up his hands. On looking he saw Ranger Hayhurst, who acting on the theory explained to him that the man was perhaps desperate, took the wise course to prevent trouble, by showing the man he had the drop on him. Sarabia did not put his hands up, explaining to the officer that he was not a bandit. He was again ordered to raise his hands, but again refused, and was finally taken to the city hall by the officer.

While in the city hall six different men entered the room in which he was placed under guard of a big man by Hayhurst, who went out, and returned later. One of these men Sarabia describes as a Mexican, but the description is such that, whether it was Consul Maza or Bareras can not be determined. He was placed in jail about 11 a.m. by the big man. After he was placed in jail, an old man, armed with a six-shooter, displayed very generously, walked up and down in front of the bars, and finally sat down directly in front of his cell. About 2 o'clock in the afternoon he asked for dinner, which was brought in from a restaurant. During the afternoon he asked to see his friends, but the privilege was denied him, and he again demanded to know why he had been arrested. He was informed that he would know later.

About 6:30 he was given supper. In the meantime he destroyed several letters which had been overlooked in searching him. These he destroyed to conceal his real name, pretending that he was Sam Moret, and hoping to bluff out the officers.

At 11 o'clock at night, two men, both of whom he thinks he will be able to identify, came to his cell and ordered him to dress. When he got out of the cell he was handcuffed, and taken through the hall of the building. As soon as he approached the entrance he saw an automobile directly in front and suspecting that he was to be rushed into Mexico, endeavored to escape, at the same time shouting "Long Live Liberty," and like expressions. He was overcome and forced into the machine, one handkerchief being stuffed in his mouth and another held over his eyes. Shortly after the machine started he again shouted out, but again was hushed. The next he knew he was taken from the automobile into a small round house, outside of which were ten mounted Mexican Rurales and five whom he believes were soldiers on foot. There was also two men in a buggy drawn by a team of horses, one whom he believes was in command of the soldiers. He was taken from the house and placed on a horse, handcuffed and with his feet tied beneath the horse, a rurale having the bridle rein, and leading the animal on which he was mounted. The party at once started out, being urged from time to time to go faster by

one of the men seated in the buggy. The cavalcade arrived at
Naco, Sonora, at about 5 a.m., where Sarabia was placed in jail
until the train left for Cananea, when again in the custody of the
soldiers he made the trip. He arrived in Cananea shortly after
noon, and was again placed in jail, where he remained two days
and two nights. He was then placed on horseback again, and in
company with six soldiers, one of whom led his horse, made the
trip to the railroad at Imuris, where he arrived at 2 o'clock p.m.,
July 3. On July 4, he was taken on the train to Hermosillo, where
he was confined incommunicado, which means that he was
allowed to see no one. The next time he was out of jail was on
Thursday morning July 11, when he was brought out and Captain
Wheeler met him after his release had been arranged, and he
was informed he was a free man to go wherever he wished. He
elected to come back to the United States, and came on the same
train Captain Wheeler did, arriving in this country at Nogales.
Last evening at 5:10 he arrived in Naco, where he remained that
night and will go to Douglas in the morning.

After finishing his narrative, Sarabia, who would impress one
as an enthusiastic boy imbued with the spirit of liberty, began
to speak of Captain Wheeler. His emotion was so intense that
he could think of nothing adequate to express his feeling toward
the man whom he had never seen before he came out of jail at
Hermosillo, but whom he knew was his deliverer.

The arrival of Sarabia at Douglas will undoubtedly clear
Ranger Hayhurst of the slightest blame, and show him to be an
officer who although well known for his nerve, would rather
prevent trouble than to hurt a prisoner. His arrival will also
undoubtedly mean the dealing out of just retribution to those
who, for want of consideration, were instrumental in perpetrating
this outrage, which had it not been for eminent ability displayed
on the part of Captain Wheeler, Governor Kibbey, in ordering an
investigation, and General Luis E. Torres in treating the matter
with the high sense of justice and a disdain for trickery might
have ended in serious complications as a result of the absolute lie
of one supposed to be a soldier and a gentleman.

—Bisbee *Review*, 1907

The *Review* in May 1908, had this to say:

Manuel Sarabia, the alleged revolutionist is at it again. He arrived in Tucson in custody of Lee Youngworth, United States marshal for the southern district of California, after his arrest in Los Angeles at the request of the Mexican authorities. The impression has been given circulation during the past few days when it was announced that Manuel Sarabia had been brought back to Tucson on his way to Tombstone that he was to be tried and if convicted that he was to be deported to Mexico. Such is not the case. The indictments found against Sarabia, Magon, Villareal and Rivera charges them with a violation of the neutrality laws of the United States under which statute they will be tried. The statutes provide for a punishment not to exceed two years in the penitentiary and a fine not exceeding $5,000, or both such fine and imprisonment.

The *Review* in October, 1908, stated:

Sarabia has been a prisoner in the Pima county jail at Tucson for five months and he has just been released on bond of $500, which followed receipt of a telegram to United States Marshal Ben Daniels, from Tombstone, stating that Sarabia's bond had been approved. He and his associates, who also are under arrest, were to await trial before the United States court at Tombstone. Sarabia was charged with being an ally of Magon, Villareal and Rivera, and other revolutionary agitators, and the Mexican government desires very much to extradite Sarabia, but these proceedings were hotly contested.

EDITOR'S NOTE: Before a jury at Tombstone court house in May 1909, Magon, Villareal and Rivera, after several days of trial, were all found guilty of violating the neutrality laws of the United States and were sentenced by Judge Fletcher Doan to serve eighteen months each in the territorial prison at Yuma.

What happened to Manuel Sarabia? He had disappeared from the scene at Tucson when he jumped his bond and headed for places unknown. It was thought he had fled to Canada.

———

DUEL TO THE DEATH

The Tucson *Citizen* of July 1, 1907, gave the following startling news:

Last night, a short distance from Child's Wells near Ajo,* a little settlement in the Sierra del Ajo range in the western end of Pima county, Ranger Frank S. Wheeler shot and killed James Kerrick and his partner, Lee Bentley, with whom he lived in Tucson. Kerrick and his companion were making away with a bunch of stock which they are alleged to have "rustled" in the Ajo hills and when overtaken by Ranger Wheeler and Deputy Cameron and called upon to surrender a fight ensued in which the keen eye and automatic gun of Ranger Wheeler proved too much for his two assailants.

Kerrick and Bentley, who had been working at Helvetia for several months past, were in Tucson about three weeks ago and when they left town it was for the avowed purpose of prospecting in the Ajo mountains about fifty miles south of Gila Bend.** A few days later they hired two Indian ponies in Gila Bend and set out southward, leaving word that they were prospecting and would return in a month. As Kerrick was known to be a cattle rustler by some parties in Gila Bend and as he and his fellow prospector carried no tools for prospecting it was quietly suspicioned that they were going out to "rustle" cattle and horses in the isolated Ajo hills.

* Ajo (äh-hō) Spanish for garlic.
** Gila Bend (hēē-läh).

Ranger Frank Wheeler, who is stationed at Yuma, but who happed to be in Gila Bend at this time, and Deputy Cameron, were put on their trail. From information that the men could gather from the ranchers in the hills it was learned that the suspicions concerning the self-styled prospectors were true; that the hills were being covered by the men and that they were leading and driving a bunch of stock, including calves and colts as they went. Wheeler and Cameron at once set out after them and anticipating trouble, prepared for the worst. They overtook the alleged rustlers at Sheep Dung Tanks, west of Ajo, where they were watering and preparing to go in camp. When Wheeler and Cameron rode up they were recognized and the rustlers must have known they were in trouble. Wheeler called out for the pair to surrender. His call was answered by a flash of pistols. It was then that Wheeler turned loose his automatic that could give three shots to his opponents' one. Cameron also fired but it was Wheeler's shots that did the work. Both Kerrick and Bentley were killed and Wheeler hurried a messenger to Gila Bend, who wired the news of the tragedy to the sheriff's office in Tucson.

Sheriff Pacheco left on the train this morning for Gila Bend, where he will take an automobile furnished by the Ajo Copper Mining company and bring the bodies back to Gila Bend. Justice of the Peace John Doan of Silver Bell, in whose precinct the killing took place, has been called to Gila Bend, where a coroner's inquest will be held this evening if it is possible to get the bodies there today. Sheriff Pacheco took ice out from Gila Bend and an effort will be made to preserve the bodies of the dead men for the inquest. Ranger Wheeler holds himself in readiness to surrender to the sheriff upon Pacheco's arrival.

Jim Kerrick was a bad man, and has a long record of deviltry and crime behind him. For years he has been alleged to be a cattle thief. He began his record by killing a sheep herder in Southern California when but a youth. An old man had been keeping a flock of about 600 sheep in a little valley between two mountain ranges in the San Jacinto mountains. Kerrick was a partner in a company that had a flock over the range. One day the old man's bones were found in an ash pile and Kerrick's herd was found to have suddenly increased in numbers. Kerrick was arrested, tried and sentenced to twenty years at San Quentin. Kerrick made a record for good behavior in the California prison and finally when friends represented that mistaken circumstances had caused his conviction he was pardoned. Immediately upon leaving the penitentiary he came to Arizona and resumed a career of thievery and crime. After being suspected of various cases of cattle rustling and of being involved in other difficulties at Yuma and all through the lower Gila valley he was hauled up and sent to the penitentiary for cattle rustling and here at Yuma he served his term of two years. When released he took up mining and since has had as a companion Lee Bentley. The men had evidently decided to try their fortunes once more in bucking law and order when their career was ended by Ranger Wheeler.

The *Citizen* later reported:

Whether or not Ranger Frank Wheeler and a deputy sheriff from Yuma county was justified in killing Jim Kerrick and Lee Bentley near Ajo some time ago while the latter were resisting arrest on a horse stealing charge is the question that will be settled by Judge Doan at a coroner's inquest to be held in Silver Bell on the thirtieth of this month.

The question of holding an inquest to investigate the killing has been agitated in this city for some time, and was settled yesterday when W. L. Bentley, brother of one of the men who were killed, appeared before District Attorney Benton Dick and asked that the move be made.

"I am not stating as a positive fact," said Bentley, "that the killing was not justified, but there is a reasonable doubt, and it would be the most satisfactory thing to all parties concerned if an investigation or coroner's inquest be held.

"The report printed in a morning paper shortly after the killing that I was going 'gunning' for the two officers was absolutely untrue. I am a law-abiding man," added Bentley.

Both the man who appeared before the district attorney and his brother who was killed were once in the Texas Ranger service. Bentley is now employed as a teamster by the Helvetia Copper Company.

The *Citizen* followed with this item:

SILVER BELL, Ariz., Aug. 13.—(Special Dispatch to the *Citizen*.)—A coroner's verdict rendered today finds Ranger Frank S. Wheeler and Deputy Sheriff and Constable John Cameron to have acted in the discharge of their duties and to have been justified and acting in self-defense at the time of the killing near Ajo of Lee Bentley and Jim Kerrick. The evidence of officers Wheeler and Cameron was fully and substantially corroborated by two Papago Indians, eye witnesses to the killing. The Indians testified that Wheeler called to Bentley and Kerrick twice and Cameron called once before a shot was fired and that Bentley fired the first shot. The officers' testimony was that Bentley raised and threw his gun into position to fire but was struck in the right arm by a bullet. He then shifted the position of his gun to the other hand, but was struck again and never had an opportunity to fire a shot. Kerrick shot once at Cameron who returned his fire, but the officers were unable to identify the actual shot that killed either men.

———

The Phoenix *Gazette* had this opinion:

That the bullion from the King of Arizona mines was the stake for which Jim Kerrick and Lee Bentley were playing when Ranger Frank Wheeler and Deputy Cameron called their hands, seems now more probable. For five burning, deadly days the officers trailed their men back and forth, from the camp by the stage road where the battle finally occurred, to the Mexican boundary. The rustlers had six fine saddle horses—the pick of the ranches about. They were heavily armed. Their camp was an ideal one for an ambuscade. When, in the early dawn of Sunday morning, Ranger Wheeler called in the name of the law for their peaceable surrender, the men sprang to their rifles and opened fire.

Had the pursuers halted and turned away from their long chase or had they delayed a day there would in all probability have been one more stage robbery with its attendant murder, and with relays of fresh horses, their route selected with care, the bandits would have been safe in Mexico before the crime was discovered.

From the circumstances surrounding the killing of Kerrick and Bentley by Ranger Frank Wheeler and Deputy Cameron, near Ajo, it is reasonable to conclude that a holdup of the bullion stage which passes from the King of Arizona mine to Sentinel on the Southern Pacific was averted.

The rustlers at the time of the killing were possessed of six crack saddle horses which they had stolen from ranchers, and they were in secret camp along the roadside which passes each week the stage which carries the bullion from the King of Arizona mine to Mohawk on the Southern Pacific railroad. As Kerrick and Bentley had every facility for a hold-up, including several brand new .33 Winchester rifles of the latest model and had familiarized themselves with the nearest and best trail by which they could make their escape across the line, it is believed their plan was to rob the stage, pack the bullion on their speedy horses and make their escape to Mexico.

———

YUMA, July 4.—In telling the story of the shooting of Kerrick and Bentley, Ranger Frank Wheeler, in an interview, said:

"I left here on June 26 and went as far as Welton, where I met Johnny Cameron, whom I had wired to as soon as I had word from Captain Wheeler to go after the men. Cameron had two horses at Sentinel, and together we struck out across the burning desert in search of the outlaws. We knew they were in the Ajo country, and we rode 140 miles in the blazing heat, tracking the horse thieves. On Saturday we rode thirty-five miles. Our horses went without water the entire day, and the water in our canteens was so hot we couldn't drink it, and you know how hot it was. Just as dawn was breaking we started in the direction we knew the men were camping, and when we had walked a mile and a half we took off our shoes and walked another mile and a half before we came upon the men sleeping beside their guns.

"Bentley's Winchester lay about a foot from where he was asleep, and as soon as he was awakened, (of course we let them know what we wanted,) he managed to load his gun before I began shooting. Four times I shot at him, but not until the fifth shot did he drop. The bullet went through his left temple and came out the right ear. Cameron got his man Kerrick with one shot. My gun was a 30–40 rifle, and Cameron carried a 30–30.

"When we were sure they were dead we put them on their own horses and rode twenty-five miles with them to the Ten Miles Wells, ten miles from Ajo. We sent word to Sentinel to wire to Pima county for a coroner. The coroner refused to come, and a wire was sent to Silver Bell for the justice of the peace, and he refused to come. So it was all day Sunday and until 2 o'clock Monday when Sheriff Pacheco arrived, before we buried the men. We did not dare leave them on top of the ground any longer, on account of the heat, so I made boxes for them and lowered them into the ground. Even when Pacheco got there the bodies were decomposed beyond recognition.

"We went back to Gila Bend, where we took the train for home. Both men were wanted for stealing Indian ponies in Maricopa county. There was no reward offered either by the captain of the Rangers or the sheriff of Maricopa county."

—Phoenix *Democrat*, 1907

TUCSON, Aug. 20.—"I never before realized what a terrible thing the act of taking a human life was until the evidence of the inquest into the killing of Bentley and Kerrick by Ranger Wheeler and Deputy Sheriff Cameron was unfolded bit by bit before my eyes," stated District Attorney Benton Dick in discussing the inquest at Silver Bell.

"According to the story told by the two officers and corroborated by two eye witnesses the killing was entirely justifiable, but it was a horrible affair, nevertheless," continued the district attorney.

"Bentley was a young man in the prime of life, about twenty-six years of age, and Ranger Wheeler said that he showed more nerve under fire than he had ever seen displayed by a man before, which is saying a good deal, as Wheeler has been in the Southwest for a good many years and has been a member of the Ranger force for the past four years, having handled a number of bad men in his time.

"Bentley was down on one knee with his rifle in hand taking deliberate aim when the first shot was fired, which struck him in the abdomen. Although five shots were fired into his body, one in the head, two near the heart, one in the abdomen and another in the lower part of the body, Wheeler said that Bentley never wavered from his position he had assumed at first until the last shot had been fired, whereupon he fell face down upon the ground, but not until after he had made a last desperate effort to recover his equilibrium."

J. D. Simmons of Helvetia and Silver Bell, who is a brother-in-law of Lee Bentley, one of the men killed, made a statement today in which he denies that Bentley fired the first shot.

"According to the statement made by the officers at Silver Bell," said Simmons, "Lee Bentley did not fire the first shot. Cameron fired first and the shot struck Bentley, who was the first one injured.

"Also regarding the ponies which it is stated they had stolen, witnesses swore at the inquest that Bentley and Kerrick had hired the ponies from Indians, paying them ten dollars for their use."

—Bisbee *Review,* 1907

JOHN JOHNS

News reached the city, says the Tucson *Citizen* in 1907, of the killing of Lariano Alvarez of El Cubo, a small Indian village about 150 miles west of Tucson on the 30th of August, the murderer being John Johns, an Indian resident of the village.

The news was contained in a letter from Tom Childs Jr., who is a brother-in-law of Alvarez, to Sheriff Pacheco, who, through the aid of the mails, deputized Childs to arrest Johns and bring him to Tucson.

El Cubo is about twenty-five miles south of Ajo, and in the Papago language means "Big Pond," after the large water hole there. It is reported here that the Indian residents of the village frequently smuggle mescal into the place from Mexico and get on drunken sprees.

No particulars of the killing are given in the letter, with the exception that Alvarez was in the camp for a few days and while there Johns got drunk, and picking a quarrel with him, stabbed him to death before any of the Indians who were present at the time could interfere.

There are numerous Indian villages in that part of the country and it is said that the residents of all of them spend a good part of their time in a drink-crazed condition.

It is not known here just when Childs will arrive with the prisoner, but it is expected that it will be within the next day or two.

A few weeks later the *Citizen* disclosed:

This afternoon, Captain Harry Wheeler of the Arizona Rangers, accompanied by eight of his men arrived in Tucson. They will be joined by Sheriff Pacheo and three of his deputies, and the combined party, armed to the teeth and prepared for a long desert trip, will leave early tomorrow morning on horseback for the Papago Indian village known as El Cubo. The trip will be made by way of Quijotoa * and Ajo.

Some time ago this paper printed the particulars of the killing of a Mexican at El Cubo by an Indian named John Johns. Later Sheriff Pacheco deputized Tom Childs Jr., of the Ten Mile well, to make the arrest. Nothing was heard from Childs for some time, until August 6th, when a letter was received by Sheriff Pacheco from him, in which he stated, "I herewith return you the warrant sent me. It is utterly impossible for one man to make the arrest as the Indians are up in arms, and threaten to kill the first white man that attempts to travel the Cubo trail."

When this letter was received from Childs, Sheriff Pacheco immediately sent the following communication to the Board of Supervisors of Pima county:

"Some fifteen days past a murder was committed at a Papago Indian rancheria called El Cubo. This rancheria is about twenty miles southwest of the Gunsight Mine in this county. As soon as I was notified of this murder I took immediate steps to effect the capture of the murderer. For this purpose I went to Gila Bend but had to return as I was unable to get necessary transportation into the Indian country. Before returning to this city, I deputized Tom Childs Jr., a very reliable man who knows the country and the Indians well, to go after the murderer. Childs, accompanied by some of his neighbors made the trip, but they were unsuccessful in accomplishing their mission for the reason that the Indians were up in arms and absolutely refused to give up the criminal. They had made the threat that any white person seen traveling over the El Cubo trail will be shot down by them.

"In my opinion these Indians must be made to respect the law, otherwise more serious complications will arise in the future. For this purpose I have made arrangements with Captain Harry Wheeler of the Arizona Rangers to accompany me together with eight or ten of his men. I will take with me all available deputies. I desire your sanction for the expenses incurred, which will be

* Quijotoa (kēy-hō tōä) Papago word meaning "carrying basket" mountain.

moderate as no compensation will be paid to any of the posse, simply supplies and incidentals. Trusting to hear from you at once as we expect to start on the 15th inst., I am, Respectfully yours, Nabor Pacheco, Sheriff of Pima County."

Upon receipt of this message from the sheriff, the board of Supervisors decided to allow the expenses incurred by the posse, and a resolution to this effect was passed by them.

This uprising by the Indians brings one back to the early days of the territory, when the redskins were out in numbers to ambush the lonely traveler of the plains. This is the first time for a good many years that the Indians have taken arms in any number to resist the laws of the White Father, and it is the opinion of Sheriff Pacheco, as expressed in his communication to the Board of Supervisors that it is best to suppress them before they are led to believe from the lack of action on the part of the officers that they are invincible and can commit their depredations and remain unmolested. To this end the posse will leave town early tomorrow morning, and will not return until they have captured the murderer and put down the threatened uprising of the Indians.

The posse left here Sunday morning, September 15, at five o'clock. They traveled on horseback all day Sunday, Monday, Tuesday, Wednesday, and Thursday afternoon at 1:30 arrived at El Cubo where Johns was supposed to be.

An old Indian was picked up 18 miles from El Cubo, who agreed to act as their guide, under the supposition that the party was bound for Gunsight. He informed Sheriff Pacheco that the easiest and shortest way to reach Gunsight would be by a small Indian village known as El Cubo. The sheriff replied with an air of indifference that they might as well go through El Cubo as any other way and told the Indian to lead the way.

The village was soon reached and Pacheco told the guide to find an Indian for them, whose name was John Johns. The fellow, realizing what the real purpose of the posse was, became frightened and refused to look for the murderer. The place, at the time the officers arrived, was deserted with the exception of a few women and several children, but before the party had been there five minutes several men came running in from nearby fields. They were placed under arrest by Sheriff Pacheco as fast as they arrived. Finally one old man came in, and after being questioned, informed the officers that John Johns, the man wanted, was in a field a short distance from the village. Pacheco and Wheeler started for the field, and as they neared it they caught sight of a man making away through the weeds. Captain Wheeler gave chase and soon returned with the man, who proved to be John Johns, the murderer. He admitted his identity.

The posse met absolutely no resistance from the Indians, but Sheriff Pacheco stated that in his opinion the only reason they were not molested was on account of their numbers. He said that if one man or even two or three had attempted to enter the village, they would no doubt have been killed by the Indians, a number of whom were armed with rifles.

Thursday night the posse camped near El Cubo, and Friday morning before sunrise the return journey to Tucson was commenced.

A news letter by mail from the special correspondent of the *Citizen* at Ajo reveals an extraordinary and astonishing state of affairs in the Indian country to the south and west of Ajo.

Sheriff Pacheco and Captain Wheeler were greatly suprised at the customs of the Indians and the apparent disregard for any civilized laws. The letter is as follows:

"An eye for an eye and a life for a life is not the custom that prevails among the Papagoes that live in the southwestern part of Pima county. They vary the ancient law so that instead of really giving an eye when one is lost or instead of having an execution when a murder is committed the family or relatives of the killed or murdered party are recompensed by a money consideration.

"It was the refusal of John Johns to pay the small sum of $75 to the widow of the murdered man, that led to all the present trouble. As is the custom of the tribe the squaw of the dead man took her claim up with the head chief in the Indian pueblo and the order was given that Johns should pay her $75. Johns balked in the payment and the squaw in her Indian understanding of her legal right attempted to force the payment of this sum. This refusal of Johns placed him under the ban of the law and it is the general belief that he would have been dealt with according to the Indian customs had not the White Man's Law stepped into the case.

"No sooner had word been received in the pueblo that the officer from Tucson wanted Johns than the whole village rallied to his support. The Indians did not at all relish the prospect of interference with their affairs and they determined to either resist with arms or to secret Johns when the officers arrive. For this reason it is believed that the officers' posse will have the greatest difficulty in discovering the whereabouts of the Indians.

"By means of communication known only to the Indians word reached the village of El Cubo within twenty-four hours after it was known in Tucson that the posse would start for the village.

"The Papago fiestas in this country are grewsome affairs and not a single one goes by without a serious cutting or killing scrape. The Indians seem to accept these things, however, as a matter of course and the relatives are always satisfied when they receive their money payment.

"It was during the last fiesta at Ajo that Rafael Vega, a Papago, mysteriously met death. It was supposed that he had perished in the flames which destroyed his shack, but there was evidence that his skull had been fractured and this strongly indicated murder. Those who are familiar with Indian adobes do not attribute the fracture to the falling of walls of the shack.

"At another recent fiesta an Indian named Juan, struck an Indian named Juaquin in the eye with a large boulder, mashing the latter's face and gouging the eye out. This ghastly scene took place at Redondo's well. The assailant settled with his victim by the payment of $75 and the two are now warm friends.

"All the depredations on the part of the Indians are caused through their becoming drunk on the vile brand of mescal which is smuggled across the border from Mexico and sold to them.

This fiery fluid inflames the Indians and it is no unusual thing for a brave to kill some member of his family and his best friend. Thus far the officers have been unable to stop the mescal smuggling and until they do the horrible scenes that mark all the fiestas will continue to be enacted.

"The Indians when sober are fairly industrious and live peacefully in their villages according to their own laws and customs. A governor selected from their ranks is the chief ruler of the village and he settles all disputes and prescribes the form of punishment for all offenses.

"It is from the tribes in this vicinity that many of the young braves and squaws who attend the Tucson Indian school are recruited. They remain in the city for several years and receive a fair education. They soon revert to their old ways and customs, however, on their return to the villages and within a short time appear to have forgotten all that they were taught in the Indian schools.

In speaking of the return trip the Tucson *Star* stated:

. . . . The posse having ridden hard that day, decided to camp with the Indians that night, a number of the force doing guard duty during the night to frustrate any attempt on the part of the Indians to rescue Johns, but not a single move was made by them.

The next morning the homeward trip was commenced and the posse, composed of Sheriff Pacheco, Deputy Mills, Captain Harry Wheeler of the Rangers, and Rangers Kidder, Stanford, Fraser, Speed, Miles, Smith, Pool, Rhodes and Bates, returned after three days of hard riding. The party returned with their man and another Indian named Citiano, whom Johns implicated in the murder. The two Indians were placed in the wagon brought along by the posse, and various members of the Rangers watched their movements on the long journey until they were placed in the county jail by Deputy Mills and the shackles removed from their legs, the irons having been applied at the time they were arrested.

Johns and Citiano were given their hearings and were bound over to the grand jury without bail, according to the *Citizen*. They were not compelled to make statements during this hearing, but both afterwards claimed that the other was guilty of the murder.

Four Indians, who were brought in from the Papago reservation, swore that they were eye witnesses to the murder and testified that it was committed by John Johns. Two others, who were also brought in for the hearing, said that Citiano was guilty of the deed. These two Indians did not see the murder, and from their testimony it appeared that their only basis for saying what they did, is the statement made by Johns after the murder had been committed, in which he said Citiano was guilty.

The four eye witnesses testified that Lariano Alvarez, who lived at El Cubo, had made several remarks to different residents of the village, concerning John Johns, who heard of these remarks which were far from complimentary and started on a still hunt for Alvarez, whom he soon found, riding on the El Cubo trail. Johns, so these four witnesses claim, pulled Alvarez from his horse, and stabbed him several times with a knife. Death resulted five days later from the wounds.

The Tucson *Star* later revealed:

The jury, after deliberating all night, one of the ballots this morning stood ten for acquittal and two for conviction in the first degree. At noon the jury came into the court room and asked to be discharged, agreeing on the fact that they could not agree. Judge Campbell, however, sent them back with instructions to get together. At 3 o'clock they asked for some information on law points, and the verdict was returned a little less than two hours later, which was guilty of murder in the second degree.

The Tucson *Citizen* in February 1908, stated:

Ten years in the territorial penitentiary was the sentence given John Johns, the Papago Indian, today by Judge Campbell.

———

EDITOR'S NOTE: The Yuma Prison records show that John Johns, convict 2725, was received February 18, 1908, to serve ten years for second degree murder. Johns was 26 years of age, 5 feet 7½ inches in height, and weight, 175 pounds. He was unmarried and his mother was left to bear the sorrow.

———

CAPTAIN WHEELER DEFENDS RANGERS

Among the visitors to Bisbee Saturday afternoon was Captain Harry Wheeler of the Arizona Rangers, who made a trip to Bisbee on matters of official business. He returned to his headquarters at Naco the same evening.

The captain stated that reports from his men in the north are to the effect that there is comparatively little breaking of the law in that section; that several cases of cattle rustling have been reported by men working in the mountains of the south near the boundary line.

Information of a somewhat definite character has been obtained in regard to the law-breakers, and there is no doubt that a part of the force will be detailed on the work.

In referring to articles written concerning the Ranger force by various magazine writers which, among other things, described the appearance of the members of the company as being that of "careless cut-throats," Captain Wheeler said:

Ranger Holmes, who, in attempting single-handed to arrest a Mexican smuggler and an Indian, was forced to kill both in self defense.

"I can assure you that neither myself nor my men appreciate any such description. We use our best efforts to uphold the laws of the territory, but I do not think we can be accused of swaggering around with the air of a desperado. It is unfortunately true that in the course of official duty it has been found necessary by members of the company to kill outlaws, but duties of this kind have always been performed with the greatest regret by the Rangers. I have not the slightest hesitation in saying that the Rangers are honorable officers, and do not resemble 'careless cut-throats' in any particular."

To anyone acquainted with the men composing the command of the Ranger captain, the absurdity of the description of the magazine writers is apparent, but unfortunately these articles are read throughout the United States, and help to keep Arizona branded as being a typical home of the "wild and woolly."

It can be said without fear of denial that there is no more polished gentlemen anywhere than the captain himself, and it would take a most vivid imagination to picture him as a "careless cut-throat." Although his personality is striking, his mode of dress would never attract attention for any "wild west style," and there is not a man who would think he had a six-shooter on his person, unless he knew he was an officer.

Including the captain of the Rangers there are nine men in the organization who never touch liquor of any kind, and drunkenness is a cause for immediate dismissal.

The Rangers never congregate in the large cities of the territory except when absolutely necessary, spending the greater part of the time riding the ranges rounding up lost, strayed or stolen cattle, or tracing some criminal. It is true they are absolutely fearless, and are marksmen of high caliber, which facts account for their being alive. But with it all they are a modest set of men, who say little and try to avoid the "tenderfoot" magazine writer, who insists on maligning them, and blackening the name of Arizona.

The days of the "wild west" are gone, and the territory now ranks with the foremost of the union, with her educational facilitiss, churches, modern cities and pretty homes. In the city, of New York horse cars are still in vogue, but in Arizona this antiquated mode of transportation has given way to most modern electric systems.

—Phoenix *Democrat*, 1907

THE CHARLES EDWARDS MURDER

Charles Edwards, one of the prominent cattlemen of the Tonto country and the oldest son of the late Judge Edwards, was assassinated yesterday while on his way home from Globe, after attending court in his capacity as deputy sheriff. Details are lacking owing to the fact that the body was found about twelve miles north of Roosevelt and telephone communication ends at that point.

The first word of the tragedy was received here at 2:30 yesterday afternoon, when a telephone message was received at the sheriff's office. It stated that a man had just ridden into Roosevelt with the story of having discovered the body of Edwards lying in the road. He did not stop to ascertain the cause of death, but rode immediately to Roosevelt to notify Justice of the Peace Evans and Ranger Holmes. Edwards' riderless horse had turned back from the scene of the crime and arrived at Roosevelt shortly after noon.

Sheriff Thompson and Gus Williams, a brother-in-law of the deceased, left Globe immediately for Roosevelt and were followed a few hours later by District Attorney L. L. Henry and Deputy Sheriff W. G. Duncan. The mere fact that Edwards had been found dead in the road was sufficient evidence to the local authorities that he had been murdered, but not until late last night was their conviction confirmed. This was contained in the following telegram sent by Ranger Holmes from Roosevelt via Phoenix:

Sheriff's Office, Globe, Ariz.:

Charles Edwards was murdered.

J. T. HOLMES.

Edwards left Globe Thursday evening for his home near Cline, after returning the night before from a trip to Phoenix in charge of two insane men. He was armed with a six-shooter when he left here, which leads to the belief that he was shot from ambush. The body will probably arrive here some time today for burial, a wagon having been sent by F. L. Jones & Son for the remains.

At the sheriff's office yesterday it was the generally accepted conclusion that Edwards had been murdered and all afternoon and evening was spent in waiting for additional details, which failed to arrive. Edwards is said to have had a number of bitter enemies in the Tonto country and it was probably one of these who assassinated him.

—Globe *Silver Belt*, 1908

A few days later the *Silver Belt* continued:

Edwards, whose body was found along the road to Cline, eleven and a half miles north of Roosevelt, last Saturday, was shot from ambush, the slayer or slayers lying in wait for him as he came up the road, behind a mesquite bush. The assassination occurred about 6 o'clock Friday evening and the body was not discovered until 10 o'clock the next morning. Travel is heavy on the road between Roosevelt and Cline and it was because the body was almost out of sight of the road, that it was not discovered sooner. Guy Solomon and a man named Miller were the ones who made the grewsome discovery and they hastened to Roosevelt to notify the authorities, after identifying the body as that of Edwards.

Edwards never had even the slightest chance to defend himself. His doom was sealed the moment he rode into Roosevelt Friday morning from Globe, and was seen by the man or men whose enmity he had gained. They started out on the river road before he did and picked out a good spot for their deadly work. They knew that following the discovery of the crime, Indian trailers from Roosevelt would be put on the scent, and they took all precautions necessary to prevent trailing, even by the most clever of the trailers. Horses were abandoned at a point some distance from the ambush, where constant travel would obliterate the hoof prints and their own shoes were muffled before they started for the point they had chosen for the assassination.

When Edwards approached the turn in the road where a mesquite bush had cleverly been converted into a "rats nest" to hide the slayers from view, it must have been about twilight, judging from the time he left Roosevelt. When he was just about 57 feet from the ambush, the first shot was fired. The horse, frightened by the shot, sprang backward and then bolted from the road, running almost a hundred feet before the rider fell. The hoofprints of Edwards' horse and the ground where he fell show this evidence.

Before he fell two more shots were fired, both taking effect, and after the rider had fallen, probably dead, the assassins, wishing to make certain of their work, fired another shot through his head. The powder marks on the face give evidence of this.

The first shot struck Edwards in the breast and the bullet came out behind the right shoulder. Another struck him in the arm, breaking the bone, and the other, fired while he was still on his horse, struck him in the side, the bullet coming out at the abdomen. The last shot was fired into the left eye, emerging above the right ear.

When Sheriff Thompson arrived at Roosevelt Saturday night, he immediately went to the scene of the killing with Ranger Holmes and several Indian trailers. The trailers could do nothing, however, the assassins having left not the slightest clue or track to follow. Several 30–30 shells were found in the vicinity, which showed what kind of weapon did the deadly work.

An inquest was held by Coroner Evans at Roosevelt yesterday morning, at which a verdict of death by the hand of some party or parties unknown, was returned.

Sheriff Thompson and Ranger Holmes were out again all day yesterday and it is presumed that the clue mentioned by the sheriff in his telephone message was discovered during the day.

And the following day in the *Silver Belt:*

No developments of importance in the Edwards assassination were reported yesterday and it was impossible to secure any information from Roosevelt. The arrests which were expected to have been made yesterday did not materialize, but there is every reason to believe that despite the precautions taken by the assassins to hide their identity and prevent trailing, they will be apprehended within a few days.

A telephone message was received from Roosevelt last evening saying that Sheriff Thompson and Gus Williams, brother-in-law of the murdered man, had left there at 2 o'clock in the afternoon for Globe and that they would probably arrive here early this morning. The message also stated that Deputy Sheriff Voris, who arrived there Monday morning, would remain, and with Ranger Jim Holmes, would attempt to run down the clues, that were in their possession. Voris and Holmes are two of the best officers in the territory and that they will accomplish something definite is confidently expected here.

At the sheriff's office, no information of any kind regarding the assassination would be given out, although it was intimated that valuable knowledge was in possession of the officers.

Later in the *Silver Belt:*

John Cline, a prominent resident of northern Gila county, was arrested last evening at Mesa for the murder of Charles Edwards, who was assassinated last Friday evening about a mile from the town which bears Cline's name. The arrest was made by Sheriff Hayden of Maricopa county, on telegraphic advice from Sheriff Thompson of this county, and Cline was immediately taken to the county jail at Phoenix, where he will remain until an officer from Gila county brings him to Globe for preliminary examination. Two sons of Cline, both of whom are boys who have not yet reached their majority, were probably arrested yesterday afternoon at their home at Cline by Deputy Voris and Ranger Holmes, who left Roosevelt at noon for the Cline ranch, fourteen miles up Tonto creek, for that purpose. Owing to the fact that telephone communication with the north ends at Roosevelt, it could not be learned whether or not the arrests had been made,

but at the sheriff's office no doubt was expressed that the officers
had not done what they were sent to do. At eight o'clock last
evening, the time at which the telephone office at Roosevelt
closes, a message from there stated that the officers had not
returned with their prisoners, but were expected at any time.

Warrants were issued by Justice of the Peace Rawlings yester-
day morning for the arrest of John Cline, Joe Cline and Jimmy
Cline, all of whom are charged with the murder of Charles
Edwards. Sheriff Thompson signed the complaints and as soon
as the warrants were issued he sent a telephone message to
Deputy Sheriff Bill Voris at Roosevelt to cause the arrest of the
two boys, having been informed that the father had left for
Phoenix Tuesday afternoon. Voris said he would leave at once for
the Cline ranch, with Ranger Holmes, and that he would be in
Globe some time today with his prisoners.

A message was sent at the same time to Sheriff Carl Hayden of
Maricopa county advising him of the issuance of the warrant
against the elder Cline and requesting him to arrest him upon
his arrival in Phoenix. Hayden did not wait until Cline arrived
there, but went to Mesa to meet him.

Just what the evidence against the Clines is, has not been
revealed by either Sheriff Thompson or District Attorney Henry,
but both state that they have a strong circumstantial case against
them. The sheriff stated to a *Silver Belt* representative last evening that he was satisfied that the elder Cline did the killing and
that he was assisted by his son Joe, a boy of seventeen, who was
indicted by the grand jury at the recent term of court for horse
stealing. Jimmy, the other boy implicated in the crime, is only
fifteen years old.

When news of the crime first reached Globe, those who were
acquainted with the affairs of the deceased, immediately suspected the Clines, as bitter enmity had existed between them and
Edwards for several years. At intervals during the past few years
there has been trouble between John Cline and Edwards, and
before leaving here last week for his home, Edwards had con-
fided to friends that he was expecting further trouble over some

cattle deals. He did not suspect or fear his enemies would try to kill him. Although a very small man in stature, Edwards was held in fear by his enemies and on several occasions he is said to have taken advantage of this fact, when trouble arose with his neighbors. The first trouble Edwards had with Cline occurred when he was acting as deputy on Tonto for Sheriff Thompson, during a former term of office a number of years ago.

At that time Cline was running a saloon which was closed on an attachment by a Globe wholesale house. Edwards executed the papers and moved a part of Cline's stock to his own home for safe keeping. When Cline settled his difficulty, he went to Edwards' house for the liquor and found fault with the way it had been kept. From that time on, various incidents led to further trouble and increased the bitterness against the two men. The arrest of young Joe Cline several months ago for stealing a horse did not tend to better the feeling against Edwards, who was accused of undue activity in securing the indictment.

When Edwards arrived at Roosevelt last Friday afternoon, the youngest Cline boy was there. When Edwards left a short time after his arrival, he told some friends he intended stopping at the Peters ranch, four miles up Tonto, on his way home. About a half hour before Edwards' arrival Felix Lann, who lives near the Clines, started north, but before leaving, asked Jimmy to go with him, but the boy said he was going to stay at Roosevelt for a week. Notwithstanding this fact, young Cline is said to have left almost at the same time that Edwards did, although he took the upper road out of town. He arrived at Cline at four o'clock. Edwards stopped at the Peters ranch, where he arrived at about three o'clock, leaving there for his home an hour later. The assassination occurred at about six o'clock.

According to Sheriff Thompson, the Clines were the only persons north of Roosevelt who knew that Edwards was on his way home and that they had learned of it only when the boy arrived home. There is said to be another evidence that Sheriff Thompson, Deputy Voris and Ranger Holmes have gathered, which tends to connect the Clines with the tragedy and which will not be divulged until the trial, but it is said that all of it forms a complete chain of circumstantial evidence against the accused.

The *Silver Belt* continued next issue:

Joe Cline, aged seventeen, and Jimmy Cline, aged fifteen, are now occupying separate cells in the county jail here and no date has been set for their preliminary examination on the charge of murdering Charles Edwards, in which they were alleged to have been implicated with their father, John Cline, who is in jail at Phoenix awaiting removal to the Gila county jail.

Early yesterday afternoon Ranger Holmes came in from Roosevelt, having in his custody the older boy. They came down on horseback and several hours later Deputy Sheriff Voris arrived with the younger boy, making the trip on the Roosevelt stage. According to the officers neither of the boys made any attempt to resist arrest and expressed no surprise when they were taken into custody, apparently knowing the reason and expecting the arrests.

Deputy Sheriff George Henderson will return tomorrow evening from Phoenix with John Cline, who was arrested at Mesa several days ago. Upon his arrival here he will also be placed in a cell in the county jail and it is the intention of Sheriff Thompson to keep the father and sons separated during their incarceration. It was rumored yesterday that the officers would make an attempt to "sweat" the two boys in an effort to secure a confession from one or the other.

That the preliminary examination will be held in Globe instead of Roosevelt, is the result of a disagreement or something worse between the sheriff's office and J. C. Evans, the justice of the peace at Roosevelt. According to the sheriff's office, Judge Evans refused to give the officers any assistance in running down the murderers of Edwards and went so far as to refuse to issue warrants for the arrest of the Clines, when requested to do so by Sheriff Thompson. It is also said that when it became certain that the Clines would be arrested on suspicion of having committed the crime, Judge Evans left the county, going to Mesa. Judge Evans' side of the story has not as yet been heard.

The arrest of John Cline and his two sons did not cause surprise or excitement at either Roosevelt or Cline, according to the officers who brought the boys in yesterday, the arrests being taken as a matter of course. Both Voris and Holmes believe that there is a strong case against the older Cline.

———

Cline was seen in jail this morning by a representative of the *Gazette*. He greeted the newspaper man cordially and expressed entire willingness to tell his side of the story. And he told a story remarkably clear in every detail, that seems to ring true in every word.

Cline admitted that he had heard the shots which probably ended the life of Edwards. This was about six o'clock Friday evening. He was at a haystack in a field, not over 150 yards from his house. According to Cline the stock had eaten deep into the stack and he was away in under the stack pulling out fodder, when he heard the first shot. The sound of this was of course rather muffled, owing to his position, but by the time the next shot came he had scrambled out to the open air and was enabled to hear clearly. He heard three shots altogether, the last two plainly.

He states that standing there near the house were his son, George, and Guy Solomon, who could see him at the haystack. His work being completed, he left immediately for the house and arrived there before the departure of Solomon. Solomon had ridden up only a few minutes before and began a conversation with young Cline. About ten minutes after the firing of the shots Solomon put spurs to his steed and galloped off down the road, passing right by Edwards' body without seeing it. No one attached any importance to the shots that had been heard, as there are several ranchers and campers in the neighborhood that do much hunting.

The next morning about nine o'clock Edwards' body was discovered. His horse came riderless to his home and a party immediately began to follow the trail of the animal backward. A rope had been dragged all the way, making this an easy matter. The body was only about fifty yards off a much traveled road and in plain sight of the passerby. Had anyone chanced to glance in that direction the discovery would have been made with even less trouble.

The members of the searching party were Lee Miller, Lum Martin, Guy Solomon and George Spears. Upon the discovery of the body the news quickly spread. Ranger Holmes was soon on the scene. Cline himself joined the crowd, riding from his ranch on horseback. He states that he mentioned the importance of tracking up the ground thereabout as little as possible, but that his warning was almost unheeded. Next day when the Indian trailers were put to work they were unable to do anything.

At that time no one suggested the arrest of Cline. Wednesday he left Roosevelt with Judge Evans, going to Fish Creek that night. Yesterday the journey was continued to Mesa, the two of them getting in there about five o'clock. After he had been there a while Cline was arrested by Marshal Burton. He says that he accepted his apprehension philosophically, slept well last night and at no stage of the game has evinced any alarm over his trouble. This morning he told the *Gazette* that it would only be a matter of time. He would have to be taken to Globe and it would take some time for him to secure his witnesses. Besides having his son George and Guy Solomon there are a number of others he wishes to summon to prove that he never got mad at Edwards, though the latter abused him on several occasions.

So far as is known the only reason for Cline's arrest is that he was not on exactly good terms with the dead man. Cline stated that Edwards had "cussed him out" a number of times and was once heard to say that he only wanted an excuse to kill him (Cline).

Cline stated this morning that the father of Edwards, the late Judge Edwards, begged him with tears in his eyes a short time before his death to keep his son out of trouble. Cline declares that Edwards has long been known as reckless, if not exactly a bad character. He was getting into scrapes all the time. Furthermore, Cline declares that he has kept his promise to his friend Judge Edwards, so far as lay in his power. He on one occasion prevented him from killing a man named Fred Golden, by knocking his gun up and pleading with him not to commit murder.

Edwards often declared, states Cline, that he was being interfered with too much and one time Edwards made the remark that he "just wanted that s— — — —h to say something so he could shoot him." This was one time when Cline and another man had a little altercation over a dog fight. They had been drinking in Cline's saloon when this customer called in a little shepherd dog of his and made him fight his host's big hound. When the shepherd dog began to get the worst of it his owner jumped in and began to choke the hound with his hands. Cline shoved him away and the two men slapped each others' face for a time or two. Edwards strolled in about that time and began to abuse Cline, who took everything in silence and refused to quarrel.

On another occasion Cline stated that Edwards used very vile language to him. This was after the effects of the latter's saloon had been attached by process of law by a firm of creditors and stored in Edwards' house. Cline settled the costs and Edwards told him to come and get his things. This Cline refused to do, saying that the stuff should be brought back to him. Finally Edwards went to Cline and told him that the things would have to be taken away, as he intended moving to Globe. When Cline again refused Edwards called him the meanest man on earth and poured out a torrent of abuse. Still Cline would not quarrel and finally his unwelcome guest departed. Cline says that friends of his who were present "guyed" him unmercifully for making no retaliation for the abuse of Edwards, but remembering his promise to the dead father he would make no demonstration.

"I haven't the faintest idea who killed Edwards," said Cline this morning. "Had they not tramped up the ground and put these Indian trailers to work right away, the murderer would have been discovered. I don't consider myself in any danger.

Indeed, I am at a loss to understand why I have been arrested. They must think they have discovered some evidence against me. But I can prove an alibi all right enough."

Cline is a rancher about fifty years of age and does not look or act like a man who would commit the crime of murder. Furthermore it is said that he has the reputation of being a man of very peaceful proclivities.

—Phoenix *Gazette*, 1908

The *Silver Belt* responded:

John Cline arrived in Globe from Phoenix Sunday evening in custody of Deputy Sheriff George Henderson, who went to Phoenix for him. Cline was locked up in the county jail, apart from his two sons, who are occupying cells.

The preliminary hearing will be held before Justice Rawlings, but as yet no date has been set for it. It is reported that while in Phoenix, Mr. Cline retained Judge A. C. Baker to defend him and his two sons, and that Attorney George R. Hill of Globe will assist in the defense. Little or nothing of the evidence in possession of the sheriff and district attorney against the accused, is known and all the officials interested are maintaining a discreet silence on the subject. In some quarters it is hinted that the evidence against the Clines is of a very flimsy nature, and that when it comes out of the preliminary hearing, it will be insufficient to justify holding the accused to the grand jury.

The Phoenix *Republican* of January 20 says:

Deputy Sheriff George Henderson of Gila county arrived in the city yesterday after John Cline. Cline has been very cheerful and confident during his stay in the jail, but last night when the deputy sheriff put handcuffs on him his eyes filled with tears and turning to the deputy he broke out into an indignant oath. He quickly recovered himself and followed it with a smile, protesting though against the irons. He had known the deputy so long that it seemed that this humiliating precaution was unnecessary. But the officer was insistent and a compromise was effected by the loosening of the handcuffs so that they would not press painfully against the wrists.

A large majority of those who know Cline do not believe that he is guilty and are confident that he will be able to establish the alibi which he says he will have. The Cline family, that is, the most of the members, have a bad name, but John Cline is said by those who know him to be the best of the lot and that he has always been straightforward in his dealings.

He has never been regarded as a quarrelsome man and it is further pointed out that if he had wanted to assassinate Edwards he would not have waylaid him within a quarter of a mile of his own house and so have invited immediate suspicion.

Concerning the examination of John Cline and sons, the *Silver Belt* says:

John Cline of Tonto Basin, and his two sons, Joe and Jimmy, appeared in the court of Judge W. F. Rawlings for their preliminary hearing. The defendant was represented by Judge A. C. Baker of Phoenix and Attorney George R. Hill of Globe, while the interests of the territory were looked after by District Attorney Henry and Attorney Wiley E. Jones of Safford, an old friend of the Edwards family, who has been retained by them to assist in the prosecution of the case.

The hearing began at one o'clock yesterday afternoon and nine witnesses for the prosecution had been examined when adjournment was taken until ten o'clock this morning. Just before adjournment the territory rested, but announced that two witnesses who had not arrived from the north had been delayed and that the prosecution would be reopened if the witnesses arrived by the time court convened this morning. It was supposed that no witnesses would be called for the defense, but counsel for the Clines stated that witnesses in their behalf would be placed on the stand this morning.

Ranger J. T. Holmes, who is stationed at Roosevelt, was the first witness called in the examination. He told of finding the body of Edwards, its location and the efforts made to pick up the trail of the assassins.

Felix Lann, who lives at Cline, testified to seeing Jimmy Cline at Roosevelt on the afternoon of January 10. He asked the boy if he were going home, but the latter said he was not, that he intended to stay with his sister at Roosevelt. He arrived at Cline's home at about four o'clock and saw George Cline, the oldest son, there. Had a conversation with him regarding Edwards, whom George said had threatened to kill him (Cline). He saw nothing of John Cline.

C. H. Gilbert, who drives the commissary wagon for the O'Rourke company between Roosevelt and the damsite, testified to seeing Charley Edwards about a mile out of Roosevelt on the afternoon of January 10. He was rising north at a walk. When he was within a quarter of a mile from Roosevelt, witness saw Jimmy Cline riding north from Roosevelt, probably a mile behind Edwards. The witness spoke to both Edwards and the boy.

Probably the most important witness of the day was Guy Solomon, one of the men who, Cline said in his story to the Phoenix paper, could prove an alibi for him. Solomon testified to meeting Felix Lann about a mile above Cline's. He was on his way to the Bar A ranch and reached the home of the Clines at about five o'clock. He talked for a few minutes with George Cline and asked him where his father was. George answered that he was down at the haystack, but the witness did not see him. Soon after his arrival he saw Jimmy Cline ride up from below. When the witness started to leave, Jimmy came up on his horse, riding bareback, and said he was going to Thompson's ranch for some coffee. While talking to George he heard shots from the direction in which the body was later found.

The next morning the witness was told of the fact that Edwards' horse had come to his home riderless with the horse which he had obtained at the Peters ranch. In company with others, Solomon followed the trail of the horses back along the road and discovered the body of Edwards. John Cline appeared there a half hour after the body was discovered when they were waiting for the coroner from Roosevelt.

Sheriff J. H. Thompson and William E. Wooten testified to ill feeling which existed between Edwards and the Clines and Wooten testified that Cline had expressed the wish to him that he would buy Edwards' cattle, as it would be a good thing for the country if Edwards were out of it.

Mrs. Fannie Edwards, the widow of the murdered man, testified concerning the return of the horses and of the trouble between her husband and the Clines.

I. M. Delbridge and John Spear were the last witnesses. Their testimony related to conversations with Cline and expressions of ill-feeling by him toward Edwards.

Two weeks later, the *Silver Belt* concluded:

John Cline, the well known Tonto cattleman, and his two sons Joe and Jimmy, who were arrested and bound over to the grand jury without bail for the murder of Charles Edwards five weeks ago, were yesterday afternoon released from custody and the case against them dismissed by Judge Frederick S. Nave, who granted the application for the writ of habeas corpus made by the attorneys for the defense. The decision of the court made after argument had been heard yesterday morning, caused considerable surprise, as it was generally expected that the writ would be denied. Mr. Cline and his sons left for their home immediately after their discharge from custody.

Judge Nave announced that the evidence was not sufficient to hold the defendants and he ordered them discharged from custody. The decision was evidently a surprise to the defense also, as Judge Baker had already made public at Phoenix his plan of defense for his clients.

It is very improbable that the slayers of Edwards will ever be brought to justice and the crime will go down into history as one of the many mysterious murders which have occurred in the Tonto country and of which the perpetrators have never been punished.

Captain Wheeler (left) and Sergeant Rye Miles. *Photo by Dale Coolidge*

RANGERS HAD A BUSY MONTH

Captain Harry Wheeler's report of the operations of the Ranger force for January has been made public. It shows that the Rangers have been busy and that their work has not been without some very important results.

The miles traveled by all members of the force total 9,855, of which 7,870 were on horseback. Thirty-eight arrests were made, of which sixteen were for felonies committed either in Arizona or elsewhere by men who were arrested in Arizona as fugitives from justice. Twenty-two arrests were for misdemeanors committed in Arizona.

Of the felonies for which arrests were made, three were for cattle stealing, five for murders, one was for burglary, two were the receiving of stolen goods, two were grand larceny, and two were highway robbery.

The Rangers in the course of their duty recovered stolen property to the value of $2,500. The captain says that every member of the force is now busy in the field or on special work.

—Tucson *Citizen*, 1908.

JEFF KIDDER'S LAST FIGHT

Three members of the Mexican police seriously wounded and Sergeant Jeff Kidder, of the Arizona Ranger force, probably fatally wounded, is the result of a clash between the Mexican authorities and Kidder at Naco Saturday morning about one o'clock. Kidder is under arrest and guard on the Mexican side, the affair having occurred about 300 yards beyond the line. There is considerable feeling on the part of both the American and Mexican inhabitants of the town, but no demonstration is being made, and the authorities on both sides of the line expect no further trouble.

At the time of the trouble there were only two Rangers in Naco, Kidder and Tip Stanford. Kidder had been stationed near Nogales for the past year, where he has made an exceptionally good record by his arrests of notorious criminals. His term of enlistment expired on the first of the month and he had just come in to re-enlist for another year when the trouble occurred.

Kidder was wounded in the stomach, the bullet, a .45, entering just to the left of the navel, and after ranging downward, came out at his back. He is under the care of Dr. F. E. Shine, of Bisbee, and Dr. Brandon, of Naco. They state that it is impossible to imagine a bullet taking the course it did without penetrating the intestines, and that while he is resting well, the best hope they can hold out for is that he has a chance for recovery. Jack O'Laughlin, of Bisbee, is acting as nurse for Kidder.

The Mexicans injured are all members of the city police. Their names are Thomas Amador, wounded just above the knee; Dolores Quias, wounded in the fleshy part of the thigh; Victoriano Amador, slightly wounded in the side. The wounds are all from a Colt's .45. That which entered the knee of Quias ranged downward after striking the bone, and imbedded itself in the calf of his leg. Dr. Shine removed it yesterday. None of the Mexicans is dangerously wounded, and unless complications set in, will recover.

The story of the shooting, aside from the different versions given, is about as follows:

Kidder had been in one of the dance halls in the evening, having danced some and taken several drinks. He left and in from one to five minutes returned and went to one of the rooms occupied by Chia, one of the girls of the house, who had just come to Naco from Douglas, and whom Kidder had never seen prior to the night of the trouble. Soon after he entered her room she called for the police, to which call two of the Mexican police, Quias and Thos. Amador, responded.

In the shooting which followed both of the Mexican officers and Kidder were wounded. The Mexicans lay where they had fallen, while Kidder got up and began to make for the United States side of the line, about 300 yards distant, his sole idea being that he would be killed if he were taken on this side. Just who his pursuers were after he left the dance hall could not be learned, but he fired at them sufficiently to keep them from coming close enough to capture him. After he had gone about seventy-five yards he fell, but rolled over for about twenty feet, still keeping in the direction of the American side, reloading his gun from cartridges which he had in his pocket, his belt being empty.

He then arose and proceeded about seventy-five yards farther, having in the meantime come up with two line riders, with whom he exchanged shots. At the same time that he came up to the fence his ammunition gave out and he was captured by the Mexican officials. He was struck on the head with the butt of a gun, and dragged in the direction of the Mexican jail, a distance of over 100 yards, the trail being plainly visible from that distance, although his own statement only says about fifty yards. There were other injuries on his body, but whether they were received in his attempts to scale the fence or at the hands of his captors could not be ascertained from their nature.

He was then taken to the Mexican jail, but on the arrival of Deputy Sheriff Ells, of the American side of the line, he was removed to a private residence, Judge Garcia having given his permission. Dr. Brandon was called in, and about daybreak Dr. Shine of Bisbee, arrived.

Although very weak from the loss of blood and the terrible experience he had gone through, Kidder, while lying on a cot, with a Mexican standing guard over him with a Winchester rifle, made the following statement of his side of the case:

"I know that a great many people think I am quick-tempered and without looking into the details will form the opinion that I precipitated this trouble. It is probable that I may die, and I would like the public to hear my side of the affair.

"In company with the other boys we came across the boundary to meet a friend coming out of Cananea, and while waiting for the train went into this house. We had been in there for some time, and this woman was in the room. There was some fooling around and we finally walked out. As I stepped outside the door I put my hand in my pocket and found that a dollar which I had was gone. I went back in and told this woman to

give me my money, as I believed she had taken it. She struck
me with her fist and immediately ran to the door and yelled
police.

"I had not had a chance to move when two Mexican police
came through the doorway with their six-shooters drawn, and
one fired, hitting me. I fell and was dazed, but knew that my
only chance was to fight while I had cartridges left. I drew my
own six-shooter while sitting on the floor and opened fire. I
believe I wounded both of the men, and they went down helpless.

"I was very weak, but was able to crawl to the door and out,
it being my intention to get to the American side of the line. I
finally got on my feet and was walking along when suddenly
firing opened up in front of me, and I saw a number of men
between me and the line armed with Winchesters. They were
directing their fire directly at me, but although I was only a
short distance away, and had an empty revolver in my hand,
they did not hit me. I noticed the fence to my left and staggered
in that direction, hoping that someone would come to my assistance. When I got to the fence I put the last six cartridges I had
into my gun. During all this time these men were firing at me,
and as I was too far away to do any good with my six-shooter
I saved my fire, until one of their number came within range
and I shot him. I then fired until my gun was empty. When my
last cartridge was gone I yelled to them that I was all in and
told them to come and get me. They came and placed me under
arrest.

"If anybody had told me that one human being could be as
brutal to another as they were to me I would not have believed it.
I could scarcely stand, but one of this crowd armed with Winchesters that was necessary to place a wounded man under
arrest struck me over the head with his six-shooter and I fell.
Between them they dragged me on the ground for about fifty
yards, and then seemingly tired by their exertions stopped and
beat me over the head with a six-shooter. They finally dragged
me to the jail and threw me in there. I suffered terrible agony,

but could get no relief until this morning, when the doctor arrived.

"I did not precipitate this trouble, and never drew my gun until I was wounded and on the floor in that house. I had absolutely no chance for my life, except to keep fighting until I was helpless. It's too bad such an unfortunate thing occurred, but if I am fatally wounded, I can die with the knowledge that I did my best in a hard situation."

Turning to Deputy United States Marshal and former Ranger John Foster, Kidder muttered:

"You know Jack, that I would have no object in telling what is untrue. They got me, but if my ammunition had not given out, I might have served them the same way."

A representative of the *Review* secured interviews with all of the wounded Mexicans, the bartender in the dance hall where the trouble occurred and with Chia, the girl, who called for the police. Their stories fail very materially to tally with each other. In the interviews with the Mexicans Frank H. Morales acted as interpreter, and otherwise offered such assistance as he could in securing the facts in the case. Judge Garcia also gave permission to interview the injured members of the police force.

The *Review* representative was told the story of Thomas Amador could be relied upon because of the reputation for veracity and soberness which he bore. As interpreted by Morales, it is as follows:

"Dolores and I entered the dance hall just after Kidder. We heard the girl call for the police and started in that direction. Kidder met us at the entrance of the door which leads from the dance hall to the girl's room. He had his gun under his coat and ordered Dolores, who had his gun about half drawn, to throw up his hands. When he said this and before any other shot had been fired, I shot at Kidder and hit him. After he fell he shot at me and hit me in the leg. I took another shot at him after I fell. He then shot at Dolores and hit him. I do not know who shot first, Kidder or Dolores. Kidder and Dolores had trouble some time ago, when Dolores did not know he was a Ranger and asked him about carrying a gun. Both drew their guns, but no shots were fired. Kidder had taken several drinks at the bar, but I do not think he was drunk. Kidder did not shoot at the bartender."

Dolores Quias' story of the affair was as follows:

"Thomas and I were at the bar when the girl called to us. I stepped to the entrance of the hall leading to the girls' rooms and was met by Kidder, who was carrying his gun under his coat. He drew his gun and ordered me to throw up my hands. I did not do so, and he shot me. I also shot at him about the same time and hit him. He then shot Thomas. After I was down he fired at me three times and I fired at him twice. I think that he was drunk, because he had been drinking during the evening. There was no hard feeling between myself and Kidder. We had never had any trouble. Kidder did not shoot at the bartender." These are the stories of the two men who were in the fight in the dance hall.

Ramon H. Telles, the bartender in the dance hall where the fight occurred, relates a story that is hard to believe, and that in many points is contradicted by the other witnesses. He says:

"Kidder had been in the hall dancing in the early part of the evening and had taken at least fifty drinks. He had spent $5 in gold and had several drinks charged. He was very drunk. He left the hall just about 12:15 and came back after going about fifty steps. He went to Chia's room and slapped her. I know this because she told me. She called for the police and Dolores went clear to the end of the hall where Kidder was. Kidder drew his gun and backed him to the dance hall. He then told him to throw up his hands. Dolores did not comply and Kidder shot him. Dolores then shot at and hit Kidder. After Kidder fell he shot Thomas. He then shot at me as I started toward him, although I had only a bottle. One of the girls pulled me away from him, but not until he had taken another shot at me. If the girl had not pulled me away I would have been killed, because I was going to him to make him stop. After they caught Kidder they brought him back to the bar-room. He called on me to protect him and drew a razor from his pocket and began waving it about. One of the men put his foot on Kidder's wrist and took the razor from his hand."

When Ramon was telling about keeping the men away from him, he was asked by the reporter if they were trying to hurt him. He said no, he was sick and did not know what he was saying. He repeated his story several times and later on said: "If it had not been for me I guess they would have killed Kidder when they brought him back to the dance hall. One of Dolores' sons had a gun and was trying to shoot him, but I knew I was responsible for what happened in the dance hall and kept them away from him."

Victoriano Amador, chief of police, who was slightly hurt, received the wound after Kidder had reached the fence in his efforts to cross the line. His story is as follows:

"I was awakened about one o'clock by the shooting and hastened in the direction of the firing. Two of the line riders and Kidder were exchanging shots. As I came up he shot me in the side. His ammunition gave out about this time and we captured him. We took him to the jail and later, upon the direction of Judge Garcia, to a private residence. He is being held a prisoner there awaiting developments. I kept the men from striking or otherwise injuring him after we got to him. Kidder was not taken back to the bar-room after he was captured, and I know nothing of his having drawn a razor."

In regard to what took place between Kidder and the girl, there were no witnesses other than the principals themselves. Kidder says that he went back to get a dollar he missed, which the testimony of the others to the effect that he had just been out a minute or so when he returned, seems to corroborate. He says that when he asked the girl for the money she hit him with her fist.

—Bisbee *Review*, 1908

Sgt. Jeff Kidder, slain in gun battle at Naco, Sonora in 1908 after serving five years with Arizona Rangers.

From the *Review* the following day was this story:

Sergeant Jeff Kidder died in Naco, Sonora, at six o'clock Sunday morning as a result of wounds he received in a desperate encounter early Saturday morning with a number of Mexican police, in which three of them were also wounded. The body is now in Bisbee and will be sent on to Los Angeles this afternoon. The local lodge of Elks have charge of the ceremonies.

An examination of the bullet wound which Kidder received revealed the fact that it was certain the intestines had been cut, and that he had practically no chance for recovery. Over and above the bullet wound, however, were the injuries he received while he was in the custody of the Mexican officers, when he was brutally beaten and dragged, although in a dying condition, a distance of more than 200 yards.

Although his chances for recovery was very slight, throughout

it all Kidder displayed the greatest courage. He talked freely
with his brother officers who were almost constantly in attendance and a number of friends who visited him from time to time.
He said he hoped to live but was not afraid to die, knowing he
was innocent of having precipitated the trouble. During all of
Saturday he did well, but during the night began to show signs of
weakness, finally sinking until death came at 6:30 o'clock.

Owing to the intricacies of the Mexican law on this point it
was impossible to get the body across the international boundary
line until late in the afternoon, when a message from Governor
Torres granting the necessary permission was received. The
remains were then brought to Bisbee to be prepared for burial.

Instructions have been received from the mother of the dead
officer, who lives at San Jacinto, Calif., to send the body there.

On Saturday evening Sergeant Tip Stanford, of the Rangers, in
command in the absence of Captain Wheeler, after having done
everything to make Kidder's remaining hours as comfortable as
possible, asked the wounded officer if he had been able to dis-
tinguish the men who had beaten him. Kidder replied it was so
dark he could not see very well, but that it was one of the men
who had a Winchester rifle.

It is probable that a petition will be sent to the department of
state at Washington by some of the friends of Kidder asking that
a request be made of the government of Mexico to dismiss the
man or men from service who beat Kidder after he was wounded
and under arrest, if it is proven that it was a man in the government service.

Sergeant Stanford sent a telegram to Kidder's mother Sunday
evening, and then wrote her a letter in which he set forth the
details. The communication speaks of the true worth and fearlessness of the dead officer in the highest terms.

Up until late yesterday it had been impossible to establish
communication with Captain Wheeler, who accompanied by
several of his men, had been following the trail of some horse
thieves for about ten days. Telegrams have been sent out, however, to all places where it is possible he will visit, and it is

expected that as soon as he receives one of these messages he will leave at once for Naco.

Although directly after the affray very bitter feeling developed on the American side of the line no untoward act was committed. For a time after it was learned on Saturday morning that Kidder was dead it also looked as if trouble would break out. The arrival of permission from the governor, however, to remove the body, did much to quiet matters.

Later the *Review* stated:

For the first time since the tragedy Captain Wheeler learned of the affair yesterday morning while riding through the Chiricahua Mountains with a detachment of his men returning from a trip after horse thieves. He was informed by two cowboys that Kidder had been killed at Naco. Immediately the party's course was changed, and instead of going to Naco, the headquarters of the company, all haste was made to Bisbee.

The commander of the Rangers went at once with his men to the undertaking parlors to view the remains. Steeled as he is to every hardship, a man who in the course of duty has seen blood shed at various times without a tremor, the sight of Wheeler as he leaned over the coffin containing the remains of his dead comrade was affecting. As he saw the wounds about the face and head where Kidder had been brutally struck with guns after he was mortally wounded, tears came into Wheeler's eyes and he gave way. Gunner, Chase and Horan also looked on the body of their dead friend and brother officer. Not one of the four men uttered a syllable. But that their grief was deep-seated, and their thoughts bitter could be easily seen in their faces.

When seen after the services Captain Wheeler said:

"This is a terrible experience for us, coming back from a trip on which we had captured a Mexican wanted across the boundary for the murder of one of their officers. Of course I have not yet had time to investigate the matter, but have heard many reports since we arrived in the city, all of which agree that Kidder had done no wrong, but made a fight for his life after he had been mortally wounded.

"Jeff Kidder was one of the best officers who ever stepped foot in this section of the country. He did not know what fear was; was a devoted son; was absolutely truthful; had rendered excellent service; and was hated by the criminal classes because of his unceasing activity in bringing them to justice. His life was in danger at every moment at his station in Nogales, because of the fact that during the past year he has arrested many highwaymen, murderers, and other criminals, yet his being killed in this manner is a terrible shock.

"We not only lose a true friend and a well loved member of the force, but Arizona loses a faithful American officer who was fearless in upholding her laws."

—Bisbee *Review*, 1908

Jeff Kidder's Dog.

A sad little cur sat in the baggage car of No. 9, last night with its big brown eyes reflecting the distress of its broken heart. It was Jeff Kidder's dog—the dog that on that terrible night at Naco, crouched on the breast of its dying master and fought with all its tiny strength against the men who shot him down. It is on its way to San Jacinto, Calif., where Jeff Kidder sleeps the long sleep and where the Ranger's aged mother lives. For the rest of its life the little dog will live with the grey haired woman and the bond of sympathy between these two will be a hallowed memory.

The dog is part Chihuahua, part plain cur. Big Jeff Kidder found it starving on a border road one day. He picked it up, made it his constant companion and won from the little beast an affection wonderful from such a tiny thing. Kidder carried the dog on his saddle and in his blouse on long trips along the border. It slept with him at night. It fed with him and played with him and shared his sorrows. Everyone who knew Jeff Kidder in recent years knew his little dog. It is not surprising that the dog had a part in the tragic closing chapter of Jeff Kidder's eventful life.

At Naco, on the early morning of April 4, the dog was at its master's heels when he began his desperate pistol battle with three Mexican policemen. When Jeff Kidder and his three opponents lay bleeding on the ground the dog crouched itself on the Ranger's breast. It fought the brutes who kicked him and beat his prostrate body. Finally it was kicked aside, but it followed its wounded master when he was carried to the jail. Later it crouched beneath his cot while in a hospital where he fought his losing battle for his life. A day later it followed the solemn little cortege that carried all that was mortal of Jeff Kidder across the line into the United States.

During the funeral services at Bisbee the little dog was near the casket. When the coffin was taken to the train to be shipped to California the cur trudged pitifully behind. Ranger Hayhurst picked up the little animal. It was first the intention that the dog be adopted by the Arizona Rangers. But it mourned and sickened. Again and again it ran away seeking the master that it could not find. Finally the matter was brought by the Rangers to the attention of Captain Harry Wheeler. He passed the hat. There was enough money filling it to have sent the dog to California in a Pullman, but of course, it went in a baggage car. And that is how a nameless little cur went through Tucson last night, the object of as much attention from the trainmen as a magnate in his private car.

—Tucson *Citizen*, 1908

Earlier, the *Citizen* had this comment:

Kidder was one of the best known officers on the Ranger force. He was also considered one of the most efficient. He was known for his daring and fearlessness and has been in several previous gun fights. He had been a member of the Ranger force for five years and was promoted to the position of sergeant on the force in appreciation of his excellent services.

Before being appointed to the Rangers, he was a resident of Nogales and served in various capacities there as an officer. He had also worked in the mines at Bisbee. Kidder was about thirty years of age and of somewhat slender build. He was reported to be the quickest man on the Ranger force in drawing a gun. It was said of him that he could allow an average man to cover him with a gun and then draw his own weapon and fire quicker than the other party. He was also one of the best shots of the Rangers, and could shoot also equally well with either hand.

NACO, Ariz., April 24.—A drastic order summarily dismissing all of the members of the Naco, Sonora, police force as well as all of the line riders in the Naco district, was received in the town just across the border line from here today. Twenty officers were let out.

A second order arrived also revoking all the saloon licenses in Naco, Sonora, and ordering all of these places, about fifteen in number, closed immediately. As a result, Naco, Sonora, will be by the end of the week a completely "dry" town.

The wholesale discharging of the Naco police and line riders and the closing of all the saloons in that town is the direct result of the fatal wounding of Sergeant Jeff Kidder in a deadly duel with Mexican officers. The promulgation of this order followed an exhaustive investigation which was made by Mexican federal authorities into the duel between the officers of the two countries.

Ugly rumors about a deliberate plot to get Sergeant Kidder into a fight and then to murder him had arisen immediately following the bloody duel fought by the officers.

The Mexican federal officials were advised of the reports that were being circulated and they determined to institute an exhaustive inquiry. This investigation has been on for two weeks. The result is given in the dismissal of the policemen and line riders and the closing of the saloons.

It is reported on this side of the line today that sufficient evidence was discovered by the investigators to allow good grounds for belief that the reports regarding a conspiracy to kill Jeff Kidder were based on facts. It is stated here also that the Mexican government would have placed a number of the Naco, Sonora, policemen and line riders under arrest had the investigators been able to secure more tangible and direct evidence against the alleged conspirators. The information obtainable, however, was considered sufficient to warrant the dismissal of the officers.

Permission had previously been given Capt. Harry Wheeler to take across the line the gun which Sergeant Kidder made his fight and the Ranger star which he wore at the time. Kidder's watch and money were not returned, however.

Kidder died two days after the fight. One of the three Mexican policemen who battled with him also died. The other two including Chief of Police Thomas Amador recovered. Amador is among those dismissed from the force today.

Kidder's friends in Bisbee were the first to circulate the report that he had been deliberately decoyed to a fight that instead of being the aggressor he had simply defended himself against overwhelming odds.

An entire new police force and bunch of line riders will immediately be put on duty by the Mexican government.

—Tucson *Citizen,* 1908

OUTLAW TAKEN IN MOUNTAINS

With a detachment of his men Captain Harry C. Wheeler arrived in Bisbee yesterday morning after having been absent from this section of the territory for twenty days following the trail of horse thieves. He had in custody a Mexican wanted at Pilares, Mexico, for the murder of an officer. The trip had been an unusually hard one, and both men and officers plainly showed the effects. In all about 500 miles had been traveled through the wildest portions of Cochise, Graham, Pima and Pinal counties, and a part of New Mexico.

Wheeler had been receiving reports from various parts of Graham, Cochise and Pinal counties to the effect that cattle "rustling" and horse stealing were going on in those sections, and about twenty days ago left Naco horseback, taking with him Sergeant Chase and Privates Horne and Gunner. The detachment rode through Cochise county, spending several days in those sections where thieves and outlaws might be in hiding or have their plunder hidden. A trip was made into a portion of Pima county, then into the mountains of Pinal, across Graham, and into that section of New Mexico in the vicinity of Rodeo.

At every stage of the trip the officers inquired of whoever they met in these wild places concerning any traces of cattle or horses, but in no instance did they meet anyone who had seen any strangers or persons who might be suspected of being implicated in the outlawry. The investigation was most thorough, but no traces of thieves could be found.

The hunt took the officers into the wildest country, where they were miles from any sign of civilization, and many times they were without food, let alone short rations. They were covering a great deal of territory and could not afford to load the pack animals too heavily.

Convinced that the cattle thieves could not be making their headquarters on this side of the boundary line, Wheeler started on the return trip, coming home by way of the Chiricahua Mountains. When his command arrived in that section the captain was informed by some of the ranchers that there was a Mexican living in a cabin in the mountains who was wanted for murder in Mexico, and who for some time past had been riding around that section armed with a rifle and six-shooters looking for trouble through which he could strengthen his record as a "bad man."

The Rangers at once rode into the mountains, and after traveling over many trails discovered a cabin perched near the summit of one of the highest peaks. They kept riding towards it, and when a short distance from the cabin met the Mexican mounted on a horse and armed with a Winchester rifle. He was placed under arrest and disarmed, after which the party returned to the valley. This was on Sunday morning just about the time that Sergeant Kidder died at Naco, Sonora, as a result of wounds inflicted by a gang of Mexican officers.

Wheeler and his men with their prisoner were riding through the Sulphur Springs Valley in the vicinity of Moore's ranch yesterday morning when they met two cowboys, who told them Kidder had been killed. In spite of fatigue as the result of the hard trip, hunger and the jaded condition of their horses, Wheeler and his men started immediately, and covered the remaining twenty-eight miles to Bisbee yesterday morning, arriving there about 11 o'clock.

The Mexican who the Rangers brought with them is Andres Marina Guelialmo. He is wanted for the killing of an officer named Silveria at Pilares, a town situated about 60 miles south of Douglas, in Mexico. He admitted to the officers having shot Silveria about a year ago, but claims he only wounded him. He stated that at the time of the occurrence the Mexican authorities pursued him, but that he succeeded in crossing the line.

He contended that he had not committed any crimes in this country. At the time of his arrest he was mounted on a bay horse with an inverted B brand on the left thigh for which he could show no papers, claiming they had been burned up. The officers believed the animal was stolen.

Wheeler and his men left here on horseback about 4:30 o'clock yesterday afternoon for Naco, taking their prisoner with them. When asked concerning the alleged cattle stealing Captain Wheeler stated that some traces would certainly have been discovered if the gang made its headquarters on this side of the line. He said he was convinced that the outlaws must be across the line in Mexico.

Although the bitterest feeling still prevails along the border over the killing of Kidder and the brutal manner in which he was treated, it is not likely that there will be any outbreak, as Wheeler is on the ground. He started an investigation last evening.

—Bisbee *Review*, 1908

HORSE THIEF PAYS PENALTY

At about 3 o'clock yesterday morning, George O. Arnett, alias George Wood, was shot and killed by Captain of the Rangers Harry Wheeler and Deputy Sheriff George Humm of Lowell. Arnett was killed about one mile from Lowell in a canyon a short distance from the Winwood townsite. The dead man had in his possession at the time of his death, and also when encountered by the officers, two horses which he had stolen from the Brophy stables in Lowell, and upon the two horses were two stolen saddles which have been missing for two or three weeks.

Arnett's death was caused by a wound which was made in his neck by one of the shots fired by the officers. The course of the bullet was through the left shoulder, into the left side of the neck and out of the right ear. Another wound was that in his left arm, the bullet passing through that member, entering below the elbow and leaving just above where it entered.

The wholesale theft of valuable horses which has been occurring in the district the past few months, and even later than this, led up to the officers suspecting Arnett, and for about four or five days, ending yesterday morning, they have been lying in wait for him in the canyon above mentioned. The officers refuse to divulge where they learned that the horse thief was to leave by that pass.

For several weeks both Humm and Wheeler have been at work on clews pretaining to the theft of several horses and also of quite a number of valuable saddles, and their patience and persistency was rewarded yesterday morning, when their man was encountered. During the four days leading up to the killing, both the officers have been keeping watch every night, and in the day time also, awaiting the appearance of the thief with the stolen property, which they had sufficient reasons to know that he would have in his possession.

At about 2 o'clock yesterday morning the officers left for the place where they would intercept Arnett, and a short time after arriving there their man made his appearance. The officers had hid behind some bushes and when he was about ten feet from them, both officers sprang up and flashed their electric bulls eye lights on him, at the same time commanding him to hold up his hands, as he was under arrest. Instead of complying with their demands, Arnett quickly wheeled his horse to the right and turned and fired two shots at the officers, who returned the fire. Arnett then passed out of range over the brow of the hill and was lost to view. The officers thought that they had missed their man, and bemoaning their ill luck in failing to capture him, returned to Lowell to secure horses in order to take up his trail at daylight. When they returned to the scene of the shooting shortly after four o'clock they found two horses standing some distance apart, but could not see the man on account of darkness. A little later the body was found, face downwards. Arnett had ridden about a quarter of a mile after he was shot. The coroner was notified and a jury was taken to the location of the corpse at about 6 o'clock. The remains, after being viewed, were taken in charge by the Palace Undertaking Company.

The full facts surrounding the killing of Arnett were brought to light at the inquest at Coroner Grier's office in Lowell yesterday afternoon when the stolen saddles were identified, and facts regarding his past life were bared. The first witness was Deputy Sheriff George Humm. He stated that the last time he saw deceased was on the trail north of the Johnson Addition at about

3 o'clock yesterday morning. He, with Captain Wheeler, had been lying in wait for Arnett for the previous four nights. They left Lowell at about 2 o'clock yesterday morning and rode over the mountains on different trails. They left their horses in the mountains and went to the trail where they expected to intercept the party. After arriving there they looked for a place to hide. In a very short time Captain Wheeler stated that he heard someone coming up the trail. He hurried back to where Wheeler was, and both hid behind the first objects they came onto, he getting behind a bush and Wheeler behind a cactus. Arnett soon afterwards came over the top of the raise. When he came to within ten feet of the officers they sprang up at the same time commanding him to halt, and flashing their lamps in his face. Arnett said "Oh," or some other exclamation and wheeled off towards the right. The officers yelled to him again, commanding him to throw up his hands, and he opened fire on them. The fire was rapid and at a distance of about twenty feet. It was very dark and Arnett was about fifty feet away when he fired his last shot, of which there were two. Humm then picked up his rifle and fired once at Arnett as he was crossing the ridge at an angle. Both officers followed him some distance, but they were on foot and their attempts would be of no use, so they returned to Lowell and secured horses at a livery stable, going there by way of the Johnson Addition. When they returned they found one of the stolen horses and later the other one. They tied their reins together and proceeded to look for the man, who they now suspected of being injured. At break of day the dead body was discovered, The coroner was then notified. On the way back the jurymen picked up the hat of the dead man and also his chaps.

Captain Wheeler was the next witness. His testimony was in nearly every instance identical with that of Humm. The officers and the fugitive opened fire at about the same time, the latter shooting a second before them. The shot from Arnett's gun struck a bush between the officers. Captain Wheeler then noticed that the second horse which he thought was a pack horse, followed at a pretty good pace, and concluded that if his man was able to get away in such good grace that he was uninjured. He tried to follow him, but saw that it was useless and too difficult to follow on foot. Then they came to Lowell and secured horses. Upon returning they found the horses and later, at daylight, found the body. When questioned by Assistant County Attorney Taylor, Wheeler stated that he is positive that the first shot was fired by the fugitive. He stated:

"I was pointing my gun at him and holding my light at arm's length to detract his aim, the light shining in his face, he fired a second before I pulled the trigger of my gun. Humm opened fire upon him at the same time I did. I would like to state that we did all we could to arrest him, allowing him to approach within ten feet, in order to show him that he had no chance whatever for escape, but he seemed to think that he had. I have heard a relative state that Arnett had said that he would never submit to arrest."

James E. Brophy, proprietor of the livery stable from which the horses were stolen on the night of the 5th, stated that he had been notified by his help that two horses had been stolen from the stables, one belonging to himself, a roan, branded "44," and the other the property of Ralph Cadwell, superintendent of the Warren electric line. The animal belonging to Cadwell was shot in two places, in both instances the bullets passing through the hind legs.

W. H. Goode, the next witness, identified one of the saddles, a bridle and a pair of chaps as being the property of Albert Christian, who lives with him. This property disappeared from his place on the night of April 23. This saddle was also identified by C. H. Dusold and J. F. Vaughan. The latter repaired it several months ago, and was familiar with the different parts.

John Gerdes, foreman of the Brophy stables, stated that he was notified of the horses being stolen when he arrived at the stables yesterday morning at 5:30 o'clock, by the night man, John Carlson. He went with the officers later in the day and secured the animals.

W. B. Maxwell identified the other saddle as being his property, and which was stolen from his barn on the night of April 21, another before that belonging to Mr. Christian was stolen. This saddle was identified also by Joseph Boyle, Wiley Fitzgerald and George Hunter.

Captain Wheeler was recalled and identified the saddles as being the same as those on the animals in the morning.

Edward Payne was the next witness. He stated that he had known Arnett for about four years. Saw him last about two months ago. Had a falling out with him regarding a family affair, and over which, Payne admitted, several shots had been fired. Had made a trip with Arnett into Sonora on a hunting and mining expedition, the only trip he ever made with the deceased. They crossed the line at Naco. The saddles were the property of Arnett, as was one horse, the other animal being borrowed from a friend of Arnett in Bisbee. He came back by train, while Arnett returned by horseback. When he returned he had the same outfit he had when he went to Sonora. This trip was made five months ago. Attorney Taylor tried to lead Payne out on several important lines, but he failed to accede to his wishes.

John Carlson, the man who was in charge of the Brophy stables at the time of the stealing, stated that he was at Warren late at night, and when he returned to the stables he noticed that two of the horses had been stolen or had strayed from the stalls, although their tie ropes were also missing. He reported the absence of the animals to the foreman in the morning. He did not rent out or loan the animals to anyone.

Frank Arnett, a brother of the deceased, stated on the stand that George Arnett was born in the United States and that his father was an American, while his mother was Spanish. He stated that deceased was about 28 years of age. He asked permission to ask questions, which was granted, and he desired to know the number of empty shells in the gun belonging to his brother. The answer was "two." He then thanked the officers for granting his request.

A witness who knew a great deal concerning the actions of Arnett was Mrs. Edward Payne, whose husband testified a short time before. She stated that the last time she saw him was about two or three months ago. She had been on friendly terms with him for some time, had visited his family and he had called at her home. He was inclined to be somewhat of a braggart and had told her of his holding up people and taking their money away from them. That in one instance he had held up a gambler at the ice plant in Lowell. He also bragged about his cuteness in keeping out of the clutches of the law in running horses over the line into Mexico. This was some time ago, just before Christmas. At one time she had asked Deputy Sheriff Frank Bauer for protection, as she feared that Arnett would keep his word and kill her and her daughter, as he had threatened to do. She stated that the reason for his making the threat is that she probably knew too much regarding his unlawful operations. On one occasion, as she was on her way to her home in Bakerville from Lowell, on a dark evening, at about 8:30 o'clock, some one had shot several times at her and she believed that Arnett had done the shooting. This instance happened about two and a half months ago, as she was returning from the picture show at Lowell. Upon being closely questioned, she stated that the cause of her being threatened by Arnett was her influencing her husband against associating with him and since that time she has been afraid of her life.

The verdict of the jury was as follows: That the deceased, George O. Arnett, 37 years of age, a native of the United States, died near Lowell on May 6, 1908, from the result of a gunshot wound inflicted by George Humm and Captain Harry Wheeler, in the discharge of their duty, and we, the jury, exonerate said officers from all blame, as they were in the discharge of their duty at the time.

The verdict was in accord with the popular sentiment. The officers had been praised on every hand regarding the way they performed their duty, and their fairness in permitting the dead man to surrender without a struggle. Arnett is suspected of committing crime by the wholesale in the district, and is credited with holding up the Chinamen in Tombstone Canyon several months ago, and for which he was arrested, but which could not be proven against him. There are many thefts of horses and saddles laid at his door, and it is the general opinion of the public that a dangerous man has met his end.

—Bisbee *Review*, 1908

CONVICT WAS DEPUTY SHERIFF

WILLIAMS, Ariz., July 21.—With a pistol pressed to his abdomen by Ranger Lieut. Old, Frank Sherlock, alias Charles Bly, recognized as a convict who rode away from the New Mexico penitentiary on the warden's horse exactly eleven years ago, exclaimed: "Guess you got me, kid," and quietly surrendered.

He was delivered into the custody of Captain Christman of the New Mexico penitentiary and immediately started on the overland train for Santa Fe, where he had two years yet to serve on a four years' sentence for horse stealing.

Sherlock was betrayed by a fellow convict whom he discharged from a position with the Grand Canyon Lime and Cement company at Nelson, Arizona, where Sherlock had taken a contract. Since his escape, he has lived an exemplary life. For eight years he had served as a deputy sheriff of Mohave county, Arizona, and in that time had run down many desperate criminals. Sherlock also served four years as livestock inspector of Mohave county.

Aware that Sherlock was a dead shot, Lieut. Old, accompanied by Ranger Wood, met him casually at the Grand Canyon Cement company's camp. Old introduced Wood and while the two men were shaking hands, Old stuck his pistol against Sherlock's stomach and cried:

"Hands up! I have a warrant for you!"

Sherlock calmly replied as his hands went up: "Guess you got me, kid."

Wood disarmed Sherlock of a huge pistol and extra clip of cartridges while Old covered him with a cocked gun.

For the first time Sherlock weakened badly and wept bitterly as the officers took him away. He admitted that he was the right man and said he had quit crooked business long ago, and wanted no more of it. He requested the Rangers to speak a good word for him, if possible, when they reached the New Mexico officials.

—Tucson *Citizen*, 1908

BILL DOWNING KILLED

WILLCOX, Aug. 5.—William Downing, in his day a noted outlaw of southern Arizona, and since last fall a resident of Willcox, was killed this morning by Ranger William Speed in the rear of the Free and Easy Saloon, of which Downing was proprietor. Ranger Speed killed Downing only after the latter had made a move as though to get his six-shooter. A coroner's jury this afternoon exonerated the Ranger. Public sentiment here also exonerates the officer for any blame in the killing. Downing had made frequent threats and boasted often that no one could arrest him.

"Bill" Downing came to Willcox early last October and started the saloon where he was killed today. He had just been released from the Yuma penitentiary where he served seven years for the Cochise station train holdup. The place is located back of the postoffice about 100 yards. It has had an unsavory reputation. Frequent robberies and brawls were reported from it. Last week Downing was prosecuted for permitting women to congregate and drink in his saloon and paid a fine of $50 for the offense.

Citizens of Willcox secured a copy of the proceedings and sent them to Tombstone with a petition to the board of supervisors that Downing's license be revoked. None of them, however, being willing to appear publicly against Downing it was decided to secure the evidence in another way. The matter was taken up with Captain Harry Wheeler of the Rangers and two officers were detailed to keep a watch on the Free and Easy, one of them Ranger Speed.

Tuesday night Downing beat a Mexican woman who frequented his saloon and she made an information against him. The warrant was given to Constable Bud Snow. The latter went to Ranger Speed and asked him to help make the arrest. The two officers went to Downing's saloon about 8 o'clock this morning. Speed carried a 30–40 Winchester. They called in at the front door of the saloon for Downing to come out. He paid no attention to the request. A second demand was made by the officers. Downing then darted out a back door. Speed went around one side of the saloon and Snow around the other. Speed reached the rear first. Just as he turned the corner Downing came out of a woodshed. The Ranger called on Downing to throw his hands up. Instead Downing made a move for a six-shooter he supposed he had in his pocket. Speed fired, the bullet entering Downing's right breast and passing through his body. He died in two or three minutes.

Downing was unarmed, as it developed later, but a six-shooter had been taken from his pocket by R. E. Cushman as he passed out the back of the saloon and when Downing reached for his gun he supposed that he still had on his person. He had been drinking during the morning and was in an ugly humor before the officers came.

In Downing's pockets at the time he was killed was over $200 tied up in a handkerchief in bills of various denominations. Frequent robberies at the Free and Easy had been blamed on Downing. He was accused of encouraging the robbery of men who frequented his saloon by women he kept about.

Downing had practically terrorized Willcox for several months. He boasted of the fact that he was a bad man, and drank much. No open complaint was made against him because he had threatened to kill whoever filed charges at Tombstone. Downing was about 50 years of age; was of rather slight build and a man of undoubted nerve. His wife who died at Tucson while he was a prisoner at Yuma, is said to have been a beautiful woman of good family in Texas.

Captain Wheeler left Naco for Willcox this afternoon.

"Bill" Downing died in a manner befitting the life which he had lived, and if the truth were known, in the manner in which he had expected to die. That he was a fearless man, at home with the wildest spirits in the early days of Arizona when it was a rendezvous for men of his class, no one who knew the least of his many deeds of daring will care to deny.

There are people in Cochise county perhaps who know what the real name of the outlaw was, but they are few. According to information which may be relied upon as accurate, Downing was the last member of the notorious Sam Bass gang in Texas, and came to this section when that gang met its Waterloo at the hands of the Texas Rangers.

Forced to leave the Lone Star state, he took the name of Downing and soon located in this section of the country, He brought with him the scars of former battles, as one of his legs in which he had been badly shot troubled him all the time. In fact, it became so bad when he was in the penitentiary that the physicians declared it would be necessary to amputate it. "Well," said Downing, "that leg and I are going to live together or die together," and the leg got better.

Downing had not remained long in this section until he was suspected by many of being implicated in numerous cattle and horse thefts, and to be known as a man who would not hesitate to shoot, and shoot to kill. Notwithstanding his shady record he secured an appointment as constable, and it was while holding this commission that he took part in the famous Cochise holdup near Willcox, in which the Wells-Fargo was robbed of $140,000. This was in 1891.

In the gang were Billy Stiles, Matt Burtt, Bert Alvord and the two Owen brothers. The robbery occurred in the fall of the year.

Sacks of Mexican coin were used as ballast on the sticks of dynamite placed over the safe, and Mexican coins are picked up to this day on the prairie in the neighborhood of the holdup. Coins lodged in the top of the car, which was blown out, and one which is kept as a souvenir was picked from the top of a telegraph pole.

After the robbery Downing, then a constable at Pearce and Bert Alvord, who held a position as deputy sheriff at Willcox, made a great bluff at capturing the robbers. Chief of detectives Thacker of the Wells-Fargo people came out from San Francisco and soon had the whole gang under arrest. It is stated as a matter well understood that the first hint of the guilty parties was received by Thacker from Stiles himself. After the arrest the Owen brothers gave the whole affair away, and were given light sentences of four years.

The prisoners were taken to Tombstone for safe keeping, and it was from there that Stiles and Alvord escaped on the night preceding their trial. Stiles was later captured, whereupon Alvord surrendered. Alvord was tried first and given two years in the pen for his complicity in the holdup. That night he and Stiles again broke jail. Alvord was later captured by the Rangers at Naco and sent to Yuma, where he served his two years.

All of the others of the gang captured, including Downing, were sent to Yuma to serve their terms. Downing drew ten years, but by good behavier was released at the end of seven years.

Shortly after his release he opened up a saloon at Willcox, which was run on the "free and easy style," that is, practically nothing from gambling to shooting up the town was barred.

—Bisbee *Review*, 1908

The Tucson *Citizen* in covering the story of Downing's death, stated:

"After Downing's arrest for robbing the mails, his wife, who was very well thought of, sold the ranch near Willcox, and expended all of the proceeds in the defense of Downing. Finding herself penniless, she went to work as a servant in Tucson. She was found dead one morning and a coroner's jury which investigated the case returned a verdict that her death was due to heart failure.

———

Sheriff Jack White, who was in the city yesterday, says the Bisbee *Review*, talked interestingly of the recent death of Bill Downing at Willcox. Among other things he stated that had not Downing been killed by Ranger Speed, he would probably have been killed in a very short time, not more than a few days at the most, by George McKitrick, who had a saloon in Willcox.

McKitrick had Downing fined on a former occasion for allowing women to come into his saloon and drink. Later when Downing was said to have beaten a Mexican woman with whom he was living the woman went to McKitrick and asked him what to do. He advised her to have a complaint sworn out against him, which she did. It was while resisting arrest on this charge that Downing was shot.

Upon learning of the fact that McKitrick was the man who had had the warrant for his arrest served, he swore that he would kill him. McKitrick learned of this and went armed with a double-barrelled shot gun loaded with buckshot. He was laying for Downing in his house in the dark when the latter came looking for him and the fact that Downing did not know which was his room probably saved the latter's life.

After the killing of Downing, McKitrick went behind the bar to let down the hammers of the shot gun, which he kept at full cock all the time. In doing so he fired one of the barrels through the wall, whereupon some bystander wanted to know if he were nervous. McKitrick is a man of undoubted courage, but he admitted that he had stayed up all night watching for Downing, whom he knew would kill him at the first opportunity. McKitrick is the man who put a Negro soldier permanently out of business at Ft. Dodge after the latter had the drop on him.

Sheriff White is of the opinion that Downing deliberately walked to his death at the time he was shot, and that he had made up his mind to that, with the intention of getting as many of his enemies as he could before he cashed in. The sheriff says that at the time of his release from the Yuma prison Downing was looking well and was full in the face. Not long afterward he was thin, worried, despondent and was drinking hard all the time.

According to the testimony of a score or more of people who saw the death of Downing, he slowly and deliberately lowered his hands after Ranger Speed had ordered him to surrender, reaching at the same time for his left hip pocket, for he was left handed. He kept his hand on his pocket and kept advancing, notwithstanding the fact that Ranger Speed begged him to put his hands up and to stop, as he did not want to kill him. He refused to obey and no alternative was left Speed but to shoot.

GOVERNOR KIBBEY'S REPORT

BISBEE, Jan. 27.—Cochise county being the headquarters of the Arizona Rangers, considerable interest has been taken here in the recommendation of Governor Kibbey in his message to the territorial legislature.

The number of arrests for the year ending June 30, 1908, is given as 1,096, which is a considerable increase over the report covering the two previous years. The total number of arrests for the two years, 1905 and 1906, is given as 1,756. These figures show that the Ranger force, although not as large as authorized by law, on account of a number of vacancies now existing which Governor Kibbey has not seen fit to fill, is evidently carrying on a more vigorous campaign against criminals.

Group of Arizona Rangers, 1908

In this connection Captain Harry Wheeler calls attention to the fact that while crime has been greatly reduced, still we have entirely too much of it, and two many criminals, guilty of the most heinous crimes succeed in escaping and going unpunished. During the past year within a radius of four miles of Bisbee four murders were committed and to this date three of them are unpunished and the perpetrator of the deed unknown. In the other case a man is being held awaiting the action of the grand jury, but the officers are far from certain that they can succeed in bringing sufficient evidence to cause his conviction. That this is a deplorable state of affairs will be recognized by every citizen of this county and the territory.

Captain Wheeler, however, is of the opinion and states positively that if the members of his force were provided with the necessary implements of their profession they could easily have captured all of the four criminals mentioned, and they could make it so hard for any criminal to escape that the incentive to crime would need be much greater to tempt the criminal element.

In discussing the remedies he mentions the following things:

"First of all, a pair of bloodhounds of the very best training and breeding could easily have taken the trail of each of these murderers. Again, had we possessed the dogs, we could have given them the trail in each case, within thirty minutes, there would have been no possible escape for the fugitives.

"I consider the question of dogs the most important of all. I refer only to the best of trained and blooded dogs, any other sort would be worse than useless. Again the extradition laws are abominable and are without sense or reason. It is next to impossible to get a criminal by means of extradition from either side of the Mexican line. The process is costly, clumsy and full of trouble, and a hundred technicalities are run against at every turn. Our criminal must have an indictment against him found by the grand jury. He may have killed a man yesterday—the grand jury will not meet again for six months. In the meantime an officer apprehends the criminal in Cananea, Mexico. They can hold this criminal forty days according to their law and then he must be released. In the meantime our grand jury is five months away. At present the laws of extradition are merely an invitation to the criminals of both countries.

"Another thing: At the present time I know of no way in which an officer can follow a criminal, if the criminal takes to the railway, unless the officer pays the fare of the road out of his own pocket. This is not to be thought of, for no officer can pay such sums of money out continuously for railroad fares. Now we can only write to some other officer, who would not know the criminal even if he saw him. Another thing, there should be a method (telegraphic) by which every officer in the territory could immediately be made acquainted with the crime, the criminal's description and all things necessary to give every officer an intelligent and clear idea as to the crime and the criminal. Yet there are no rates for officers and even so there is no way for an officer to pay these telegraphic charges.

"The principal reason, however—the one which if rectified would do the most good—is the lack of the very best trained bloodhounds that money can buy. Grant us the dogs, railroad transportation particularly for those officers who are compelled to travel most, and fix for us the extradition laws so that they offer some hope to the officer instead of an inducement to the criminal, and I am positive that I voice the sentiment and the belief of all the officers of Arizona, when I promise and guarantee a decrease of the murder crimes and those of robbery 50 per cent and in general all crime 70 per cent to 80 per cent."

These recommendations of Captain Harry Wheeler, who is noted for his conservation, should be given more than passing thought by the members of the legislature, which is now in session, and if, after due investigation, they find that it is possible to provide the things which Captain Wheeler speaks of as being necessary, and in their judgment it will make Arizona a safer place in which to live, then they should provide them without delay and at any reasonable cost.

There are many people throughout the states who regard Arizona as hardly a safe place to live. There are many people in our own midst who share this idea and carry with them daily, contrary to the law, dangerous weapons for their own protection. Our officers are doing their best to deter men from a life of crime and it is the duty of the territory to see that they are properly equipped.

Doubtless some of the things Captain Wheeler would like to see brought to pass cannot be accomplished until we are granted statehood, but it is possible in some cases to so enact laws as to materially aid the members of the Ranger force, and in other cases Congress should be memorialized to give us the proper relief. We hope that this matter will receive earnest consideration by the territorial legislature, which is now in session in Phoenix.

—Globe *Silver Belt,* 1909

EDITOR's NOTE: It will be seen by the foregoing item and this item, published two weeks later, that the plea of Captain Wheeler with the approval of the press, was to no avail as far as improving the Ranger organization was concerned.

———

As stated in yesterday's *Silver Belt*, a petition is being circulated in Globe asking the legislature to reconsider its action in attempting to abolish the Rangers in Arizona. A counter petition was started yesterday and there will undoubtedly be a lively scrap in the legislature for attempting to eliminate the Rangers was prompted by the belief—and there was ground for this conclusion—that it was merely a political shot aimed at Governor Kibbey.

The question is now being argued on its merits. The *Silver Belt* believes, as it previously stated, that if there was ever a necessity for a company of Rangers in Arizona that conditions have not sufficiently changed to modify the necessity.

Arizona is far from being densely populated. There are sections visited by the Rangers not frequented by other officers, and that they do offer protection cannot be successfully denied.

It is also true that since the formation of the Ranger company crime of all kinds has been reduced to a minimum in these isolated places and train robberies are incidents fast fading from our memories, as far as they pretain to this territory. That this protection is still needed goes without saying. If it can be more cheaply secured in the employment of some other brand of officers, well and good. The people should be safeguarded before the protection that is now given is removed.

It is held by those who would banish the Ranger company that only three counties in the territory are benefitted by this annual expenditure of about $30,000. This is only partially correct. It is true that most of the offenders are captured in the border counties, but isn't this a compliment to the efficiency of the Ranger force? The criminals are apprehended right at the gates of Arizona, and are either driven back into Mexico, or are incarcerated and punished for their depredations. Should we take down this barrier and permit them to overrun the entire territory? Shouldn't the people of all Arizona be willing to stand for the expense of this good work? The people in the border counties are compelled to bear the expense of their convictions, as well as to pay their pro rata of the cost of maintaining the Rangers.

In New Mexico, a territory with a greater population than Arizona, a Ranger company was organized for the protection of the people. The people of New Mexico state that they were prompted to take this action because the Rangers of Arizona had driven all the bad man into that territory and that the ordinary peace officers found it impossible to cope with them. In order that the criminal classes might have some peace of mind and eternally green fields for browsing, Arizona should now remove the bars and permit them to enter this territory!

At a recent meeting of the members of the boards of supervisors of the respective counties of Arizona, we are informed, that a resolution was passed by a large majority—almost with unanimity—asking that the Ranger company be abolished. Cochise and Pima counties did not join in this request. The opinion of these gentlemen, paying all due respect to the exalted positions they hold—is of no more weight than that of the ordinary observing layman. It is doubtful if they correctly mirror the sentiment existing in their respective localities.

The matter of abolishing the Ranger company was a surprise party for the people of the entire territory. It might be interesting to know at this particular time how the matter happened to come up for consideration at this territorial conclave of county representatives. Surely there had been no surface agitation. But, as the *Silver Belt* has stated, if the Ranger company is an expensive worthless luxury, abolish it. No definite action should be taken, however, until the question is thoroughly canvassed.

—Globe *Silver Belt*, 1909

The Tombstone *Prospector* in February, 1909, stated:

No matter whether the ultimate result of the fight on the Rangers in the legislature should be the retention of the service, Harry Wheeler will tender his resignation to the governor. Already he has tentatively resigned, but, awaiting an answer to a telegram sent to Phoenix, he has not formally tendered his resignation to the governor.

———

EDITOR'S NOTE: Governor Kibbey vetoed the bill abolishing the Arizona Rangers. The veto message covered twelve typewritten pages in defense of the Ranger service and claimed the legislature was actuated by political motives in abolishing same.

The bill was passed over the governor's veto and the Arizona Rangers ceased to exist on February 15, 1909.

Wheeler immediately upon the receipt of news of the action of the legislature, telegraphed orders to his men giving them their discharge and his own discharge was at the same time signed by the governor and the ex-Ranger left for Naco.

———

OPEN LETTER OF RANGERS TO PUBLIC

Former Captain Harry C. Wheeler of the Rangers in the following letter expresses the appreciation of the men of the organization for the hearty interest and support given the service in years past by the public:

Editor Bisbee Daily Review—I say for myself and my boys that the sting and bitterness of defeat so recently suffered by us, is forgotten and lost sight of in the knowledge which has come to us, individually and as an organization, of the good will and appreciation of our people, our friends and neighbors. To all our friends we extend our sincere gratitude. They made a fight for us, which from force of circumstances we could not make for ourselves. We are grateful to every man, woman and child in this and other counties, for petitions and letters sent to the Territorial fathers in our behalf.

We would not care to dwell upon the Act of Repeal, passed by the 25th Legislature Assembly of Arizona, were it not for a few statements made by individual members of that Honorable body.

We do not question the motives of a majority of those who dealt us our death blow as an organization. Having been so long guided ourselves blindly at times, from a sense of duty, it is not for us to question of others the motives actuating them, and therefore we do not question, but feel assured that by the majority the actual dictates of conscience were followed and carried out. We feel no bitterness toward any who honestly fought us; we trust that in the end will be proved the wisdom of the Act abolishing us, however much we doubt this will be so.

We believe our representatives Fred Sutter, Oscar Roberts and Ben Goodrich would have saved us had such been within their power. Had Mr. Goodrich and Mr. Sutter both been of the Assembly, instead of being in opposite houses the governor's veto would have been sustained, but it is useless to argue "what might have been." The Rangers are no more. The wisdom or unwisdom of the Act of Repeal will be evident to all in the near future.

Yet, while we are not bitter toward those who killed us, as an organization, there were some, who seemingly not satisfied with their work (The Act of Repeal had been passed before speeches) arose and needlessly, and falsely attempted the assassination of the personal characters of men who have never in any way harmed them. It was a cowardly and a cruel thing, this attempted ruination of the characters of a faithful body of men; men who having been denied the right to be heard, being denied the right of self defense, little expected to be made the victims of a personal attack.

I, being the captain of the company, for my boys' sake requested to be placed before a committee of investigation; we feared no possible interrogation and I was to resign my captaincy regardless of whether the Rangers lived or not. We were not, however, accorded any hearing. No investigation was permitted, no chance of self defense allowed. We judged from this no attack would personally be made upon us, nor upon anyone connected with us. We were deceived for we were doomed to suffer an attack, from Mr. Thomas Weedin of Pinal county. Mr. Weedin arose and publicly stated that the Rangers had been assessed by the governor for $3,000 of their salaries for campaign purposes. Just think of that statement! Think of all it means! Only men without honor would either demand such a thing or submit to such a thing were the demand made. Further when you consider that of the twenty Rangers eighteen are Democrats, the shame of the assertion, were it true, becomes more manifest. Men of one political faith buying their positions from another administration.

Be that as it may he who was guilty of falsehood when he made his statement regarding the assessing of the Rangers for any purpose. Mr. Weedin appears to be a man of force and should have some character. A false and malicious statement coming from him, might injure, therefore I believe it a duty to myself, my boys and our friends to state publicly that Mr. Weedin apparently did deliberately and maliciously make a false statement in saying the Rangers were ever assessed or ever gave any money or thing of value for any political purpose whatsoever.

As to Governor Joseph H. Kibbey, he will always rank first in the heart of every Ranger. He was like a father to us, fair, just and kindly in all things. We dared perform our duties against all alike, the high and the low, the mightiest and the lowest. All he ever demanded of us was "Be sure you are right." If there ever was a noble man 'tis Governor Kibbey. We were with the people and of the people before we were Rangers; now we are of the people and with the people still. We are citizens of Arizona, have our families and our homes, and here we shall remain.

The organization of the Arizona Rangers is indeed dead, but the same spirit which made of the boys, faithful and efficient officers, will make of us loyal and earnest citizens.

We will do our part as citizens, help bear the burdens of citizenship and we will share in all the pride and pleasure and the glory of simply being Arizonans and living in Arizona.

For the Rangers and by them.

HARRY C. WHEELER.

—Bisbee *Review,* 1909

A. F. Chase and John Redmond, two former members of the now disbanded Ranger force, stationed under the regime of that body at Florence, were in Bisbee yesterday on their way to Courtland (the new town just opening up). Both, while indignant at their summary dismissal, refused to speak at any great length upon the subject.

"I was out chasing outlaw horse thieves for five days after the force had been disbanded," said Redmond. "Luckily I forced them into another man's territory and he gathered them in. It would have been a pretty 'how-dy-do' if I had been killed or had killed one of them after my commission had been taken from me."

—Bisbee *Review,* 1909

Col. Emilio Kosterlitzky of the Mexican Rurales

5

COL. EMILIO KOSTERLITZKY

THE SCOURGE OF SONORA

IN ALL THE flaming annals of the wild country below the Arizona-Sonora border there is nothing more vivid than the record of Col. Emilio Kosterlitzky.

Gaunt, eagle-eyed, tireless, remorseless as doom in bringing authority and justice to a bandit-scourged land which had known no more of law than the stone age before he came, he is already becoming a myth among the thousands whose fear of that stern law-bringer was balanced by their trust in him; for whenever he rode at the head of his terrible *cordada* throughout that vast realm he moved civilization a full century ahead.

Visionary sentimentalists have dwelt overmuch upon what they have called his ruthlessness and have shuddered at tales of his cold killing of killers and plunderers; but, as is the habit of their kind, they have overlooked the fact that the Russo-Mexican cavalry leader's fantastic, disordered environment called for different concepts and laws; they have ignored the age-old reign of terror, wholesale slaughter of pitiful families, the brutal rape and rapine which had made of Northern Sonora an inferno before Colonel Kosterlitzky's inexorable control wrought order out of chaos.

As Harry Carr has written, after Kosterlitzky had imposed his relentless justice upon the land "you could trundle a wheelbarrow loaded with diamonds from the border to Mazatlan without fear of molestation."

But if Kosterlitzky was implacable as fate toward the murderers and pillagers, he was nevertheless true as steel to his soldier's code. Not even Mexico's president was able to draw him into any of the stealthy assassinations which some rulers have at times "justified" by their devious sophistries. Often, Emilio informed his commander-in-chief, grim duty had compelled him to order execution of outlaws; but, he proudly and stubbornly declared to the man in Chapultepec Castle, never had he, nor ever would he, kill an enemy except upon the field of battle.

The man's innate faculties made him a perfect leader for the irregular campaigning by which alone the widely scattered and elusive bandit crews of his far-flung district could be outmaneuvered and cornered. Adroit to a clairvoyant degree, quick thinking, amazingly skilful in emergencies, more than once his nimble brain turned imminent disaster into surprising victory.

Yet along with his natural aptitude for desultory, unorganized strategy there was academic training in the art of war; for he was the scion of a long line of distinguished cavalry leaders and had been educated along the lines of his fighting forebears. He was born in a military barracks, where his father was hetman (colonel) of a regiment of Cossack cavalry. The elder Kosterlitzky had lost a leg in the Crimean war when the British, French, Sardinians, and Turks were battering the Czar's legions at Balaklava, where the immortal charge of the Light Brigade occurred.

But with that reluctance of many to have their sons follow their own trade, Emilio's father ignored the boy's passionate desire to become a Cossack cavalryman and sent him to the Royal Naval School at Moscow. There the young Kosterlitzky applied himself assiduously to his studies, but his deep-rooted desire to be a cavalryman lingered.

Sailing on his midshipman's cruise around the world he was regarded by his superiors as excellent naval material. His mind was keenly receptive to all matters pretaining to the art of war, physically he was tough as a mesquite root, tireless at his sailor's duties as member of the old square-rigged man-o'-war's crew. But ever his mind wandered to horses, which he continued to love more than the sea.

When they weighed anchor at the first Mexican port of their voyage several of the Russian cadets went ashore and beheld the stirring maneuvers of a dashing regiment of that country's dragoons. Midshipman Kosterlitzky was thrilled. He promptly deserted from the Muscovite navy and became a cavalryman beneath a guidon that bore the Aztec eagle.

At this point in this remarkable man's history occurs the only discrepancy, if such it be. Some who knew Kosterlitzky well along the border declare he was at one time a trooper in Company E of the Third U. S. Cavalry, and that he deserted at Fort Huachuca and crossed the line to begin his gallant career in the service of Mexico. If so, this country lost a brilliant military man when Emilio decided to change his allegiance.

To his friend Arthur Hopkins, sergeant in the Arizona Rangers when Ranger Captain Tom Rynning was helping Kosterlitzky make border history, the expatriated Russian told the story of his desertion from the Czar's sea forces. Hopkins, now dwelling in peaceful Santa Monica, cut Kosterlitzky's trail many a time in the Sierras and along the Sonoran plains in the years when the Rangers and the *Cordada* were quartering that wild land in quest of outlaws.

But these conflicting accounts possibly are reconciled by a story, or rumor, that during his first service with Porfirio Diaz' legions Kosterlitzky's fiery nature brought about a clash with his superior officers that led him to quit them and join the United

Lieutenant John J. Brooks

Left to right, Arizona Rangers Lieut. John Brooks, Sgt. Arthur Hopkins, and Capt. Thomas H. Rynning, meeting with Col. Emilio Kosterlitzky and two Mexican Rurales near the border

States Cavalry, and that subsequent dissatisfaction with comparative inaction on this side of the line impelled him again to try his fortunes with our sister republic.

The first definite word of his presence in the wilds of Northern Mexico is that given by Tom Rynning, then a member of the Eighth U. S. Cavalry but detached as a packer under General Crook in Sonora during the Geronimo campaign. That was in 1886. Tom was riding hard o' nights as he dodged hostile Apaches, carrying dispatches for Crook from the village of Bacuachi up near the Sierra Madre crags to Gen. Luis Torres down in Hermosillo, a bridle-path canter of 190 miles.

As Tom followed along the Sonora River he came upon a camp of *rurales* and met Captain Emilio Kosterlitzky, then serving under Colonel Fenochio. In later years these two iron soldiers were to cooperate as leaders of hard-riding columns along the Arizona-Sonora border, to clash bitterly, then to become fast friends to the end.

His resolute nature and instinctive military skill carried Emilio rapidly upward in the service of his adopted country. Long before the Madero revolution in 1910 he was a colonel of the *gendarmeria fiscal* (*rurales* or *cordada*), recruited from the fiercest bandits in Mexico, though commanded by regular cavalry officers on detached service. Just before Diaz was overthrown Kosterlitzky had become a senior colonel in command of cavalry on the west coast. As near as I have been able to learn, the words "*rurales*" and "*cordada*" are synonymous, but for some reason Emilio's flying column, made up of the hardest riding and most efficient mounted men in all Northern Mexico, was always known as "The *Cordada*."

Kosterlitzky's rapid rise in rank was no chocolate soldier's experience. His service was one long series of desperate clashes, of lion-hearted expedients that pulled him out of seemingly hopeless corners. He was wounded by arrows, slashed by sabers, shot many times. Once he was grievously shattered by an exploding shell and lay on the battlefield many days, his wounds becoming infected and filled with maggots, but he was finally picked up at death's verge and his rawhide constitution and wonderful vitality pulled him back from the valley of the shadow to fight many another fiery engagement.

Yet despite his fierce life, the necessity of ever being ready to kill or be killed, Emilio Kosterlitzky was far from being the ruthless tiger many have assumed him to be. More than once he spared a bandit's life because of some extenuating circumstance in the latter's bad deeds, although in such cases the culprit always had to choose between the firing squad or service in the *cordada*.

And he had a streak of justice and even of consideration for the misery of others that many a man of less violent life lacks. I recall one incident that will illustrate my assertion. It occurred in La Cananea, William C. Greene's great copper principality of Northern Sonora, back in 1901.

Another hard-rock miner and myself had been working in the Oversight Mine high up in the Cananea range. Just at quitting time, as Merrill was loading the round of holes we had finished drilling, a fall of rock broke his leg an inch or so below his hip. Taking him down the rough mountain in a delivery wagon (there were no ambulances in Cananea yet) was agony for him. At the hospital in Ronquillo the indifferent doctors just dropped his leg into a metal cast and left it that way. It was late and they wanted to get home.

About two or three next morning the clear notes of a bugle cut the frosty air. The *cordada* had ridden in from the south. A few moments later Colonel Kosterlitzky came in, cussing his usual blue streak. It was his way of being sociable. Following him was a member of his force carrying a basket filled with oranges and other fruit from the *Rio Azul*. The hard-bitten war dog never forgot to bring some such delicacies for whatever miners might be in the hospital.

Recognizing me he came over to where I was sitting beside the suffering Merrill and asked what was the matter with the groaning miner. He gave Merrill's shoulder a rough squeeze, as great a display of any tender emotion as the stern fellow ever achieved. But when I told him of the doctor's failure to set the injured miner's leg there was enough emotion of another kind to melt the snow on the hospital roof. How Emilio could cuss! My childhood was passed within hearing of bullwhackers and Mule-skinners in the Arizona hills, but all of those blue-sky orators were linguistic paralytics by comparison with the *cordada's* leader. And he could handle expletives fluently in eight languages!

But his pirate talk lasted only a few moments. Turning to the soldier who bore the basket of fruit he told him to summon his lieutenant. If my memory serves me right the latter's name was Mendez. When the officer came Kosterlitzky barked out orders for him to take a squad of *cordada* and dig one of the doctors out of bed, *pronto!*

And when the agitated surgeon arrived at the hospital he was tersely and profanely informed that if he didn't get the miner's leg set "as quick as hell would let him" he himself would need a lot more than bone setting. It is needless to say that Merrill's leg received prompt and efficient attention.

The Madero revolution flared up so quickly that Kosterlitzky, to quote his own words, he didn't know where he was at. He had been a favorite officer of Porfirio Diaz, was generally supposed to hold *carte blanche* from that president. Anyhow, he never got along with his nominal superior, General Torres, military governor of the State of Sonora, and wouldn't take orders from him. The revolution didn't extend to the west coast, but Kosterlitzky resigned, retiring with the rank of senior colonel of cavalry. He didn't wish to serve under Madero.

But later, much against his wishes, he was called back to the service by President Madero and ordered to report to the latter at Mexico City. When the grim *cordada* leader conferred with Diaz' successor the latter told Emilio he wanted him to go to the state of Morelos, then controlled by the anti-Madero leader Zapata, gain the confidence of that fierce bandit-general and kill him.

It was then that Kosterlitzky dared President Madero's wrath and disdainfully told him that when he, Emilio Kosterlitsky, killed an enemy it must be on the field of battle. As a result he was retired by Madero as northern chief of the *gendarmeria fiscal* and succeeded by Juan Cabral.

But not Juan Cabral nor any other than Emilio could hold down the wild bandits of the north, and Kosterlitzky was again called into service. When Huerta succeeded Madero, Kosterlitzky had reached the rank of general. From then on parts of his history are nebulous. In the end Kosterlitzky and Pedro Ojeda remained in command of two remnants of the once terrible *rurales* of Northern Sonora. Ojeda and his small force came across the border at Naco. Kosterlitzky, defeated by Obregon, led his faithful few across the line at Nogales and were interned at Fort Rosecrans.

The Mexico he had served so long and faithfully was torn by constant internecine strife, its leaders seemed a disorderly procession of political opportunists to the orderly mind of the soldierly Kosterlitzky. In profound disgust he quit the banditti-overrun and leaderless land below the border, decided to become an American citizen.

His friend, Tom Rynning, leader of the Arizona Rangers when Emilio's *cordada* had kept order across the line from him, risked his life to see if he could save anything from the wreck of Kosterlitzky's beautiful home in Magdalena. But when he got there everything of value had been looted and horses were stabled in the fine rooms once occupied by the Kosterlitzky family.

Captain Rynning and Captain Charles T. Connell talked their friend's prospects over. Connell, through his connection with the government, was able to get Kosterlitzky placed with the Department of Justice in Los Angeles, thereby doing his country a big service, for the keen and resourceful ex-*cordada* general, speaking eight languages fluently, knowing nearly every outstanding adventurer in the world, having close knowledge of the many fellows who had been conspiring in Mexico for undoing of the United States during the early days of the World War, was able to lay his finger on many an alien enemy who otherwise would have remained free to plot against the allies and practice sabotage in this country.

Kosterlitzky's cleverest disguise in Los Angeles, one that never was penetrated, was that of a German doctor. Speaking the language as flawlessly as any man born in Deutschland, he easily passed himself off amongst the plotters as a violent enemy of the U.S.A. During the days of his clever posing the spies and *saboteurs* were bewildered by the inevitable exposure and arrests that frustrated all their conspiracies. When they complained to Kosterlitzky he appeared just as worried as the next one, urged them to greater care in their plans, to the deepest secrecy concerning their meeting places and the codes used in their communications—all of which he knew so thoroughly and was using so effectively against them.

When the war was over he remained with the department here, but his restless soul could not brook the humdrum ways of peace. He was a soldier by birth and lifelong training. He craved action.

The banditry and utter disorder below the line where he had so long held sway caused him deep unrest. He decided to organize a revolution and take over control of Sonora. And with his super military training, his exact knowledge of that country, intimate understanding of its people and the certainty that they would follow wherever he led, it is quite possible that his contemplated move would have been successful. More than that, no longer owing allegiance to any of the leaders of the Mexican republic, his revolt might have swelled into a tide of marching men that would have overthrown the whole Mexican government and left Emilio dictator of the land of the Montezumas.

He often talked his plans of conquest over with his friend Harry Carr. In fact he planned to make Harry his chief of staff. Whether that newspaperman agreed to join his fortunes with the dynamic Kosterlitzky is more than Harry ever told me. But if he had followed that wild soldier of many flags it's a cinch Harry wouldn't be the plump columnist he is today. Campaigning in the Mexican hills on *frijoles* and *tortillas* is not conducive to curves.

At least Harry agreed to collaborate with Emilio in the life story of that great soldier of fortune, but just as they were ready to begin the work Kosterlitzky was stricken with his last illness. What a pity the history of that man of tremendous action was not written down before he answered the last bugle call! He lived so fast and so furiously that even his own intimate friends' knowledge of his meteoric career is but a series of glimpses through battle smoke and the rush of charging horses.

To Carr, Hopkins, Rynning and others he has told of exploits that would hardly merit belief, were it not that his reckless courage and daredeviltry in tight corners was not open to question, and that many of the Kosterlitzky doings viewed by Hopkins and Rynning were just as unbelievable.

Once he had a running fight with Villa. He cut repeatedly at the bandit leader with his sword, but Pancho was mounted on a

fresher horse and drew away from his dreaded opponent. Kosterlitzky dared Villa to halt and fight, hurled his sword at him,
and when his empty gun snapped threw that also at the fleeing
bandit, shouting deadly insults at the wild man of the north.
But Villa put spurs to his horse and outdistanced the *cordada's*
chief.

Once when his command had been scattered he rode alone
over a hilltop almost into the arms of a small detachment of
the enemy. Turning in his saddle he shouted orders to an imagi-
nary force behind him to halt. Then he rode forward and disarmed the scared soldiers before him.

At another time he had the wild Indian chieftain, Geronimo,
surrounded, at his mercy, but drew off his force rather than
interfere with the United States troops who were in Sonora to
negotiate with the vicious Apache for his and his follower's
surrender.

And Kosterlitzky's remarkable luck nearly always held. Had it
not, he never could have lived through such constant peril. The
late Bill Sparks, one of Captain Rynning's most remarkable
Rangers, tells in his writings of Kosterlitzky, then a captain of
rurales, having a hair-raising encounter with Apache Kid and
his bunch down in the Sierra Madre. The *rurales* had blundered
into a trap. It would be fatal for them to retreat, equally suicidal
to hold their position.

So Captain Kosterlitzky led an impetuous charge against the
rocks behind which the Indians were concealed. Many of the
Mexican soldiers must surely have fallen were it not for unex-
pected good fortune. A dog belonging to the *rurales* had followed
a rabbit to a point behind the entrenched Apaches and when he
began barking in their rear the Indians thought they were surrounded and fled in wild panic, leaving three of their band dead
among the rocks.

But for all his desperate courage Emilio Kosterlitzky had a cool
head, always had complete control of himself. The only time he
ever declined an invitation to fight illustrates that trait in his
character.

Back in 1906 a strike of Mexican miners in La Cananea, fifty miles below the border, had suddenly flared into a race war. Ranger Captain Rynning led 300 Bisbee miners across the international line as a civilian force. At Naco they were sworn in as soldiers in the Mexican army by Military Governor Torres and Civil Governor Ysabal of Sonora and reached Cananea after 150 lives had been snuffed out, and the torch applied to lumber yards and buildings. Rynning, cool-headed and efficient from his many years of soldiering, soon had things in hand.

In the afternoon of the second day Kosterlitzky and his *cordada* came loping into the district. They had been riding hard from Magdalena for twenty-three hours. Both Kosterlitzky and Rynning were dog tired, nerves touchy. Emilio rode up to the Ranger captain and said "Get to hell out of Mexico, Tom, or I'll shoot you out!"

That came mighty close to touching off some international fireworks. "You Russian - - - - - - - - - -," roared Tom, "get your troops up in those rocks where you can put up a fight and I'll show you one that'll make you think you never were in one before!" And Kosterlitzky took it.

When Tom got back across the line he was still puzzled. "What do you suppose he took that for?" he kept asking.

Perhaps Kosterlitzky felt, intuitively, that any kind of a fight between *gringos* and Mexicans might have resulted in a movement of Americans across the border that would have cost Mexico at least a part of the State of Sonora. If so, he was right in his deductions. Such a move was set on a hair-trigger just then, as has since become known. But that's another story.

Years afterward Kosterlitzky said to Rynning, "I figured I had to run that sandy on you for its effect on my troops. I thought perhaps you'd take it." Anyway they respected each other as good and fearless soldiers and were fast friends up to the day of Emilio Kosterlitzky's death.

—*Touring Topics*, August 1932

EDITOR'S NOTE: The foregoing biographical sketch of Col.

Kosterlitzky was written by Joe Chisholm, prominent Arizona pioneer who died in 1937. His books on Arizona include *Gun Notches*, the life story of Thomas H. Rynning, ex-Ranger captain; also *Brewery Gulch:* frontier days of old Arizona. Chisholm also wrote numerous articles pertaining to Arizona history.

———

An International News Service wire from Los Angeles, July 14th, announced that after devoting more than half his life in law enforcement work in this country and in Old Mexico where he was known as former President Porfirio Diaz' "mailed fist," while in command of a brigade of regular Mexican troops and later of a regiment of cavalry, due to ill health and advanced age, General Emilio Kosterlitzky has announced his retirement. Hero and winner of scores of battles with Mexican bandits and revolutionists, and Uncle Sam's right bower here during the searching out of German spies and unfriendly aliens, today retired from the government service as an agent of the department of justice.

It was soon after his flight to this country in 1914 that the colonel entered the service of the United States, becoming attached to the department of justice because of his wide knowledge of Mexican and German affairs. He spoke fluently the languages of Spain, Germany, France, Russia, Poland, Italy, Sweden, Denmark, the United States and other countries, and because of his knowledge of these languages and their speakers, he became a most invaluable aid to the government, especially during the period this country was at war with Germany.

At the conclusion of the World War Colonel Kosterlitzky's principal activities were to keep this government informed in Mexican affairs. His intimate acquaintance with Mexico, its officers and people, coupled with his ability to "read" the mind of Mexicans and Mexico, was said to have enabled American officials often to steer clear of embarrassing complications.

—Phoenix *Gazette*, 1927

The Flagstaff *Sun* in 1928 announced:

General Emilio Kosterlitzky, one of Mexico's greatest soldiers, died at his home in Los Angeles on March 2, 1928, being 75 years of age. He was a native of Russian Poland and had deserted from the Russian army. Coming to Mexico he became a citizen of that country and during his many years there was known as one of Mexico's best military men. He was proud of his Mexican citizenship, a good friend to Americans and highly respected on both sides of the international boundary line. A widow and six sons and daughters survive him. He was buried in Calvary Cemetery, Los Angeles, California.

APPENDICES

ROSTER OF THE ARIZONA RANGERS

(Listed only in highest ranking achieved)

Burton C. Mossman	Captain	August 1, 1901 to August 31, 1902
Thomas H. Rynning	Captain	September 1, 1902 to March 20, 1907
Harry C. Wheeler	Captain	March 21, 1907 to February 15, 1909

Name	Rank	Age at Enlistment	Where Born	Occupation
John Foster	Lieutenant	34 (1906)	S. Carolina	Officer
William D. Allison	"	42 (1903)	Ohio	Peace Officer
John J. Brooks	"	36 (1903)	Texas	Ranger
William A. Old	"	32 (1904)	Texas	Ranger

Name	Rank	Age at Enlistment		Where Born	Occupation
Dayton Graham	Sergeant	43	(1902)	Ohio	Peace Officer
John E. Campbell	"	36	(1901)	Pennsylvania	Farmer
Arthur F. Chase	"	31	(1908)	Illinois	Clerk
Alex R. MacDonald	"	39	(1903)	Isl. of Mauritius	Cowboy
Frank S. Wheeler	"	31	(1902)	Mississippi	Cowboy
James T. Holmes	"	30	(1902)	Denmark	Cowboy
Arthur A. Hopkins	"	26	(1903)	Colorado	Soldier
Tip Stanford	"	29	(1903)	Texas	Stockman
James E. McGee	"	34	(1904)	Arkansas	Carpenter
William Speed	"	35	(1906)	Texas	Stockman
William Sparks	"	42	(1903)	Iowa	Cowman
Jeff P. Kidder	"	28	(1903)	S. Dakota	Stockman
Clarence L. Beaty	"	28	(1903)	Indian Terr.	Stockman
Oscar McAda	"	26	(1907)	Texas	Stockman
Lew H. Mickey	"	37	(1905)	Nebraska	Stockman
J. T. Miles	"	41	(1907)	Texas	Stockman
Anderson, Robert M.	Private	36	(1902)	Tennessee	Stockman
Baggerly, Roy	"	31	(1906)	Texas	Stockman
Bailey, James D.	"	33	(1903)	Kentucky	Cowboy
Barefoot, Fred S.	"	41	(1901)	Mississippi	Cowboy
Bassett, James H.	"	34	(1902)	Texas	Cowboy
Bates, W. F.	"	24	(1907)	Texas	Ranger
Black, Samuel C.	"	45	(1908)	W. Virginia	City Marshal
Brooks, Ross	"	42	(1904)	Texas	Stockman
Burnett, Reuben E.	"	42	(1905)	Texas	Cattleman
Byrne, Cy	"	42	(1907)	Ohio	Dpty. Sheriff
Carpenter, William L.	"	41	(1908)	California	Stockman
Clarke, John R.	"	22	(1906)	Arizona	Blacksmith
Coffee, Garland	"	29	(1905)	Arkansas	Dpty. Sheriff
Davis, Wayne	"	28	(1906)	Arizona	Cattleman
Devilbiss, George W.	"	31	(1904)	California	Cowman
Doak, Boyd M.	"	39	(1905)	Texas	Stockman
Ehle, A. E.	"	29	(1907)	Arizona	Stockman

Name	Rank	Age at Enlistment	Where Born	Occupation
Ensor, William	"	39 (1904)	Texas	Dpty. Sheriff
Eperson, Charles A.	"	26 (1903)	California	Cattleman
Farnsworth, Clark H.	"	31 (1905)	Illinois	Stockman
Felton, Oscar	"	27 (1902)	Oregon	Stockman
Ferguson, William F.	"	44 (1903)	Texas	Cowboy
Ford, Frank A.	"	22 (1907)	Kansas	Stenogrphr.
Foster, William K.	"	36 (1903)	New York	Dpty. Sheriff
Fraser, J. A.	"	28 (1907)	Texas	Peace Officer
Gadberry, M. Tom	"	40 (1909)	Texas	Stockman
Gray, Henry S.	"	47 (1901)	California	Stockman
Greenwood, John F.	"	45 (1905)	Texas	Stockman
Grover, Herbert E.	"	33 (1901)	Kansas	Peace Officer
Gunner, Rudolph	"	35 (1907)	Texas	Peace Officer
Hamblin, Duane	"	38 (1901)	Utah	Farmer
Hayhurst, Samuel J.	"	32 (1903)	Texas	Cattleman
Heflin, C. W.	"	30 (1908)	Texas	Stockman
Henshaw, Samuel	"	37 (1903)	Texas	Stockman
Hickey, Marion M.	"	(Served 1½ months only— resigned)		
Hicks, O. F.	"	36 (1905)	Missouri	Peace Officer
Hilburn, J. R.	"	41 (1904)	Texas	Peace Officer
Holland, Thomas J.	"	28 (1901)	Texas	Cowboy
Horne, R. D.	"	26 (1907)	Pennsylvania	Clerk
Humm, George	"	34 (1908)	Ohio	Dpty. Sheriff
Johnson, Don	"	22 (1901)	Texas	Peace Officer
Jorgenson, Louis	"	32 (1903)	Utah	Cowman
King, Orrie	"	37 (1908)	Texas	Stockman
Larn, William A.	"	33 (1907)	Texas	Cowman
Lenz, Emil R.	"	27 (1908)	New York	Officer
McDonald, James P.	"	37 (1905)	Texas	Peace Officer
McGarr, Charles E.	"	35 (1905)	Arizona	Miner
McGee, E. S.	"	32 (1907)	Texas	Peace Officer
McKinney, Joseph T.	"	47 (1906)	Arkansas	Ranger
McPhaul, Henry H.	"	40 (1906)	Texas	Peace Officer

Name	Rank	Age at Enlistment	Where Born	Occupation
Mayer, George L.	"	41 (1907)	New York	Stockman
Moran, James	"	29 (1904)	California	Cowboy
Mullen, John Oscar	"	24 (1903)	California	Cowboy
Neill, Reuben L.	"	28 (1904)	Arizona	Peace Officer
Olney, Benjamin W.	"	34 (1906)	Texas	Stockman
Page, Leonard S.	"	25 (1901)	Texas	Cowboy
Parmer, William C.	"	25 (1908)	Texas	Peace Officer
Pearce, Joseph H.	"	30 (1903)	Iowa	Cowman
Pearson, Pollard	"	34 (1902)	Texas	Stockman
Peterson, William S.	"	38 (1902)	Texas	Cowboy
Poole, Travis B.	"	28 (1907)	Texas	Stockman
Redmond, John McK.	"	24 (1908)	New York	Ranchman
Rhodes, John	"	55 (1906)	Texas	Stockman
Richardson, Frank	"	40 (1901)	Oregon	Stockman
Rie, Charles	"	31 (1903)	Pennsylvania	Blacksmith
Robinson, McDonald	"	33 (1901)	Texas	Stockman
Rollins, Jesse W.	"	34 (1906)	Utah	Carpenter
Rountree, Oscar J.	"	27 (1903)	Texas	Peace Officer
Scarborough, Geo. E.	"	23 (1901)	Texas	Peace Officer
Short, Luke	"	33 (1908)	Texas	Peace Officer
Shute, Eugene H.	"	22 (1905)	Arizona	Student
Smith, James	"	32 (1907)	Texas	Stockman
Splawn, C. T.	"	31 (1905)	Texas	Stockman
Stanton, Richard H.	"	30 (1901)	New York	Waiter
Stiles, William L.	"	32 (1902)	Arizona	Cowboy
Tafolla, Carlos	"	36 (1901)	New Mexico	Peace Officer
Thompson, Ray	"	30 (1905)	Nevada	Stockman
Warford, David E.	"	36 (1903)	New York	Forest Rngr.
Warren, James	"	37 (1901)	Illinois	Cattleman
Webb, William W.	"	33 (1902)	Texas	Cowboy
Wilson, Owen C.	"	29 (1903)	Texas	Stockman
Wilson, W. N.	"	35 (1906)	Arkansas	Stockman
Wood, Herbert E.	"	27 (1908)	Arizona	Cowman
Woods, Leslie K.	"	29 (1906)	Arizona	Stockman

Appendix B

AN ACT

By the Arizona Territorial Legislative in 1901, to provide for the formation of a company of Rangers:

Section 1. That the governor of this territory is hereby authorized to raise and muster into service of this territory, for the protection of the frontier of this territory, and for the preservation of the peace and the capture of persons charged with crime, one company of Arizona Rangers, to be raised as hereinafter prescribed, and to consist of one captain, one sergeant and not more than twelve privates, each entitled to pay as follows: Captain to receive one hundred and twenty ($120.00) dollars per month; sergeant to receive seventy-five ($75.00) dollars per month; and privates fifty-five ($55.00) dollars per month, each; and the pay herein provided shall be full compensation in lieu of all other pay and compensation for clothing for both officers and men.

Section 2. That the requisite number of officers and men for said company shall be raised, if possible, in the frontier counties of this territory.

Section 3. That the governor is authorized and empowered, when in his opinion the public emergency shall require it, after the passage of this act, to appoint competent persons as captain and sergeant, and to enroll, as set forth in this act, the requisite number of men for the company; the captain shall return to the governor the muster roll and the report of the condition of the company, and the governor shall thereupon commission the said officers of said company, supply said company as under the provisions of this act he may deem proper and necessary, and order them upon duty in accordance with the provisions of this act.

Section 4. Said men shall be furnished by the territory with the most effective and approved breech-loading cavalry arms, and for the purpose the governor is hereby authorized to contract in behalf of the territory for ten stands of arms, together with a full supply of ammunition, the same to be all of the same make and calibre, and each member of the company to be furnished with the arms to be used by him at the price the same shall cost the territory, which sum shall be retained out of the first money due him.

Section 5. That each member of said company shall be required to furnish himself with a suitable horse, six shooting pistol (army size) and all necessary accoutrements and camp equipage, the same to be passed upon and approved by the enrolling officer before enlisted, and shall any member fail to keep himself furnished as above required, then the officer in command shall be authorized and required to purchase the articles of which he may be deficient, and charge the cost of the same to the person for whom the same shall be provided: *Provided,* That all horses killed in action shall be replaced by the territory, and the cost of horses so killed in action shall be determined by the captain.

Section 6. That said officers and men shall be furnished by the territory with provisions, ammunition, and forage for horses when necessary and when on duty.

Section 7. Each member of said company is hereby authorized, when in pursuit of criminals, to take horses when necessary to continue the chase, wherever he may find them; said horses to be returned to the owners as soon as possible afterwards, and the same to be paid for by the territory.

Section 8. That the men shall be enrolled for twelve months, unless sooner discharged, and at the expiration of their term of service others shall be enrolled to supply their places, in case the governor deems such action necessary for the protection of the frontier, or for the preservation of the peace, or the capture of persons charged with crime.

Section 9. That no enlisted men shall be discharged from the service without special order from the governor, nor shall any member of said company dispose of or exchange their horses or arms without the consent of the commanding officer of the company while in service of the territory.

Section 10. That the captain of the company shall use his own discretion as to the manner of operations, selecting as his base the most unprotected and exposed settlement of the frontier.

Section 11. That the troops raised under and by virtue of this act shall be governed by the rules and regulations of the army of the United States, as far as the same may be applicable, but shall always be and remain subject to the authority of the Territory of Arizona for frontier service.

Section 12. The captain of such company shall have authority to concentrate all of such company, or divide into squads for the purpose of following and capturing any outlaws, law breakers, marauding Indians, or bands of hostile Indians, or for the purpose of carrying out any measure that may contribute to the better security of the frontier; but the entire force raised under the provisions of this act, shall be at all times under and subject to the orders of the governor, and shall be exempt from all military, jury or other service; and that the governor shall direct all the arrangements necessary to carry out the intention of this act, with full power to remove any officer or man for incompetency, neglect of duty or disobedience of orders.

Section 13. Members of said company shall have full power to make arrests of criminals in any part of the territory, and upon the arrest of any criminal, shall deliver the same over to the nearest peace officer in the county where the crime is committed.

Section 14. It shall be the duty of the auditor of this territory to draw his warrant on the territorial treasurer at the end of each month for the pay of each officer and man in said company, and to forward the same to the captain of said company, and also a warrant for the amount of provision, ammunition and forage; but the food of each officer or man in said company shall not exceed in price the sum of one dollar per day and such forage shall not exceed the sum of fifty cents per day per horse; the same shall be forwarded upon the receipt by said officer of an itemized account from the captain of said company, to be signed by such captain and certified by him, and which shall be carefully scrutinized by such auditor, and should the same or any item therein be found unlawful or unreasonable, he shall suspend payment of the same and refer the same to the governor, who shall pass thereon and certify the same for the payment in such sum as he shall find correct and reasonable; and it shall be the duty of the territorial treasurer to pay such warrants out of the general fund as other warrants are paid.

Section 15. That the captain shall be authorized to purchase all necessary pack animals to be furnished said company for transportation purposes, but not exceeding four in number; to purchase all necessary supplies to be delivered by contractors at the place to be designated by the captain of the company; and all accounts and certificates of such agent shall be examined and allowed by the captain of the company and certified by him, as the accounts for the payment of men, food and forage.

Section 16. The governor shall have power to disband said company or any portion thereof when in his opinion their services shall no longer be necessary for frontier protection.

Section 17. That there shall be annually levied and collected in addition to all other taxes authorized by law, a tax of five cents on the hundred dollars of taxable property in this territory to be placed in a fund by the territorial treasurer, to be known as the Ranger fund, and upon which fund all warrants and payments made under any of the provisions of this act, shall be drawn and made. Said tax shall be levied and collected in the same manner, at the same time and by the same officers as other territorial taxes.

Section 18. That no portion of said troops shall become a charge against the territory until organized and placed under orders.

(Took effect March 21, 1901.)

(NATHAN OAKES MURPHY, Governor.)

The Territorial Legislature in 1903 repealed or revised certain sections of the original law, increasing the Ranger force to consist of one captain, one lieutenant, four sergeants, and not more than twenty privates, making a total of twenty-six men. The salaries were changed as follows: the captain, one hundred and seventy-five dollars per month; lieutenant, one hundred and thirty dollars per month; sergeants, one hundred and ten dollars per month, and privates, one hundred dollars per month. Along with salary increases the new law also provided that, instead of the territory furnishing pack animals, each member of the company was required to furnish his own pack animal as well as his own horse. A new provision was included, that all members injured while in the performance of their duties, shall have medical treatment and care at the expense of the territory. In case of a deficit in the Ranger Fund, the territorial auditor was authorized and directed to draw his warrant on the general fund.

The new law also provided that the captain shall provide and issue to each Ranger a badge, uniform in size and shape, with the words "Arizona Ranger" inscribed thereon in plain and legible letters, which badge shall be returned to the captain upon the said Ranger going out of service.

The revised Ranger bill was signed into law by Governor Alexander O. Brodie, March 19, 1903.

Attempts were made in subsequent legislatures to abolish the Ranger force, but without success, until 1909. The law abolishing the Arizona Rangers is as follows:

AN ACT

Repealing the Act Establishing the Ranger Force of the Territory of Arizona.

Be it Enacted by the Legislative Assembly of the Territory of Arizona:

Section 1. Act No. 64, Session Laws of the Twenty-Second Legislative Assembly of the Territory of Arizona, and all amendments thereto are hereby repealed.

Section 2. All Acts and parts of Acts in conflict with the provisions of this Act are hereby repealed.

Section 3. This Act shall be in force and effect from and after its passage.

This Bill having been returned by the Governor, with his objections thereto, and after reconsideration, having passed both houses by two-thirds vote of each house, has become a law this 15th day of February A.D. 1909.

                                        GEO. W. P. HUNT,
                                        President of the Council.

SAM F. WEBB,
   Speaker of the House.

Appendix C

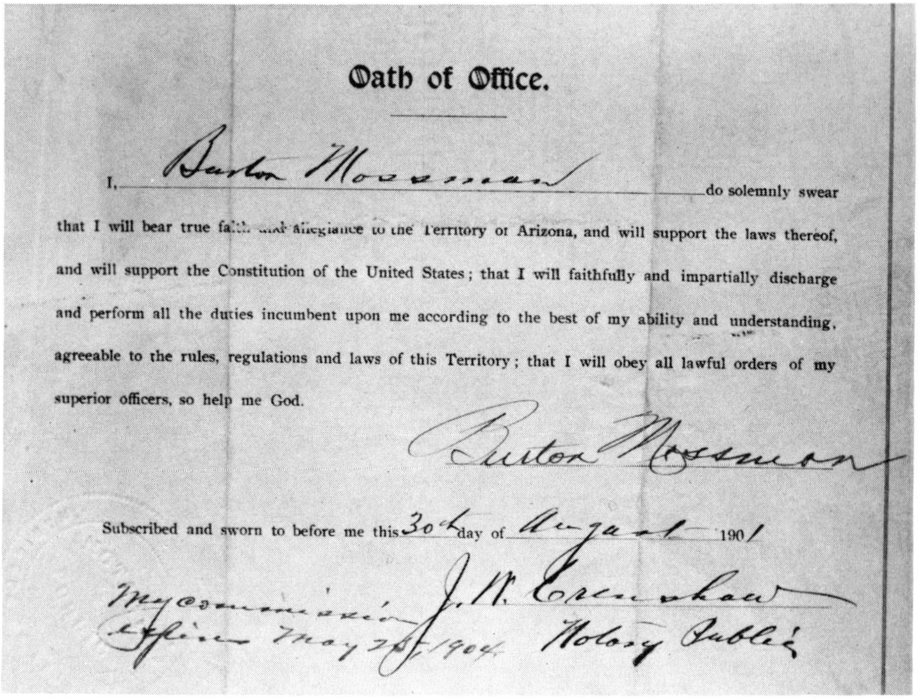

Oath of Office.

I, Burton Mossman do solemnly swear that I will bear true faith and allegiance to the Territory of Arizona, and will support the laws thereof, and will support the Constitution of the United States; that I will faithfully and impartially discharge and perform all the duties incumbent upon me according to the best of my ability and understanding, agreeable to the rules, regulations and laws of this Territory; that I will obey all lawful orders of my superior officers, so help me God.

Burton Mossman

Subscribed and sworn to before me this 30th day of August 1901

My commission expires May [illegible], 1904

J. W. Crenshaw
Notary Public

Specimen—Oath of Office

Appendix D

Territory of Arizona.

County of *Apache*

City or Town of *St. Johns*

I, *Carlos Tafolla* _____ born in *Cubero*

in the State of *New Mexico* _____ aged *thirty five* years and

months, and by occupation a *Peace Officer* DO HEREBY ACKNOWLEDGE

to have voluntarily _____ enlisted this *tenth* day of *September* 190 *1*

as a soldier in the ARIZONA RANGERS OF ARIZONA, for the period of ONE YEAR,

unless sooner discharged by proper authority. And I do solemnly swear that I will bear

true faith and allegiance to the Territory of Arizona, and will support the laws thereof, and

the Constitution of the United States ; and I will faithfully observe and obey all laws and

regulations for the government of the Arizona Rangers of Arizona, and the lawful orders of

all officers elected or appointed over me, so help me God.

Carlos Tafolla

Subscribed and sworn to before me this *tenth* day of *September* 190 *1*

Burton C. Mossman

Captain Arizona Rangers.

Recruiting Officer.

Specimen—Enlistment Paper

Appendix E

ARIZONA RANGERS

To all whom it may concern:

This is to Certify that *Jaff P. Kidder.*

a *1st Sergeant* of the Arizona Rangers, who was

enlisted the *1st* day of *April* one thousand nine

hundred and *Seven* to serve *One Year*

is hereby Honorably discharged from the service of the Territory in

consequence of *Expiration Term of Service*

Given under my hand at *Naco* this *8* day

of *April* one thousand nine hundred and *Eight.*

Harry C. Wheeler

Brave, honest and faithful.

Captain Arizona Rangers

CHARACTER

Excellent

Harry C. Wheeler

Commanding Company

4/14/08

Jos. H. Kibbey

Governor

Specimen—Discharge Paper

Appendix F

... *Report of* ...

CAPTAIN BURTON MOSSMAN

of Arrests Made by

ARIZONA RANGERS

from

October 2, 1901 to July 30, 1902,

OCTOBER, 1901.

DATE		NAME.	CRIME.	PLACE OF ARREST.
Oct.	2	Andrew Griffin	Murder	Huachuca Mts.
Oct.	2	Hete O'Connor	Murder	Huachuca Mts.
Oct.	9	Frank Hollis	Horse Stealing	Black River

NOVEMBER, 1901.

Nov.	11	James R. Head	Cattle Stealing	Chiricahua Mts.
Nov.	11	Wm. Williams	Cattle Stealing	Chiricahua Mts.

DECEMBER, 1901.

Dec.	7	Martin Woods	Grand Larceny	San Carlos
Dec.	12	John Ruth	Grand Larceny	Cochise
Dec.	31	Cruz Figuerra	Murder	Huachuca Mts.
Dec.	31	Ramon Moreno	Murder	" "
Dec.	31	Trinidad Ariola	Murder	" "
Dec.	31	Francisco Hemandez	Assault, intent to kill	" "

JANUARY, 1902.

Jan.	5	Zeck Day	Cattle Stealing	Barbacomari
Jan.	5	March Day	" "	"
Jan.	7	Joe Roberts	" "	"
Jan.	7	Francisco Moreno	" "	Metcalf
Jan.	9	Wm. Grummell	" "	"
Jan.	19	Ed. Lerue	Assault on Woman	Cochise
Jan.	19	Unknown Man	Horse Stealing	Animas Valley, N.M.
Jan.	19	Unknown Man	" "	Animas Valley, N.M.

FEBRUARY, 1902.

Feb.	4	George Cook	Highway Robbery and Murder	Blue River
Feb.	4	Witt Neill	Highway Robbery and Murder	Blue River
Feb.	4	Joe Roberts	Highway Robbery and Murder	Blue River
Feb.	8	Dura	Murder	Wilcox
Feb.	17	Jas. Mitchell	Horse Stealing	Safford
Feb.	20	Charles Dwyer	Burglary	Bisbee
Feb.	20	Frank Rogers	"	"
Feb.	22	Walter Trimbell	Rape	La Cananea, Mex.
Feb.	22	E. Trimbell	Rape	" "
Feb.	23	Clarence Hawkins	Horse Stealing	Mud Springs

Specimen—Periodic Report of Arrests

MARCH, 1902.

DATE	NAME.	CRIME.	PLACE OF ARREST.
Mar. 3	Martin Diaz	Highway Robbery.................	Naco
Mar. 3	Alphonse Armento.....	Highway Robbery.................	Naco
Mar. 5	Joe Belcher...............	Assault with Deadly Weapon.	Bisbee
Mar. 6	Hugh Drake...............	New Mexico Fugitive............	Sulpher Spring Valley
Mar. 27	Chas. Hull................	Selling Intoxicants to Indians	Don Luis
Mar. 27	Andres Pino...............	Disturbing Peace.................	"
Mar. 27	Juan Chico	Disturbing Peace.................	"
Mar. 27	Nelson Kisto............	Disturbing Peace.................	"

APRIL, 1902.

April 7	Simon Montoya.........	Grand Larceny...................	Eagle Creek
April 7	Valicute Perie...........	" "	" "
April 7	Francisco Florez........	Grand Larceny...................	Eagle Creek
April 7	Feliz Martinez...........	Grand Larceny...................	Eagle Creek
April 7	Rosalio Herrera.........	Grand Larceny...................	Eagle Creek
April 7	Bartelos Sandoval......	Grand Larceny...................	Eagle Creek
April 7	Manuel Mendosa.......	Killed Resisting Arrest.........	Eagle Creek
April 15	S. Dominguez.............	Smuggling......................	Sanoyta River
April 16	John Shaw	Larceny (Fugitive)	Clifton
April 16	Raymond Martinez.....	Horse Theft and Smuggling....	Greaterville
April 17	Jesus Escalante.........	" " " ...	"
April 17	Fiburcco Bartillo	" " " ...	"
April 20	Unknown Mexican....	Assault on Womau	Nogales
April 23	Angel Lara...............	Jail Breaking......................	Clifton
April 25	Lincoln Freeman	Robbery	Clifton
April 25	J. J. Mundell.............	Robbery	Clifton
April 25	Jack Cary	Robbery	Clifton
April 27	J. W. Smith .... alias Sam Bass.....	Robbery and Murder	OL. D. Ranch, N. M.

MAY, 1902.

May 7	Sim Neighbors.........	Cattle Stealing	Pinal County
May 7	John Richards...........	Cattle Stealing	" "
May 11	John Van Winkle......	Violation Live Stock Law......	Dos Cabazes
May 11	Bob Van Winkle..	" " "	" "
May 11	Walter Bruce	" " "	" "
May 20	Levrow Marcia.........	Horse Stealing	Mammoth
May 28	Frank Cowser...........	Horse Stealing	Blue River
May 30	Ed. Halderman.........	Cattle Stealing	Cochise
May 30	Frank Halderman......	Cattle Stealing	Cochise

JUNE, 1902.

June 1	Mann Powers	Horse Stealing	Safford
June 10	John Nobe...............	Horse Stealing	Huachuca Mts.
June 12	Jesus Moreno...........	Horse Stealing	Naco
June 24	Joe Brockman...........	Horse Stealing	La Cananea, Mexico
June 30	Francisco Para..........	Murder	Bisbee

JULY, 1902.

July 17	Bert Wayne ....) Walter Hester........ } John Bowman.......)	Horse Stealing...................	Chirichua Mts.
July 27	Jesus Valensula.........	Cattle Stealing	Santa Cruz County

Specimen—Periodic Report of Arrests

Appendix G

HEADQUARTERS ARIZONA RANGERS

DOUGLAS, ARIZONA, January 1, 1905.

Hon. Alexander O. Brodie, Governor of Arizona, Phoenix, Arizona—

Sir: In obedience to instructions contained in your letter of December 9th, 1904, I have the honor to transmit herewith report of the operations of the Company of Arizona Rangers for the two years ending December 31, 1904.

At the beginning of the year 1903, this organization under the laws of 1901, consisted of a Captain, a Sergeant, and eleven privates, which organization was in effect until April, 1903, when in accordance with the acts of the 22nd Legislative assembly it was increased to consist of one Captain, one Lieutenant, and not more than twenty privates. I have been in command of the Company for the past two years and have been assisted by Lieutenants Foster, Allison and Brooks, in turn.

Headquarters have been established at Douglas, Cochise County, on the Mexican line, as the greater part of our work has been in those counties along the border; however, have had Rangers working in every county in the Territory. Have operated extensively in Cochise, Graham, Pinal, Gila, Pima, Yavapi, Coconino, and Santa Cruz. The counties of Yuma, Maricopa, Mojave, Apache and Navajo have not required the presence of as many Rangers as the other counties. We have, however, covered every part of the Territory.

Our principal work has been on the ranges in connection with the live-stock interests of the Territory. We have worked in conjunction with the Live Stock Sanitary Board, The Arizona Cattle Growers Association, and the various county cattle growers' associations, from all of which organizations we have received the most valuable assistance and support.

The Rangers usually operate in squads of two or more, as I have found this to be the most effective, except in cases requiring secret or detective work, I have kept men constantly riding the ranges and attending round ups and patrolling those parts of the Territory not easily accessible to other peace officers, which has resulted in a great saving to the various counties, as we do not draw fees or mileage.

Have had a number of men performing extra duties, six rangers acting as Live Stock Inspectors, several as Deputy Inspectors. This has resulted in a large saving to the Territory in salaries. Several of the Rangers have held commissions as Field Deputy U. S. Marshals, which has facilitated our work especially in making arrests outside of the Territory. We do both the Inspection and U. S. work in conjunction with our other duties.

We have recovered and restored to their rightful owners, a great many strayed and stolen cattle, horses, sheep and goats, as well as quantities of other stolen property.

The present live stock laws are accomplishing much good, and under their operations cattle stealing has in the past two years been pratically wiped out in Arizona, the last of the gangs of cattle rustlers has been broken up, and there is now no organized cattle rustling or smuggling in Arizona.

We have captured and turned over many fugitives from justice from other States and from Mexico; also many U. S. offenders, principally smugglers, Chinese unlawfully in the United States, persons selling whiskey to Indians, and others have been captured and turned over to the U. S. authorities.

The most cordial relations exist with the Mexican authorities, who have at all times assisted and co-operated with us in the pursuit of criminals and the recovery of stolen property taken into Mexico. We have always followed fugitives into Mexico and the International line is no longer a protection for criminals from Arizona. Lieutenant Colonel Kosterlitzky has been especially active in his co-operation, and to him our thanks are especially due.

The conditions throughout the Territory are most gratifying. Law and order prevail. There has not been a train robbery, bank robbery, nor lynching in the Territory during the past two years; the old gangs of rustlers, smugglers, and wandering outlaws have all been broken up; there has been but one case of strike rioting, that in Morenci in June 1903, which was however averted without the shedding of blood or the destruction of property.

But two men have been killed resisting arrest during this period, which I consider a remarkable record considering the great number of arrests made on serious charges. They were John Robinson (negro) at Naco, and Joe Bostwick in Tucson. In both of these cases the Rangers were fully exonerated.

I have at all times endeavored to secure the very best men obtainable, and by the elimination of those found incompetent, have now secured a body of officers especially qualified for this class of work.

Complaints filed with the Governor or sent direct to this office are promptly investigated by men detailed for that purpose. I am constantly in receipt of petitions from citizens of various communities, stockmen, and requests from local officers, asking that Rangers be sent into their districts or into towns on some special occasion, or to do some special work, all of which are complied with as far as possible.

The total number of arrests reported during the past two years is 1059; of these, 297 were made on felony charges and 762 on misdemeanor charges. This is not complete as the Rangers have not always reported all petty misdemeanor cases. Of the misdemeanor cases reported 16 arrests were for petit larceny, 37 concealed weapons, 25 assaults, 9 selling whiskey to Indians, 39 violation of stock and butcher license laws, 5 violations of game laws, 23 for keeping and frequenting opium resorts, 7 running bunco games and gambling games without license, 266 for disturbing the peace and drunk and disorderly, 339 other misdemeanors and vagrants.

I would most respectfully recommend that some steps be taken providing for the compiling and publishing of a list of fugitives from justice, similar to that published by the State of Texas. It is a most necessary aid to officers, and many fugitives would be apprehended through its agency.

I would further recommend that the amount allowed for incidentals and office expenses be increased to the actual expenses incurred and receipts submitted, but not to exceed fifty dollars ($50.00) per month. I have found that the twenty dollars now allowed will not cover the actual expenses. I append a list of the arrests made on felony charges during the past two years.

Respectfully submitted,

THOS. H. RYNNING,
Captain Arizona Rangers,
Commanding the Company.

Specimen—Report to the Governor

HEADQUARTERS ARIZONA RANGERS

Douglas, Arizona, **February 28**, 190 6

Muster and Pay-Roll of Arizona Rangers for Month of   February   . 190 6.

NAME	RANK	TIME	AMOUNT DUE		TOTAL	
Thomas H. Rynning	Captain	Full month	175	00		
Harry C. Wheeler	Lieutenant		130	00		
William Sparks	1st Sergeant		110	00		
Arthur A. Hopkins	2nd Sergeant		110	00		
William A. Old	3rd Sergeant		110	00		
James E. McGee	4th Sergeant		110	00		
Robert M. Anderson	Private		100	00		
Clarence L. Beaty	Private		100	00		
Reuben E. Burnett	Private		100	00		
Wayne Davis.	Private		100	00		
Charles A. Eperson	Private		100	00		
John F. Greenwood	Private		100	00		
James T. Holmes	Private		100	00		
Jeff P. Kidder	Private		100	00		
J. Porter McDonald	Private		100	00		
Charles E. McGarr	Private		100	00		
Joe T. McKinney	Private		100	00		
Harry H. McPhaul	Private		100	00		
Lew H. Mickey	Private		100	00		
Reuben L. Neill	Private		100	00		
Ben W. Olney	Private		100	00		
Oscar J. Rountree	Private		100	00		
Tip Stanford	Private		100	00		
Ray Thompson	Private		100	00		
Frank S. Wheeler	Private		100	00		
	Private		$2645	00		

I hereby certify that the above account is correct.

Thos H. Rynning

Captain Arizona Rangers
Commanding the Company

Specimen—Monthly Payroll

Appendix I

LIEUTENANT W. A. OLD.   WILLIAMS
1st SERGEANT T. STANFORD. PATAGONIA
2d SERGEANT R. GUNNER.   NACO
3d SERGEANT O. McADA.   FLORENCE
4th SERGEANT L. MICKEY.   TUCSON

Headquarters Arizona Rangers

NACO

HARRY C. WHEELER
CAPTAIN

~~September~~ October 1"1908.

Mr Sims Ely,

Territorial Auditor,

Phoenix,Arizona.

Dear Sir:-

Enclosed you will please find three dollars upon the fund
here which I keep to pay the expenses of ammunition etc.

You may remember that I kept five dollars out of a mans ammunition
money to pay for a lost star,or badge.This mans name was Fraser.

Ordinarily these stars cost four or five dollars,however in this
case,the jeweler,being friendly to the Rangers,would not charge
over the actual cost,which amounted to two dollars.

I cannot find this man Fraser now,I understand that he went back
to Texas,where I sincerely hope he will remain.

Not knowing where to send him the three dollars and not knowing
what else to do with it,and feeling anyway that a Ranger who is so
careless as to lose his star,should be punished anyway,I decided to
return the amount left over to the Ranger Fund.

We leave within thirty minutes for Willcox and vicinity,so please
send our checks there,I will await them at that place until the seven
seventh anyway.I will send them to the men from there and than go on
with our scout.

Very truly yours

Harry C. Wheeler

Captain Arizona Rangers.

Self-Explanatory Letter

INDEX

Crook, General George, 56
Cuen, Tranquilino (Mexican cattle inspector), 42
Cummings Cattle company, 41
Cushman, R. E., 212

Davis, Young (witness), 130
Delbridge, I. M. (witness), 186
Diaz, Porfirio (president of Mexico), 151
Dick, Benton (district attorney), 161
District court at Holbrook, 21
Doan, Judge Fletcher, 44, 46, 53, 155
Doan, John (justice of the peace at Silver Bell), 157
Douglas, Arizona, 4, 5, 25, 58–60, 64, 83, 85, 91, 92, 96, 119, 133, 147–149, 154
Downing, William "Bill", 211–216
Downing's saloon, (Willcox), 212
Duncan, W. G. (deputy sheriff), 173
Dusold, C. H., 207

Eagle Creek, 14
Edwards, Charles (cattleman), 172–187
Edwards, Mrs. Fannie, 186
Eight-hour law (1903), 68
El Cubo (Papago Indian village), 163–170
Ells, ——— (deputy sheriff), 190
El Paso Southwestern Railroad, 6
El Paso, Texas, 5
Empalme, Sonora, 112–114
English, Allen R. (attorney), 63
Epley, ——— (deputy sheriff), 70
Evans, ——— (coroner-Globe), 175
Evans, ——— (justice of the peace), 173

F. L. Jones & Son (undertakers-Globe), 173
Ferguson's undertaking parlors (Douglas), 129

Ferguson, W. C. (court stenographer), 63
Fish Pond saloon (Bisbee), 47
Fitzgerald, Wiley, 208
Florence, Arizona, 44, 45, 225
Fort Grant, 70
Fort Huachuca, 70
Fort Huachuca, Arizona, 124
Fort Sumner, New Mexico, 46
Foster, John (ex-Ranger, deputy marshal), 192
Fountain, Lt. Samuel, 56
Fraser, J. A. (Ranger), 168
Free and Easy saloon (Willcox), 211, 212
Frisco River, 72, 73
Furken, Arturo, Cananea, Sonora, 89

Galbraith, ——— (American consul), 124
Garcia, Adolpho (Mexican criminal), 148
Garcia, Judge (Naco, Sonora), 190, 192, 194
Gerdes, John (foreman Brophy Stables), 207
Gila Bend, Arizona, 156, 157, 161
Gilbert, C. H. (commissary wagon driver), 185
Gilchrist, Alex (witness), 63
Giles, Bob (cattleman), 42, 43
Globe, Arizona, 5, 104, 105, 172–184, 220
Gonzales, ——— (outlaw), 114, 115
Goode, James (witness), 63
Goode, W. H. (witness), 207
Goodrich, Ben (legislator), 223
Graham County, Arizona, 4, 24, 29, 30, 51, 53, 66, 68, 74, 102, 202
Graham, Dayton (ex-Ranger, constable), 61
Grand Canyon Line and Cement company), 210
Gray, Henry (Ranger), 45